D0122074

DANGEROUS GROUND

Also By M. William Phelps

Perfect Poison

Lethal Guardian

Every Move You Make

Sleep in Heavenly Peace

Murder in the Heartland

Because You Loved Me

If Looks Could Kill

I'll Be Watching You

Deadly Secrets

Cruel Death

Death Trap

Kill for Me

Love Her to Death

Too Young to Kill

Never See Them Again

Kiss of the She-Devil

Bad Girls

Obsessed

The Killing Kind

She Survived: Melissa (e-book)

She Survived: Jane (e-book)

I'd Kill for You

To Love and to Kill

One Breath Away

If You Only Knew

Don't Tell a Soul

DANGEROUS GROUND

M. WILLIAM PHELPS

KENSINGTON BOOKS
Kensington Publishing Corp.
http://www.kensingtonbooks.com

Some names have been changed to protect the privacy of individuals connected to this story.

KENSINGTON BOOKS are published by

Kensington Publishing Corp.
119 West 40th Street
New York, NY 10018

All Kensington titles, imprints and distributed lines are available at special quantity discounts for bulk purchases for sales promotions, premiums, fund-raising, and educational or institutional use. Special book excerpts or customized printings can also be created to fit specific needs. For details, write or phone the office of the Kensington Special Sales Manager. Kensington Publishing Corp., 119 West 40th Street, New York, NY 10018. Attn.: Special Sales Department. Phone: 1-800-221-2647.

Library of Congress Card Catalogue Number: 2017940675

Kensington and the K logo Reg. U.S. Pat. & TM Off.

ISBN-13: 978-1-4967-0952-3
ISBN-10: 1-4967-0952-7
First Kensington Mass Market Edition: August 2017

eISBN-13: 978-1-4967-0953-0
eISBN-10: 1-4967-0953-5
Kensington Electronic Edition: August 2017

10 9 8 7 6 5 4 3 2 1

Printed in the United States of America

For my immediate *Dark Minds* family:

Collette Sandstedt, Peter Heap, Jared Transfield, Jeremy Adair,
Andrew Farrell, Geoff Fitzpatrick, John Kelly, Jeannie Vink

&

of course, my readers.

CONTENTS

AUTHOR'S NOTE

This is a work of nonfiction. Everything in this book is based on interviews, letters, diary entries, individual memories, and other primary and secondary sources. Scenes and conversations are, at times, built around those sources and also witness accounts.

The childhood and familial life of the serial killer in this book is told, mainly, by the use of over six hundred pages of separate recollections (beyond thousands of pages of letters) he wrote to me over a five-year period, hundreds of interviews I conducted with him over those five years, Video Visits (recorded Skype conversations), and in-person visits. This is *his* account of those years and the life he lived.

In instances where there would have been an exorbitant amount of ellipses in quoted dialogue or letters excerpts, I opted not to include them (to keep the flow of the narrative moving), providing those deletions did not affect context or meaning of the statement.

The book is a bit of a departure from the type of journalism I generally write. I consider this book a hybrid: somewhere between a memoir (my story) and biography (the killer's story). All of the thoughts, reflections, and quotes from the serial killer in this book are his and his alone. There are many occasions where the only source available to explain a particular scene/occurrence is the killer.

It isn't so different, the way we wander through the past. Lost, disordered, fearful, we follow what signs there remain; we read the street names, but cannot be confident where we are. All around is wreckage. . . .
—Julian Barnes, *Flaubert's Parrot*

PROLOGUE

SHE IS DEAD.

On a metal slab. A sheet covering her body. A tag hanging from her big toe. Manner and cause of death will be determined soon.

Murder by strangulation.

He is, contrarily, alive. Standing in my kitchen.

I walk in.

He appears to be waiting for the *ding* to tell him the Howard Johnson's Macaroni & Cheese dinner in the plastic frozen boat he placed inside the microwave has been fully nuked. But I notice the carousel inside the oven is not making that squeaky noise it does when it is on. Also, he is not moving. His head is bowed, as if he's trying to touch his chin to his chest, the folds of his neck fat exposed like rising dough. His eyes are closed. His right hand is on top of the microwave; his left by his side. The familiar-smelling richness of the melting cheese is not there, and this is an aroma that permeates the kitchen air whenever he cooks this meal. In a strange moment of reflection, I don't see my oldest brother nodded out in a methadone-induced coma while standing erect in front of the microwave, but a corpse—a dead man standing. All he cooks is mac-n-cheese and those baked stuffed clams, full of bread crumbs, in the half shell. He lives off pills, methadone, beer, cheese, and gluten.

"Mark?"

He does not answer.

"Mark?"

Nothing.

I toss my keys on the kitchen table. Walk over. Shake him.

It is April 12, 1996. I am twenty-nine and separated from my wife for the past two years; I will be officially divorced in a few months, remarried six months later, on New Year's Eve, to a woman I haven't yet met. Mark is living with me in a house the bank is about to foreclose on; we're both biding our time, waiting for the sheriff to come and tell us to leave. He has recently split with his "wife," Diane, who is living in Hartford, Connecticut, on Garden Street, not far from Asylum Hill. A forty-one-year-old woman was murdered the previous year on Huntington Street, just a mile away. Unbeknownst to any of us then, a serial killer is on the loose in the Asylum Hill section of Hartford, plucking women off the street, raping, beating, and killing them. Hartford is twelve miles from my house.

Last I hear, thirty-four-year-old Diane (her actual name is Diana, but we all call her Diane) is pregnant. Mark isn't sure if it is his child—and this tears him apart. He tells me he's done with her, for good this time. It's over. Yet in the twenty years they have been together, we have all heard this: after each fight, after each one has had the other arrested, after they hit and scratch and berate each other in front of their kids at retail stores, restaurants, and all sorts of other public places.

"Hey, man, wake up," I say, and shake him again.

Mark is thirty-nine. That's young, I know. But he looks fifty, maybe older. The life he's led has taken its toll. "The silent killer," hepatitis C, is coursing through his veins.

"Mark . . . wake up, man."

A snotlike length of drool hangs from his mouth.

After he comes to, figures out where he is, acclimates himself to his surroundings as if he is on a boat, trying to manage large swells, he takes his half-cooked mac-n-cheese and heads down the five flights of stairs to his space in the house. He mumbles something I cannot understand. I can decode what he says about 20 percent of the time. Later on, I will have to clean up after he spills the macaroni all over himself, on his bed, the floor, before passing out again. The used boat his food came in will be on his lap, now an ashtray, and the juxtaposition of the ashes and leftover cheese, a cigarette butt stabbed into a piece of elbow macaroni, will remind me that life is, in the end, about choices.

SEVERAL HOURS LATER, DAYLIGHT has given itself to night. Mark is standing in my kitchen again, staring out the window, waiting, anxious as each car drives by the house, headlight beams like a Hollywood premiere strobing across the wallpaper. He is somewhat coherent. His belly full of cheese and pasta, the methadone and pills have worn off. After he leaves, it will occur to me that as he stood in the kitchen, an image of his face reflected in the windowpane as he waited for a ride, I saw myself standing in the same spot, at fifteen years old, waiting for my friend, older and able to buy liquor, to come and pick me up so we could go get loaded.

"Shopping," he says after I ask. "A friend is on her way."

"Don't come back all drunk and high," I warn. "I won't let you in."

He looks at me. Doesn't respond. Lifts his cigarette up to his mouth, his fingers stained Listerine-yellow from the nicotine, hep C, or both. He inhales deeply, blows what's left of the smoke at the windowpane, fogging it up.

His disability check and food stamps allow him to feed himself, but he also trades some of the food (or sells the food stamps at a 50 percent loss) for booze and Newports. As a kid, I liked the Newport package with the upside-down Nike symbol. However, stealing and smoking his cigarettes came with a tic tac–like, cold burn in my lungs, so I wound up switching to Marlboro.

He'll be broke in two days, eating my food, calling and begging our mother for money. She'll give it to him. He'll buy pills with that money because his methadone is regulated. A taxi—paid for by the State of Connecticut—picks him up every morning, brings him into Hartford, and returns him home. At the clinic, they give him his dose of "Kool-Aid." Sometimes he stores up several doses so he can go on a bender. It is a cycle, one we've been on most of our lives. No one tries to stop Mark anymore because we can't.

It is while he is shopping that I get the call—the fucking call that will not be a shock to most in my family, but will change Mark forever, send him on a new course, and initiate a suicide that will take him eight years to complete.

Several days before the call, Mark came upstairs. I asked him to sit down. "I need to tell you what I have told you a dozen times since you moved in." As calm as I could, I explained: "I know that while I am at work, Diane is coming over." Knowing Diane all my life, I was confident she was rummaging through my house, looking for things to pawn or information about me to hold over my head. "I don't want her in the house. She cannot be in this house."

He said something about being the older brother, more experienced in life, and how I should respect that. "And you never have. I love her. We're getting back together."

It's hard, however, for me to look up to a man with burn marks all over his chest from nodding out while smoking, all his shirts with tiny burn holes on them, the bed he sleeps in and his sheets the same. Mark is a man who spends fifteen hours a day basically unconscious, takes opiates and methadone together, while drinking cans of Busch beer, and has not been a father to his three kids since they wore diapers. I love him, but I am perpetually furious with this man. He gave up on life long ago for reasons I do not understand.

For a response, I go to my emotional childhood bank and withdraw something our father would have said in this same situation: "But this is *my* house, Mark. My rules if you want to live here. And I don't want Diane over here."

He is nodding as we speak. In and out. His eyes languid, tired, Marty Feldman–bulged. His skin is slithery; the shiny texture of a salamander, with a subtle hue of yellow, like a healing bruise, same as the whites of his eyes, a strange, dull urine color. He is sickly-looking, gaunt, and emaciated. At times, he resembles a Holocaust victim staring back at me through an invisible fence between us. He has an anesthetic smell to him, same as a patient in a hospital. You walk down into the area of my split-level, ranch-style home where he lives on the bottom floor and it reeks of a rich, cigarette-butts-stuffed-inside-a-can-of-beer, stale tar odor that is part of the house forever. He sleeps on one of those pullout couch beds, with the springs that stick into your back. There are empty see-through-orange pill containers all over the place. Beer cans. Dishes. Drinking glasses. Old newspapers. Greyhound racing programs. Pencils. Pens. Two-liter Coke bottles, fruit flies hovering. Cigarette butts. Silver-gray ashes. So many ashes: the remnants of his smoking covers everything, like dust. The carpet around where he sleeps is dirty and worn. There are small burn holes all over the area surrounding his Archie Bunker chair and they look similar to tiny craters on the surface of the moon. I have installed four smoke detectors in an area the size of a one-car garage. In this moment of our lives, if there is one thing about my brother I can count on, it's that his addiction runs his life and has him on a strict schedule. When I was growing up, and he lived with Diane and the kids, everything about their lives was unpredictable; you never knew what they were going to do next. At this point, my brother is, if nothing else, confined to some sort of controlled insanity only he comprehends and visible in his physical destruction: abnormally and enormously bloated hep C stomach; frail arms; old-man, saggy-skin legs, the wires of his tendons exposed; white fingernails; dry lips, cracking and sometimes bleeding; his greasy, black hair from not showering regularly.

"Did she kill that man?" I ask after we agree that Diane cannot come into the house ever again.

He stares at me. Looks down at the kitchen table. He knows what I'm talking about.

A few years before this conversation, a man was found stabbed to death inside Diane's vehicle. She had driven him to Hartford on the night he was murdered. It is unclear what happened. He was a man she met at a bar while she was living with my brother at a nearby scuzzy motel. Diane was not in the car at the time the man was murdered, she claimed.

"Not talking about that with you," he says. "She would never kill anyone."

Mark leaves to go shopping. I put on some music and relax.

The phone rings.

That fucking call.

It's our other brother, Thomas (whom we call Tommy). He and I are closest in age and get along same as good friends. Tommy lives a few miles away—two of Mark and Diane's kids live with him. First it was me and my soon-to-be ex-wife; now Tommy is their official foster parent. Their other child, the oldest, lives with an aunt in a neighboring town.

"She's dead," Tommy says. "Strangled to death."

It doesn't register. "What do you mean—who's dead?"

"Just heard. Ma called me. She heard, too. Someone murdered Diane. Where's Mark?"

"Shopping . . . shit, dude. Are you sure?"

"Yeah, we're sure."

"What are you going to tell the kids?"

"I don't know."

I COULDN'T HAVE KNOWN at the time, but fifteen years after that phone call, my relationship with a man who had strangled eight women to death would set me on the road to resolving some of the issues I faced when my familial and personal worlds unraveled. That early evening my brother Tommy called and told me Diane had been murdered was the Phelps family's introduction to the ripple effect murder would have on all of us forever. Like so many other families I'd become involved with through my work, as murder became part of our lives that night, we would never be the same people.

"You mentioned a little bit about your loss," my serial killer tells me one day. "A death wakes up the family. Maybe some good can come of it. Maybe a Scared Straight course for the Phelps clan."

In September 2011, I wrote to this man, one of the nation's most notable, nicknamed serial killers. My goal at the time was to convince him to act as a consultant, an anonymous profiling source on my Investigation Discovery television series, *Dark Minds*. Concerned about glorifying his crimes or revictimizing the eight females he murdered, his identity remained secret throughout his tenure on the series and after. He was known to audiences only as "Raven," a disguised voice on the telephone explaining what was going through the mind of the serial killers I hunted and profiled each week. But as the series aired and our relationship progressed, something happened.

We became "friends."

"I can help you look at your sister-in-law's murder," he continues, "and offer my understanding. Hard to believe a convicted serial killer has something valuable to say, but what I offer is insight into the mind of how this killer thinks. I see through cases because I have witnessed this kind of evil firsthand, lived with evil twenty-four hours a day."

I had no idea how to respond to this.

He encouraged me to "listen and learn."

As we began, the true emotional, physical, and spiritual impact this relationship would have on my life, or how his "insight" would affect my everyday thinking, on top of the relationship with my family, was hidden—a series of blows I could have never imagined.

"Sorry for your loss," he says. "Don't make excuses for her. She was doing what she wanted to do." We play at a cost. Then someone dies and we look at ourselves for answers.

My five-year friendship with a serial killer, same as my relationship with Mark and Diane, would not only change who I was, but break me.

THERE HAD BEEN TOO many times to count when all of us—my brothers Tommy and Frankie, mother and father and stepfather, wives and cousins and uncles and aunts and friends—had said, *I wish Diane would go away for good.* For me, personally, I'd considered a number of times how I wished to hell someone would take Diane out. She'd caused our family so much pain, so much grief, it was drama every day with her. We all wanted her out of our lives.

And now, suddenly, just like that, she was

"I'll tell Mark when he gets back," I explain to my brother Tommy.

The details are hard to come by in a day and age without Internet and cell phones, but with a few calls, I piece together that someone put a pillowcase over Diane's head and strangled her with a telephone cord. At least that's what has been reported. She was found inside the Hartford apartment she'd been living in since her split with my brother. She was, it had been confirmed, five months pregnant.

After hanging up and sitting at my kitchen table, I go back to the previous night. Mark had been out—all night. A recluse, saddled by his addictions, he *never* went anywhere other than to the methadone clinic, liquor store, and market to get his mac-n-cheese and clams, Coke, cigarettes, and thirty racks of Busch beer. But last night, he was gone. If the cops come around my house asking questions, there's no way I can vouch for his whereabouts.

I walk downstairs into Mark's section of the house. Stare at his belongings, not sure what I'm looking for. This house, which I have lived in since I was thirteen years old in 1980, raised two kids of my own in, is nothing more than a body without a soul. It's empty besides Mark and me. Vacant and soiled. All of this mess down here, the remnants of his life, is beyond sad. A few trinkets, a few photos of Mark's kids and Diane, his *TV Guide,* his New York Giants pennant and hat, his remote control and television, a few Hefty bags of clothes, is all he has left. The anger I feel toward him comes from the fact that I'm his caretaker. He is the older brother, the one I should be going to for advice and security, but I am all of that and more.

Before he returns home from shopping, I have to decide how I will tell my brother that his wife, a woman he has known since she was a teenager, is dead—as it occurs to me that he might know already. I have this sick feeling. I don't know what it is. But it's real and it is gnawing at me.

PART ONE

FRIENDS

1

MEETING MY "FRIEND," THE PSYCHOPATH

"Well, evil to some is always good to others."
—Jane Austen, *Emma*

*T*HE CHECK-IN ENTRANCE FOR A PRISON VISIT AT OREGON STATE
Penitentiary looks, ironically, similar to the facade of a downtown
Chicago, 1930s-era, gangster hotel. There's a canopy overhanging
two sets of concrete stairs, each fanning out in opposite directions, like praying mantis legs. The stucco wall leading to the
door is grimy, the color and texture of cantaloupe skin, chipped
and covered with mold in places. Walking in, you are overwhelmed
by the potent smell of sweat, stale perfumes, and mildew.

Once inside, I couldn't help but notice a young pregnant
woman with lots of tattoos, a disappointed look on her face, sitting alone, staring at the floor.

"Denied access," the guard behind the counter explained after
looking up and asking for my photo ID. "She's been here for
hours. Name? License? Who are you here to see?"

I tell him.

He taps away at his computer. Turns to me. "You cannot wear
those clothes. You'll have to change. Or you cannot go in."

My blue jeans and button-up shirt were not part of the dress
code. Any clothing similar to what an inmate wears is off-limits.

The day had begun on a high note, with baby-blue skies, soft
white cumulus clouds, warm air radiating from the tar in hazy
waves. It was Friday afternoon, September 14, 2012. The coast-to-

coast journey from Connecticut was exhausting, plagued by air-port idiots causing unnecessary delays. I didn't know it then, but after my prison visit, I'd be robbed in downtown Salem of my passport, iPad, phone, rosary beads, and other personal posses-sions by a meth addict bearing an uncanny resemblance to one of the Backstreet Boys. By the end of the night, I'd be staring at the ceiling of my Portland hotel room, a warning a dear friend gave me before I left keeping me tossing and turning: "If the Devil knocks at your door and you invite him in, you had *damn* well better be prepared to dine with him."

After sorting out my garment issue, a guard walked me and sev-eral others through a metal detector, then down an incline simi-lar to a handicap ramp, where we stopped at a set of barred doors. A guard sat behind tinted glass in a kiosk to our left. The smell here was heavy, stuffy, and wretched: think of a laundry hamper full of dirty clothes. Ahead of us were a series of old-fashioned, iron prison doors that made loud, echoing, steel-against-steel latching noises as they snapped and locked shut. I'd been in over a dozen prisons. It is the supermaxes, like OSP, that have a sticky coat of scum on everything.

As I entered the visitor's area, it was loud and noticably humid. Everyone spoke over one another. Women fanned themselves with their hands and newspapers, like they do in the South on Sundays in church. I scanned the room and saw him waiting for me on the opposite side. He was a human being who was hard to miss, clocking in at about three hundred pounds, give or take. He stood six foot six and sported gray-black hair, military buzz cut, hazy blue eyes, the beginning of cataracts. He wore a pair of off-trend, 1970s-era, large-framed glasses, which reminded me of Peter Fonda's character in the film *Dirty Mary Crazy Larry*. This massive, handsome man, representing the polar opposite of everything I believe and promote, smiled and waved me over.

We sat across from each other on stiff, wooden chairs. He looked at me with the smooth, glassy shimmer only a psychopath can invoke. The depth of evil was inherent and natural—same as the slight, nervous smile he maintained throughout our conversation. All of it reminded me that a serial killer is a craftsman, a professional, in so many ways.

This was a man who had killed for purpose and reason. Every act and every thought and every word and every lie was carefully structured around an agenda, planned and thought out. Contrary to the public perception that most serial murderers are white males in their thirties living in their parents' basement, serial killers actually fit no particular stereotype. All are different. This man I sat in front of shredded the common myth that the serial killer psychopath is a solitary figure, a loner, a person without social skills who is afraid to allow anyone inside his head, or get close to him.

His hands are the size of pot holders. He had them cupped over his knees, feet away from my throat. I stared and thought: *Those are the same hands he killed eight human beings with*—all females, all strangled to death, one beaten bloody and unrecognizable, another allegedly secured with rope and dragged underneath his truck for twelve miles (according to him), until all identifying markers (teeth and fingerprints) and "even her chest cavity" were gone.

The person in front of me was a monster. He and I both understood this. I made no secret about my feelings: I despise him. I view him—and those like him—as scum that cannot be rehabilitated and will reoffend at any given chance. This man killed females for sport and enjoyed it. And these opening moments of our first visit became an existential, enlightening realization, putting the reason why I'd made the trip to begin with into perspective.

"Could you kill me?" I asked him after we exchanged pleasantries.

"If I had to," he said, pausing and laughing, before pushing his glasses up the bridge of his nose. "I need to be clear with you about something. Despite what people say, I never raped any of them—I never needed to." The tone of his voice, something I'd come to realize is a way for him to express his deepest feelings, sounded as though he'd done his victims a favor by *not* raping them. He was a "fair-minded killer" for not sexually assaulting women. It's a skewed piece of logic, I knew, something psychopaths rely on to make themselves feel better about what they've done: justification. Every single report led me to believe that he was motivated by sex and had raped many of his victims. Yet he sat staring back at me, telling me no, never.

"That is *not* who I am."

The reason I'd asked about murdering me was because we'd known each other by then over a year. I felt uncharacteristically comfortable sitting in front of this man. We'd spoken by phone over one hundred times so far. I'd received no fewer than one hundred letters, amounting to over two thousand pages of text in that time. He'd become quite fond of me. He was on the fringes of trusting me. I was his last hope, he'd often say, for telling a part of his story the way he'd wanted it told. He'd been down sixteen years and change, sentenced on November 2, 1995, to two life terms. His earliest parole date on paper was scheduled for March 1, 2063. He was fifty-seven years old the first time we met in person. This serial murderer—Keith "Happy Face" Jesperson—will never feel the sunshine on his back again as a free man. As he should, Jesperson will die alone, a convicted, incarcerated murderer, in one of the oldest, dirtiest, roughest prisons on the West Coast.

"If you ever got out, would you kill again?" I asked, knowing that 60 percent of psychopaths released from prison go on to reoffend. Those are not good numbers.

"I'd tell you no because that is what you want to hear," he said. "And I would never want to come back to this place. But the truth is, I *don't* really know."

I made note of his comment: *I* don't *really know.* I sensed a fleeting jolt of honesty in his response.

Prison for Happy Face was easy, as long as he did the time and did not allow the time to do him. On a day-to-day basis, infamous serial killers in prison are either revered or have targets on their backs. Which illustrated a point: so much of this for him was unknown, part of a subtext that many serial killers structured their lives around. You wake up feeling inadequate and angry, maybe not even planning to kill anyone. But the urge to take a life, I would come to find out, is omnipresent, something you can never escape. Much like a dope addict, it becomes all you fantasize about.

That next fix.

He wore a blue, button-up dress shirt, state-issued, and denim blue jeans, same as every other inmate around us (the reason why I had been asked to change clothes). He had a sour smell, same as a musty basement. Two of his top teeth were missing. "I'm in the middle of some dental work, excuse how I look."

As I sat and listened, he struck me as a country bumpkin. Not that I mean he was dumb, or some sort of Lennie parody from Steinbeck's *Of Mice and Men*—an oversized adult with the brain of a small child. In some respects, Jesperson was a smart man. One study of 252 serial killers found that their intelligence quotient (IQ) numbered from 54 to 186, with a medium score of about 86, with 85 to 114 being a standard average. Jesperson's IQ fell slightly above average at 115. An artist (colored pencil/charcoal on paper), he is a voracious reader, with strong, vocal opinions about what he reads.

Still, he had this strange, hospitable manner about him, which felt inviting, easy to trust. I'd sense the same temperament from locals I'd meet a week later in British Columbia, where he's from. As I sat before him, I was on my way into the mountains of a town called Smithers to hunt a serial killer. It's a regional dialect, I'd soon learn. Jesperson came across the same way: laid-back, slowed pace, comfortable in his own skin. I could grasp how he might have charmed an unsuspecting victim into his comfort zone.

He asked me why I was so late. I'd made it to the prison on time, but it took three attempts at changing my clothes before guards approved me to go in. I'd never read the regulations (like directions, who does?). No jeans. No sweatpants. I ended up wearing a pair of shorts I borrowed from my cameraman, Peter Heap, who, with the rest of my *Dark Minds* crew, waited in the parking lot.

Though it was clear to me by then that Keith Jesperson suffers from acute systemic paranoia, he did not seem to worry about much with regard to the lack of morality surrounding his eight known murders. He'd committed his crimes, given himself up. He was contented serving time for his "debt" to society. To him, he was paying for what he'd done; and the public, because of that, should not condemn him for the choices he made in life. It's a common theme I've heard within the context of my research surrounding other serial killers: Most are able to wiggle their way out of the death penalty by withholding information about their crimes until a deal is offered. Most are afraid of death (Jesperson included). All have a complex regarding what society thinks of them; they fear and loathe being judged. For example, "I dragged a woman underneath my truck to get rid of her teeth and palm prints, but I never, listen to me, I never strangled any kittens," Jesperson told me. "That's the Hollywood prototype my daughter has parlayed for herself into a career writing books and being on television."

As I began to learn about his crimes (not what has been written about him in books and on the Internet or portrayed in the fictionalized films made about his life—but the admissions he would make only to me over five years and the exclusive documents I'd soon obtain), I realized I was dealing with a complicated, evil human being (a description he would laugh at), who does not care about humanity. Not because he doesn't want to, but sympathy and empathy are not part of his biological makeup. He is a man who murdered women as if their lives did not matter, as if he'd been authorized by some unknown entity to decide how, why, and when they should die. He was a murderer who had killed for years with no thought about the consequences or pain those deaths would cause his victims' loved ones, or the mere fact that taking someone's life because of your own preconceived notions, issues with women, anger, a need to control, obsession, fantasy, or any reason, is unethical and just plain wrong. He knew what he did was immoral and criminal, yet he had trouble understanding society had the right to hate and judge him for those actions.

"I did her family a favor," he rhapsodized about a young victim who was "supposedly" pregnant and asked him for a ride. According to Happy Face, she was on her way to trick a man into thinking he was the father of her child. "There was no way I could allow her to ruin this man's life and have him raise a child that was not his."

"So you killed her?"

"Yes—*and* her baby. She deserved it. I put her out of her damn misery."

As an active killer, and perhaps even more today, Jesperson believed his own ethos. He assumed that playing God with his victims' lives was a choice *he* could make. This brings up a point one needs to bear in mind moving forward: Jesperson lives within a bubble of his own truth, a moral relativism defying explanation or reasoning. He thinks we should listen to him and take what he says as gospel because it is how he "feels." He believes the eight lives he took *needed* to be snuffed out. His victims had been at fault, deserving their fate (always), and that karma played a role in him crossing paths with each victim. Most interesting, he is certain that anyone put in a similar position, under the right conditions and circumstances, would have responded to the situation as he had.

"We are all capable of murder," he told me. "And once you cross the line and do it once, you're one murder away from becoming a serial killer like me and killing two and three and so on."

He said I had within me the capability of evil, of taking a human life—that we all do, adding, "You need to understand this. Hopefully, I can educate you. Look, I got away with my first murder. Two people were arrested, prosecuted, and convicted for a murder *I* committed. Then I attacked a woman, was arrested for it, and got a slap on the wrist. I was free to kill."

Despite everything we talked about, however, the main thrust of any discourse or soliloquy he delivered, the one objective always on Jesperson's mind, was a law enforcement and judicial fiasco following his first murder and what led to two innocent people being arrested and convicted for it. Jesperson had a detailed narrative he needed to make known to the world, one that a few before me had tried to get right, he complained, but failed. Correcting the record was a refrain and motive for him to participate in my research. "A wrong that was committed against me," he reiterated. "I need you to make it right."

Imagine: A serial killer was upset that, in his opinion, there had been an injustice (he called it a "cover-up") within his criminal life that had gone unchecked and unchallenged. He wanted me to commit to "investigating" this facet of his case and report my findings.

I promised to tell that part of his story. But sharing the facts of his case, I explained, while digging into his life and childhood, his relationship with his kids and father, and exploring why he killed, was how I'd planned to get there.

"I hope you're ready," he warned as guards rounded everyone up to leave. It was loud in the room and we had to speak over the crowd noise. There was an unspoken, handshake deal between us, as if we'd cut fingers and shook a blood oath. "Because it is going to get messy. I'm going to share things with you I've told no one—and not everyone is going to accept or like what I have to say." He winked.

I left.

2

A MURDER OF CROWS

"The only lies for which we are truly punished are those
we tell ourselves."
—V.S. Naipaul, *In a Free State*

*K*EITH JESPERSON PACED INSIDE HIS CELL. NOW, HOURS AFTER dinner, he and his fellow inmates had been put to bed for the night. It was the end of September 1996. He'd been down just over a year. A bit squirrelly still, not quite used to the daily grind of everyday prison life, Happy Face knew he would not find sleep on this night.

Incarcerated serial killers have fans (groupies) sending them money, food, nude and clothed photos, letters, all sorts of odd things. Days before, a groupie had sent Jesperson a copy of an article written about his first "official" murder—the murder he claims released the Devil inside and initiated an attack on a woman (months later) who got away, thus sparking a killing spree of seven additional victims over the next four years. As he read the article, "A Question of Guilt," written by *Los Angeles Times* national correspondent Barry Siegel, published in the *Times* magazine on September 1, 1996, Jesperson was struck by the "depth of deception" and overwhelmed by how far the prosecutor, Jim McIntyre, had gone to "make [the state's] case against two suspects, Laverne Pavlinac and John Sosnovske, who had been arrested, charged, convicted and sentenced for a murder [Taunja Bennett] I had committed."

The article was not a surprise to Jesperson; the *Times* had visited him in prison that February for "a photo shoot," he said. "But that was all that had come from the visit." After snapping the photos, they left. "Seemed what I had to say didn't matter."

Hearing him explain this as we started talking on a regular basis, I couldn't help but ask myself, *Does it matter what a serial killer has to say? Furthermore, should we listen? Should we even care?*

As he read the article several times throughout that sleepless night, the only conclusion Jesperson could come to was: *Are you kidding me?*

He felt rage bubble inside him as the night wore on. That anger, surprisingly not so prevalent in most serial killers, is a known motiving factor in only 7.8 percent of all serial murders—but a familiar emotional trigger that led to all of Jesperson's kills.[1]

Drawn from Jim McIntyre's point of view, the *Times* story is an in-depth, multilayered piece focused on how McIntyre got it wrong and how embarrassed he was by such an investigatory and judicial debacle, thus sending two innocent people to prison for four years.

Jesperson claimed that after reading the story for the first time, he'd finally understood the dynamics of the case the State of Oregon had made against Laverne and John (as Jesperson would commonly refer to them). Jesperson had always assumed—from the time they were arrested until that night in his cell—two people had been wrongly convicted for a murder he committed.

"That it was a mistake," he quipped. "I watched a lot of *Matlock* and *Perry Mason*. Maybe these cops, just like on those shows, simply made a mistake in their investigation. They arrested the *wrong* people. Put them in prison. Then this bad guy serial killer comes forward and admits to the crime and gets them out of prison with his admissions."

Indeed, after admitting the Bennett murder, along with seven

---

[1]Unless otherwise specified in the narrative, all statistical data is derived from the FBI and its comprehensive study of serial killing in the United States since 1900, which can be found on its website.

others, going through the judicial process of cutting deals in all of his cases, Jesperson had written the incarceration of two innocent people off as an error in judgment.

"I thought it was that simple. But this article someone sent me," he concluded, "well, let me just say, it changed *everything*."

In his view, this was where I came into the picture.

HUMAN INSTINCT BECKONS MOST to place a label on, and try to understand, the nature of evil. It's part of what drives the obsession many of us have with true crime in the United States today. We desire to know what the psychopath is thinking and what "made" him bad. One of the mere tenets of philosophy would lay claim that a person cannot be evil unless, at some point, he embodied good—or, at the least, there is good in the world in which he lives. This was not the premise of which I worked as I stepped into the role of employing a serial killer to help me explain why people kill; yet, in the end, it became a mystery I needed to solve, simply because I'd come to believe it.

Approaching Keith Hunter Jesperson to correspond with me was something I set out to do as part of my research for the type of television I produced from 2011 to 2014. Jesperson was known as Raven, the telephone voice on my former Investigation Discovery television series. A good friend, mentor, and colleague, John Kelly, encouraged me to seek out Jesperson for this task. Knowing me, Kelly, an addiction therapist, was confident I'd untangle complicated, maybe even hidden, emotional mysteries within myself by talking to someone like Jesperson. At the least, "You'll understand your weaknesses." What's more, a multiyear, all-inclusive study of Jesperson's crimes, childhood, mind, and motives was a unique vein of serial killer research, untapped by many. I could get from Jesperson what few journalists had from any other serial killer: a true understanding of why he killed and what was going through his mind before, during, and after each murder, not to mention how he felt each time he took a life, and what made him continue to kill. This would become the fundamental thesis of my work: figuring out what Keith Jesperson *meant* by his crimes. Every criminal tells us something about him/herself by the crimes he or she commits. A pedophile says, for example, that he was abused in a similar fashion as a child; a burglar may tell us he is perhaps a dope addict and needs to steal in order to survive another day; a "one-off" murderer might be saying with her crime of passion that she surrendered to all of the anger built up over a period of time, and that one spur-of-the-moment act of violence was her way of releasing the pressure valve.

What was the implied psychology behind Jesperson's murders? What was he saying with his crimes? I understood that when he killed for the first time (Taunja Bennett), he unleashed a narcissistic, violent psychopath already present within him. I learned quickly that he can justify his crimes and believes his truth is the only truth; that he takes pleasure in being the infamous "serial killer" he became, Happy Face. But what was behind the emotional high that he took away from each murder? What did *he* get out of it? What made him cross the line the first time and allow him to kill seven additional victims?

With those questions in front of me, early into our relationship, as I was doing more listening than digging, I asked him.

"Look, I'm not downplaying who I am or making excuses for the eight murders I committed," he clarified. "I can explain the way I am and the way I think in this manner. When I got divorced and we were in court, I looked at my kids and they were in pain. But here's the thing—it made me feel warm inside to know that I was responsible for that pain. I actually was *happy* that they were suffering and would continue to suffer from the divorce."

Left there, this statement would feel, as it should, cold and callous. The urge is to write him off as *sick*. Twisted. A sadistic sociopath who enjoys lighting a match and watching the world around him burn. Yet, as Jesperson finished his thought, the true mind of the psychopath emerged.

"I cannot tell you why I felt this way," he concluded. "I just did. When my mother died, I felt nothing. It's like there's a dead zone inside of me."

After his divorce, Jesperson isolated himself. He felt lonely and ostracized by those closest to him. When he was young, he said, his father, Les, shouldered the blame unto him for whatever had gone wrong. As an example, he claimed, his father once put the shovel of a backhoe through the side of a house. Young Keith was working with Dad at the time. Dad, Jesperson insisted, went in and told the homeowner that Keith had done it.

"And that is just a small example," he told me. "As we get to know each other and build a trust, I'll explain more sinister and even deadly instances regarding Les."

With a failed marriage, a girlfriend who had taken off on him, unemployed, thinking about a job that would place him in the cab of a truck 24/7, Jesperson held a strong emotional connection to someone who had been kicked out of the world or tossed aside, a common delusion many mass murderers (which he is not) would share.

I wanted to understand what went on in the deep recesses of a serial killer's mind and the psychological torment these types of people wrestle with daily as they contemplate taking a human life. I read mostly all material (clinical, journalistic, highly creative, true or not) available about Jesperson. In those days before I reached out to him, I'd made up my mind about Happy Face, judging and hating him with an intensity I made clear on *Dark Minds*. I decided he was bad, evil, broken, however you want to put it. I felt he should be included in a group the central Alaskan Yup'ik Eskimos call *kunlangeta:* males within the tribe who rely on lying, stealing, cheating, and sexual exploitation of females to guide them through life.

As I got to know him, however, I never expected to come to the place I did with Jesperson and learn things about myself, my family, about his crimes and motivations, his thoughts about other crimes and killers, his philosophy about life and art and culture. Nor had I planned to interview him for five years.

"Be ready," John Kelly, also a certified forensic therapist, warned. "You better be ready emotionally when you pick up that phone or write a letter or sit in front of this man. Don't let him catch you off your guard. Always be the brand, M. William Phelps, with him. Never be Mathew."

Kelly, who had been corresponding with and talking to a serial killer for ten years by then, helped me understand I needed to play a role when speaking to Jesperson. Be his "friend," if he needed one. His confidant. His conduit and connection to the outside. His Clarice.

"You will become the surrogate 'good' father he never had," Kelly explained. "But there will be psychological issues that you will have to deal with yourself—a price to pay. Don't fall for his charm. It will break you."

I kind of laughed inside at Kelly when he said this. I thought I was tough.

THROUGHOUT OUR FRIENDSHIP, WHENEVER an issue with prison mail not getting to him arose, or maybe the phones not working correctly, a crackle or hiss on the line while we spoke, or even when he was disciplined for bad behavior, Jesperson maintained that "the man" was trying to stop him from telling the "real Taunja Bennett story." He believed there was some sort of conspiracy to keep him from telling his truth.

"They don't want it out," he said.

It got to the point where he would begin to qualify a rant about corruption or censorship with, "Call me paranoid, Phelps, but . . ."

Hearing this, I'd roll my eyes. The reality is that the type of wrongful conviction involved in the Bennett murder happened. Not often. But no court of law is 100 percent flawless. It is part of the course of justice. Both Laverne Pavlinac and John Sosnovske admitted to killing Taunja Bennett. They provided evidence. They gave statements about evidence cops had not released publicly, and Pavlinac, as cops brought her out to where Jesperson had dumped Bennett's body, pointed to within "ten feet" of where Bennett had been found. In court, on the witness stand, Pavlinac admitted to murdering Bennett with Sosnovske.

Jesperson had heard stories from fellow inmates accusing cops of abuse and corruption. The chatter inside a prison about law enforcement and the court system is, as one might suspect, abundantly negative. On top of that, we've all seen death row inmates released after some miracle DNA analysis came through. But this *Times* article had set Jesperson on a different path, supposedly giving him a clear view of his case (six years hence), one of which he'd not seen before that moment of so-called clarity in his cell. He believed an injustice had occurred, not a mistake. He felt, after reading and re-reading Barry Siegel's article, there was no end to how far "they" had gone to make a case against Laverne and John. When I came on board, his entire narrative was built around this argument.

"Understand this. After reading Siegel's article, I knew their arrests and convictions were *not* a mistake," Jesperson said. "And the problem is, if you go back into this case and look at how it developed"—he meant the investigation and prosecution—"you will see they *knew* what they were doing when, in my opinion, they went *after* [Laverne and John]."

From the moment he agreed to take part in *Dark Minds*, Jesperson sent me page after page, letter after letter, debasing Oregon politics and judicial incompetence. I'd open these letters, sit in my office, and sometimes read for hours.

His first murder, he maintained, and everyone involved on an investigatory and prosecutorial level, became an abyss of venality. What's important within the context of his narrative is that Jesperson would often tell me that had he been arrested for the Bennett murder—or an attack on a woman months later—in 1990 and charged with either crime, seven of his victims would still be alive. He was, effectively, blaming the wrongful prosecution of two people for the murders of seven women.

Was he looking for someone—the incompetence of law enforcement—to shoulder the blame for his crimes? I thought. It seemed about right.

I explained to him whenever we spoke that there were major problems in accusing cops and prosecutors of wrongdoing and bias in the Bennett case: Namely, Laverne Pavlinac and John Sosnovske had admitted to the murder and were convicted by a jury. What cop would not take a confession with details of the crime and facts about the crime scene from two suspects claiming they had committed it? "I didn't plan to kill her," Laverne Pavlinac had said during her trial while crying on the witness stand. "I didn't mean to. . . . It's my fault. . . ."

How much more evidence does a cop, prosecutor, or jury need? Pavlinac came across as a grandmother: fifty-seven years old, gray hair, large tortoiseshell glasses, a calm and gentle demeanor. After Bennett's body was found and the media reported it, she first told police while calling in an anonymous tip that Sosnovske had "bragged about the crime" to her. Then, after failing to get the re-sponse she desired (Sosnovske's arrest), she met with investiga-tors and told them flat-out Sosnovske had murdered Bennett, whose body had been found near the bank of the Columbia River Gorge. Bennett had been strangled and beaten to death, a liga-ture tied around her neck. Her face had been so brutalized the medical examiner (ME) could not at first tell if she was male or female, Caucasian or African American. Her pants were down around her ankles, her panties still on. Some reports claimed she was raped. ("There was some vaginal trauma," the prosecutor, Jim McIntyre, told me.) A piece of her jeans—the button fly—had been cut out and Pavlinac had produced what appeared to be that missing piece of Bennett's jeans, along with Bennett's purse, which Pavlinac claimed to have found in the trunk of her car after Sosnovske had used it on the night Bennett went missing. She told police she and Sosnovske met Bennett at a Portland bar, and Sosnovske forced her to help him rape and kill Bennett and dis-pose of her body.

When Jim McIntyre heard Pavlinac utter those words in open court, he pointed at her and told jurors: "You listen to those words and that emotion and you will look at Laverne Pavlinac and see the face of a murderer."

Every piece of evidence, at least from the jury's perspective, fit. Laverne Pavlinac was tried and convicted in 1991. John Sosnovske, scared of facing the death penalty, took a plea bargain months later.

"And I had a free ticket to continue killing," Jesperson told me. "I saw this on the news [in 1991] and could *not* believe it. I had killed this woman and these two had not only admitted to it, but were in prison for the murder."

3

A DARK MIND

"The answer is that we don't choose our freaks, they
choose us."
—Steve Almond, *Candyfreak*

*I*NTRODUCED MYSELF TO JESPERSON IN A LETTER DATED SEPTEMBER
5, 2011. Between then and late 2016, I maintained consistent and
constant contact with him, resulting in over 600 letters he wrote
to me, culminating in approximately 7,000 pages of text. I have
received twenty to thirty pages of letters per week (some of which
remained unopened until I started writing this book, simply because I did not have the emotional fortitude or time to keep reading the ramblings from a mind unhinged). We spoke on the phone
weekly for most of the five years, sometimes three or four times per
week.

Serial killers suck the life out of the people around them. They
harbor an effortless capability of donning what psychopathy pio-
neer and psychiatrist Hervey Cleckley coined in 1941 as "the
mask of sanity." It was Cleckley's work before his death in 1984
that flexed Canadian psychologist Dr. Robert Hare's mental muscle enough to develop his Psychopathy Checklist (PCL-R): twenty
characteristics defining psychopathic behavior. Used properly,
the PCL-R checklist is an accurate way to determine the psychopath from the non-psychopath.

At first, it was difficult for me to toss out any preconceived notions—*He's just plain evil*—I had about Happy Face and enter into

a new way of critical and clinical thinking. What I realized during those early months while talking to him was that Jesperson, a teenage coal miner (among other blue-collar jobs he held) from Chilliwack, British Columbia, Canada, loved who he has become in the spectrum of American crime history. He relished his identity of being known in and out of prison as an infamous serial killer, a label that both defines and gives him an identity of celebrity status many serials crave. He projected the notion that his story is *the* serial killer story all others should be modeled after and studied. The obsessive nature of his personality was obvious in the way he steered nearly every comment and analysis about justice and the legal system toward his argument that "two innocent people were arrested, convicted, and sentenced for a murder *I* committed" because of manipulation and a cover-up. That so-called injustice was the point of launch for Jesperson's entire existence today.

As Jim McIntyre pointed out to me during a conversation, without the controversy surrounding Jesperson's first murder and two people being arrested, convicted, and sent to prison for four years for a crime he committed, the Happy Face moniker (a total media creation, according to Jesperson), and additional misconceptions about what he's done, Keith Jesperson is just another serial murderer doing time. He would be a Mr. Nobody, a pathological liar, and a con. After all, there are over one hundred serial killers, sans nicknames and notoriety, unknown to most, serving time in American prisons. The arrest and conviction of Laverne and John, Jesperson agreed, turned him into Happy Face, the diabolical serial murderer, and forced him into behaviors he would have never considered, including the "Happy Face" letters he wrote to the media, the cat-and-mouse ploy with law enforcement that followed, many of his big lies, and, especially, the smiley face he doodled on a letter one day that has become his legacy.

I asked Jesperson if he considered himself a freak of nature, abnormal.

"No," he said. I could tell the question made him mad.

"Explain."

"Freaky people are people out of the norm. A misunderstood

person is someone who is different than someone else. We [serial killers] have our way of looking at things, and if we don't look at things the way 'normal' people do, we're considered an off-lander, a freak."

I asked if he thought he was misunderstood.

"All the time."

"In what way?"

"I look at things differently than a lot of people do because I have an open mind—I *don't* have a closed mind. A lot of people have this closed idea of what life should be. I've seen both sides of it. I feel that I understand it differently."

"How is it that I misunderstand you?"

"Well, you're not a murderer. You take the stance of law and order. You cannot understand a killer's concepts one hundred percent. You try to, but you are caught between a rock and a hard place because you never crossed that line into murder."

Utterly ridiculous, I thought, without telling him.

I'd hang up the phone on days such as this and feel the need to take a walk with my black Lab, Ava. She'd run in a nearby cornfield while I contemplated what in the hell I had gotten myself into. After only a few months in and I had begun to suffer bouts of anxiousness, my heart racing, subtle pains pulsing in my stomach, butterflies I sensed would one day manifest into something more severe.

Beyond his work on the television series, I allowed Jesperson to bang on about his first victim, Taunja Bennett, and his absolute fanatical need to make sure the public understood how the facts of that crime (according to him) had been, right down to the smallest detail, misconstrued and lost in the embodiment of a culture and media obsessed with glorifying murderers.

"The Bennett case," he said—within the context of the psychopath's grandiose way of trying to convince me how superior his case is to any other serial killer case in history—"will have a serious impact on the death penalty in Oregon, if not the whole United States."

My aim in the beginning when listening to his gibberish was

not to get in the way and counter with the obvious pushback. Instead, I let him say what he needed. Through that, I could better understand whom I was dealing with and design a plan to get out of him what I needed.

Further, he said, "We can only hope we killers can get someone to write the story as it is *meant* to be told . . . [but] a general consensus is that we never agree with what is [written] about us."

During the first year, save for his *Dark Minds* analysis, the Bennett case was all Jesperson talked about. As he explained his position, I asked myself if what Jesperson was so obsessively stuck on could hold any validity. What if he *was* right? I had to be open to the possibility, despite thinking he was nothing more than a twisted psychopath looking to further his fifteen minutes and take a poke at the justice system in the process, using me as a bullhorn.

"I will point you in the right direction," he explained before oddly switching to the third person, adding, "and let you dig to your heart's content to see if Keith is telling you the truth." He promised that "sooner or later" a "lightbulb" would turn on inside me and I'd experience an "Oh my God" moment as it pertained to the Bennett case. "Just be patient, Phelps. Open to it."

In January 1991, while Bennett's real killer was on the loose, preparing to strangle more victims, a jury convicted Pavlinac of "felony homicide." Weeks later, her "coconspirator" in the murder, the alleged muscle behind the brutal beating and alleged rape of Bennett, Pavlinac's live-in boyfriend, John Sosnovske, pleaded "no contest" to the same charge. They both received life sentences, were sent upstate to prison, and long forgotten about.

It seemed almost ludicrous to believe that a convicted, admitted serial killer, known to lie about himself and his crimes, years later, after his arrest and admission of eight murders, would still anchor such a deep-seated need to initiate a campaign against the *Times*, Jim McIntyre, and the detectives involved, to undermine all that had been said. And why, moreover, did it even matter what Jesperson now claimed? Why should anybody care?

Getting the Bennett case right, Jesperson told me, was the sole reason why "I haven't slit my throat or hanged myself in prison."

As our correspondence and phone calls kicked into high gear during production of *Dark Minds,* Jesperson explained, "It is time for the public to find out exactly what took place here with the murder of Taunja Bennett, conviction of Laverne and John, and the injustice that followed. I'm responsible for *my* crimes. I need others to do the same."

I started to listen more attentively.

"Every time I pull out the L.A. *Times* story," he wrote, "I see the same thing." In this instance, he focused on dates, explaining that one of the detectives in the case had gone over to see Laverne on October 4, 1995. "But is it October fourth for real?"

This seemingly minor discrepancy revealed itself to him when he realized the day he was polygraphed in the case had been "Friday, October 6," and the article referred to the detective interviewing Laverne "on the following day." So it could not have been October 4. "And what is stranger," he added, "they *knew* I was scheduled to be tested. Why go see Laverne *at all* just before the test?"

His answer: "To try to get her to include me in their murder story—come up with a deal to save face."

According to Jesperson's lawyer, Thomas Phelan, the prosecution, at one time, "wanted to make a case that Jesperson and John and Laverne killed Bennett together."

It's a generous leap: from making a mistake on a date to accusing law enforcement of corruption and coercion. But that is the epicenter of Jesperson's Bennett argument: coincidences and errors and mistakes become grander and more conspiracy-minded as one delves deeper into the case. According to Jesperson, it's not only about Jim McIntyre and his cops. In his paranoid mindset, Jesperson believes a conspiracy took place at the highest level in order for the prosecution of Laverne and John to move forward.

"You could say Oregon has a double standard in dealing with the press and me."

The Bennett murder details are no secret, at least those that have been made public. Jesperson never went to trial, so the only source is his personal testimony, any evidence left behind, available law enforcement reports, hearings, and interviews with those involved. This murder, arguably Jesperson's first, is the egg from which seven others are hatched. I wanted a detailed account of this crime, from the moment he woke on that day until he dumped Bennett's body along the Columbia River Gorge and considered taking his next victim. I asked for his story backward and forward, from the middle to the end, from the end back to the middle. The truth, I've learned from interviewing hundreds of sources throughout my career, is not something one can lie about repeatedly and get right. The truth is absolute. It never changes. To catch a liar, you ask him or her to tell the story over and over. Cops do this with the proverbial, *Okay, let's go through it one more time.*

Now, while we could argue for and against Jesperson's motivations in wanting to tell the Bennett story and, following along with his delusional way of thinking, charge that a conspiracy to railroad two innocent people took place, the murder itself tells us a tremendous amount about who Keith Jesperson—the serial killer—is. For one, serial killers fall into two categories: organized and disorganized. The organized killer leaves behind his unique mark of logic and planning, carefully and methodically, over a period of time, he puts into the crime. He cautiously chooses his victims, selecting only those he deems the perfect fit for whatever fantasy runs on an endless loop inside his head. All of his victims are easy to handle and he can get them into his comfort zone without much resistance: kids, prostitutes, homeless, elderly, and the sick. The organized killer is in control throughout the entire process: from the hunt to the ruse he uses to abduct or convince his prey he is harmless, until the kill itself. He is cautious about leaving evidence behind and meticulous about cleaning up after himself. He conceals his victims' corpses with the utmost attention and perfection and will tend to leave his victim in a posed state, however obvious.

The disorganized serial killer, on the other hand, kills in the heat of the moment. His victims might fight back because he did not choose well. He's sloppy and dumps his victims without thinking about where, or any potential (or subsequent) consequences. He might abduct or kill in "high-risk" environments. He has little control over himself, his impulses, or his anger.

With Jesperson's first murder, he fell somewhere in between organized and disorganized. The murder itself, his victim of choice, and the location of the kill were disorganized, while everything he did afterward was somewhat organized. It was as if once he set that killer inside free, the knowledge to complete and conceal the job was there and, after being called upon, kicked into action. He knew what to do.

"My beginning as a serial killer," Jesperson explained, "started on Saturday, January 20, 1990, when I met Taunja Bennett. Before that day, I did not plan on killing anyone—and never thought about becoming some sort of diabolical, evil, infamous serial killer the media has turned me into. It didn't happen that way."

"You did embrace who you became, however?"

"Embrace?" He laughed. "I *am* that person."

4

SOME SICKNESS

"Evil would never bring Good, however much they wanted
to believe that it would. By the time they discovered the
truth, it would be too late."
—Paulo Coelho, *The Devil and Miss Prym*

H̲E SLEPT IN THE LIVING ROOM, A MATTRESS ON THE FLOOR. THIS
morning, the television was flickering, a pulsating, snowy storm of
tiny dots and strobes, which eventually woke him. He'd fallen
asleep while watching a late-night movie. Opening his eyes, adapt-
ing to this day where, by its end, he would go to sleep a killer,
Keith Jesperson felt different. The moment he got out of bed on
any morning, Jesperson said, was his favorite part of the day. A
fresh twenty-four hours lay ahead. Anything was possible. The
past was gone. The present there in the moment. The future unknown. A new day offered a chance to start over.

On this particular morning, the fog hovering over Portland,
Oregon, gave him a peculiar feeling. The sun, as he recalled, was
"trying to break through," but couldn't quite manage. When he
got up from the floor mattress and opened the front door, a cold
rush of northwestern air struck him. He didn't mind. But there
was, as he called it, a *"Groundhog Day"* sense to his life recently, a
feeling of déjà vu he had a hard time shaking.

"Each morning had become . . . just like the other," he said.

Jesperson was not a drinker. In contrast to a majority of serial killers, Jesperson maintained that—save for killing—he had no addictions.

On Saturday, January 20, 1990, Jesperson was living alone in a small one-level ranch-style home at 18434 NE Everett Street in downtown Portland. He'd moved into the house with his girl-friend, Pamela Madison (pseudonym), who had run off with an-other man, a trucker, he said, to Tennessee in the weeks before he met Bennett. The house, owned by Pamela's mother, was not far, "just five blocks," from the B&I Tavern on Stark Avenue in the east end of Portland.

Early afternoon, Jesperson found his way to the B&I Tavern to "shoot some pool." He'd spent the morning roaming through town on foot, stalking a few women, checking the lay of the land, a need for sex driving every step. He liked to jog or walk most places. Growing up in British Columbia amid acres of farmland, it was in his nature to be on foot as much as possible.

I asked how he felt that day. I wanted a sense of what was going through his mind. Anger? Rage? A sexual desire so strong he could not suppress? Was he upset? Was he missing Pamela? Think-ing about his ex-wife? Mad about something in particular? What *was* it?

"Right or wrong, guilty or innocent, it is no longer black or white, but gray," he said.

This was in response to a direct question I'd ask many times throughout our interviews: *Did you rape these women you murdered?* You read anything about Keith Jesperson and rape is part of the narrative. Yet, he told me many times he never raped any of them. I was under the impression—though I didn't share my thoughts at this time—that his idea of rape and the actual crime hold dif-ferent meanings.

"Rape is not about anger," he said. Anger being, without a doubt, Jesperson's foremost trigger in committing any act of violence. "It is about sex. Period. But society has gotten used to blaming it on some sickness."

On days like this, after speaking with him, my chest tightened, my stomach twisted in knots. I'd suffered issues with digestion most of my adult life. As I allowed Jesperson into my head, those disorders, for which I'd always had a handle on, became more profound and difficult to manage. He was getting to me.

While we discussed what he has learned in prison from the rapists around him, his ex-wife, Rose, came up. Jesperson's ex-wife is a focal point of his psychosis. He builds many of his arguments and defenses, including justification for the murders, around the dissolution of his marriage, his divorce, a self-proclaimed nonexistent sex life the last two years of his marriage as the impetus, claiming all of it contributed to him becoming a serial killer.

During January 1990, he explained, he'd experienced sweaty nightmares depicting friends having sex with Rose. He felt as if Rose had replaced him too fast by remarrying within "months" after their divorce, at a time when he still loved her. There were behaviors on Rose's part, he added, during their later years together, which he hated about her, but he understood that they had taken place within the ebb and flow of a long-term commitment and marriage. The one aspect of their marriage during its final phase that bothered him most was Rose shutting him off sexually. "Go stick it in a keyhole" was a common Rose statement, he claimed—one that made him angry every time she uttered it. He would then be "forced" to masturbate angrily, while blaming his wife for the need he developed to seek other women and frequent prostitutes.

"Rose said 'no' to me a lot," he said. "And no meant *no*! So if I wanted to get off, I had to masturbate—or find some woman that didn't say no—and we pay for sex for a reason. We *know* we will get what we pay for."

THE GIRL STANDING AT the bar when Jesperson walked into the B&I that January afternoon was attractive in a no-frills sort of way: dark hair (more brown than black), pretty eyes (reassuring and playful), a coy, charming smile. The one drawback—or maybe it wasn't in the end for Jesperson—was that she came across as scatterbrained and distracted. Jesperson didn't like this about her from the get-go. It was a turnoff. He was thirty-four years old. He

didn't know it in that moment, but twenty-three-year-old Taunja
Bennett's seemingly carefree, "loose" nature was due to what a
family member told me was a "retarded condition" she developed
from not receiving enough oxygen at birth.

Jesperson described Bennett running up to him as soon as he
bellied up to the bar, throwing "her arms around me in a hug," as
if they'd known each other.

She became aggressive, clingy. He could smell the consequence
of smoking cigarettes and drinking draft beer on her. It was rank,
pungent. Still, as Bennett hugged him, he "got a hard-on" and felt
"sex was in the air."

She likes me for some reason, he thought. *But why is she being so
friendly?*

He looked over at the bartender for insight. The bartender
twirled her index finger in a circle next to her head, indicating
she thought Bennett was "crazy." Which gave Jesperson even more
reason to believe Bennett was going to wind up in his bed by the
end of the afternoon.

There can be no doubt Jesperson views most women inside a
prism of what they can do for him. He has no respect for females.
He sees women as a means to an end, and that end generally involved sex, either bought and paid for, consensual, or forced.
Cautious with Bennett, however, during the early afternoon of
January 20, Jesperson felt she was looking to swindle drinks out of
him, nothing more. He soon judged her as the type of woman he
was uninterested in. Looking around the bar, he felt "angry eyes"
glaring back at him whenever he met the stare of the other men.
This made him even more uncomfortable. Bennett was a pawn,
he considered, sent over to play him.

"She's not all there," the bartender told Jesperson after Bennett walked away.

Bennett sat at a table with two men. Jesperson "saw no reason
to chase after her when she had two [guys] already wanting to get
into her pants. . . ."

He walked out of the bar, around the corner, out of sight, on
his way back to the house he shared with Pamela Madison.

At home. Bored. Jesperson made a pot of coffee and took a shower while it percolated. He thought about where to go out that night. He couldn't stay home. Waiting for Pamela to finish screwing her latest conquest and come home to him was not going to work. Pamela could be back in the morning, a week, a month, who knew?

Married on August 2, 1975, to Rose Pernick, though the relationship had been over long before, their divorce was finalized in April 1989, just under a year before Jesperson ran into Taunja Bennett. "I didn't really want to divorce my wife, but I didn't like the way it was going," Jesperson said. "Once we were separated, it was a foregone-conclusion kind of thing. I didn't . . . want it to happen this way, but I had no control over it."

His life—postdivorce, leading up to meeting Bennett—"started spiraling." He "lost sight of what was important. . . . I wasn't seeing my kids. I was just creating a bad situation around me and I was getting angrier at the fact that here I am, I'm working, I am continuing to work, and every time I try to work a little harder and push forward, I am being pushed back."

In the middle of a winter layoff (that pushback), Jesperson had nothing but free time.

Sex with Rose became "nonchalant," Jesperson further explained. "It became an issue that probably two years before [the divorce] *wasn't* an issue." Not having sex with Rose was a turning point. "I short-circuited."

Home that afternoon, he thought about what to do for the rest of the evening. He perceived Bennett as an easy conquest, one he could persuade into coming back to the house for some drinks and sex. So he designed a plan. "Pick up Bennett [with the hope of] being able to seduce her into a sexual episode. I saw her as sex only." With Pamela gone, "My hope was to have a willing woman to share a bed with me for a while."

I'm going back, he told himself, getting up off the recliner, that pot of coffee swishing inside his belly. It was almost 5:00 P.M. He drove to the B&I this time.

Although he claimed all of this was random and he was only

looking for a "one-night stand" because he and Pamela had a history of "falling apart and making up," Jesperson understood his limitations. In a letter to me, his first objective in heading back to the B&I, seeking out Bennett, was to "get her in my car." He'd spent that late afternoon at home building up an invented scenario around Taunja Bennett. He wanted a woman waiting for him anytime he desired her. Bennett was now *that* target. She was someone who could fulfill this fantasy. It wasn't about a one-night stand. Until Pamela was back home, begging him to forgive her, he said, "Anyone [could] satisfy my wanting of a woman in my bed."

First, though, he needed to get Bennett into his comfort zone— that car he was driving, which he'd borrowed from a friend. "Once I did that, I felt my charm would carry me. . . ."

5

THE IMPATIENT MANIAC

"Idleness is fatal only to the mediocre."
—Albert Camus

*P*SYCHOPATHS HAVE AN EXTREME NEED FOR STIMULATION. ONE OF
the core struggles for the imprisoned psychopath is that if nothing is happening within a repetitive, structured environment, he tends to initiate action of some sort. The psychopath is quickly bored with life (in general) and cannot sit idle and watch the world pass by; it's not in his nature to "relax." He needs to be continually doing something. What's more, most serial killers are hypersexual, overactive needs of which can be attributed to a number of causes: sexual abuse as a child, being exposed to violent pornography at an early age, sexual experimentation with siblings. As for Keith Jesperson, he has upheld that he was never sexually abused, but as a child he had exposed himself (after being asked) to an adult male neighbor and spent many a night listening to his parents engage in sexual intercourse in the room next to his.

I wondered if Jesperson's victims, as he lived life behind bars, were a part of that need for perpetual stimulation, either sexually or otherwise. Books, Hollywood, and unscripted true-crime television have given us the clichéd image of the serial killer in prison, arms folded behind his head, lying in his cell, reliving his crimes, while getting a high (sexual or otherwise) from the memories. Does a serial killer, in fact, go back to those intense, violent moments when he took a life and relive them for his own personal and/or sexual gratification?

"You ever dream or flash back to the moment when you killed one of your victims?" I asked. Jesperson's manner of murder was personal; with the exception of Taunja Bennett, he strangled his victims, which meant he stared into their eyes and watched them die. He'd said things to me while talking about the moment of death: "She pissed herself" or "She shit her pants" after "I put her out of her misery." She "foamed at the mouth" and "spit on me." This meant he was there with them, in the moment, at the point of death. What was it like for him being incarcerated for twenty years? Were his victims still a part of him? Was he scared to go back? Had he put them out of his mind completely and purposely? This would become a contentious issue between us later as I began to work on identifying two of his Jane Does, asking him to recall faces, features, details, names, and demand he draw a portrait of a particular victim in Florida. But early into our interviews, while I was gathering information and listening more than questioning, he provided what I believed then to be an honest answer.

"I don't think I actually go back to that point in time where I kill the victims. I remember mostly about what we were doing, what we have done. And some of them I don't ever try to get back into their world. I don't *want* to remember. After I murdered them, I wanted to forget them. Therefore, for a long time, I just kept pushing the memories out of my mind. Only after I was arrested did I have to start owning up to the fact that I *did* this. Then I had to come up with the story line for my lawyer."

We discussed a comment he'd once made, which I considered a predetermined, calculated delusion he'd devised to face the reality of murder and the monstrosity behind his crimes: *There are no coincidences in murder.* One of his catchphrases, Jesperson used this line with me on many occasions.

"Everyone thinks there's . . . that the solution to murder is like a map," he explained. "You follow a road and that all roads lead [you there]. Well, I don't think all roads lead to murder. There's no coincidence in the fact that things happen and people say things happen for a reason."

This was one of the ways in which he justified the horror he'd brought upon his victims and their loved ones. He needed to preserve a clear-cut image and answer (a way out) for the trajectory his life took; he needed to feel that it was not by his doing alone he happened upon these women and they wound up dead.

I would hear him say things like this and want to reach through the phone; I grew angrier each time he tried to take the sting out of what he'd done and reobjectify his victims. Still, I stuck to my early plan of allowing him to say what he needed, knowing I would confront him about it all at a later time.

He broke into a rant about a divine being, noting God was not what he meant. He laughed at how some people believe life has a grand design, and others have faith that there is life after death.

"You're a Catholic, aren't you, Phelps?" he said with his snarky, sarcastic, characteristic laugh, which made me seethe with hatred for him. "Your God controls everything you do, am I right?"

I'd never said anything to him about my religion. He was fishing. "We're talking about you," I responded. "Let's keep the focus on *you*."

"Oh, right. Sorry. . . . That I am acting on behalf of a playwright named God and just doing His will," he continued in a flippant tone. "So *I* don't have any choice in the matter. I do not believe in that. We *have* a choice. And whether this person is expected to be the one I kill or the one I *don't* kill, I do not know. Timing is everything." He dropped his voice, paused. I could tell he had taken himself back to the moment of violence, perhaps reliving it. Then, in a near whisper: "That's just the way . . . it . . . it works out."

THE PARKING LOT OF the B&I was full when Jesperson drove around the corner and pulled in. Finding himself at the same bar now for the second time within twelve hours, he parked at a spillover lot on a side street nearby. As he opened the door into the bar, a burst of crowd energy struck him. The atmosphere was far different from earlier that day when, as a local gin mill, dark and quiet, nothing more than a few regulars and a bartender polishing glasses filled the space. Now it was lively, boisterous: patrons yelling, tipping back beers, clanking glasses and bottles, a haze of cigarette smoke lingering. Every pool table was filled, players waiting in line, quarters stacked up on the railed, green felt.

The plan was to "sweet-talk," while shooting a game of pool, either Bennett, if she was around, or another woman "into a romp in either her car or mine." Jesperson played down the idea that as he left Pamela's house and drove back to the B&I, he had Taunja Bennett exclusively on his mind. But in several of our follow-up conversations, he told me that, in fact, he was hoping on Bennett being there because he knew she'd be easy to charm out of the bar and get alone.

Normally, he would have never hung around a bar. But being laid off, no wife, and now no girlfriend, Jesperson found himself with idle time, unable to tolerate the redundancy of his life and that relentless sexual drive inside him. For a guy like Jesperson, with so many negative thoughts constantly running on a loop inside his head, downtime was the enemy; it allowed him to focus on his failed marriage or, he said, his tenuous and abusive relationship with his father, Les Jesperson.

"You're nothing—a piece of shit on a stick," his father had allegedly said more times than Jesperson claimed he could recall. "I was his whipping post. His faults in life were my doing. He blamed me for everything."

At the time that he met Bennett, Jesperson was an out-of-work heavy-equipment operator, collecting unemployment. He'd been labeled an over-the-road trucker near this period of his life. But that was a job he would not take until after he murdered Bennett.

All of his free time was an itch; his inactivity a scab. Jesperson felt inferior. He hated himself and his life.

Compared to Jesperson, Bennett was a peanut. "Petite," he called her. But anyone, essentially, was *petite* when put next to this enormous man.

Standing by the bar, Jesperson spied Bennett, now alone, standing by herself, digging through her purse. All that week, he'd obsessed about a recurring fantasy of making a woman his sex slave. It had been some time since he'd had sex. It was an admission that played into a fact that once stalking is set in motion, planning and purpose grow, the fantasy deepens, and this new reality, however contrived, feels genuine, becoming the psychopath's new normal. Impulse can be difficult to suppress, particularly right after a broken love affair or marital collapse. Jesperson faced both. Princeton political scientist George Kateb once explained it this way during one of his lectures: "You begin by telling a story, and the longer you tell it, the louder you say it, the more you're taken in by the deception that you thought you were putting over on someone else. It's now being put over on you by yourself."

When the same fantasy blows up in your face, in other words, that rejection becomes like acid.

Bennett seemed drunker. But she didn't have a drink in her hand.

Perfect, he thought.

As he studied her, Jesperson explained in a rather telling letter to me, he gave away how he viewed Bennett in this instance as his possession: "My crazy girl was done [partying] and leaving the building."

Thus, an opportunity presented itself.

Bennett walked toward the exit.

Claiming it was "something inside" that "made me jump . . . and go out into the parking lot to follow her," Jesperson decided to "make a move . . . to play upon her earlier expression of hugging me . . . [and] reconnect."

He saw Bennett "half drunk" and—as he would later describe all of his victims in the same degrading manner by placing the onus and blame on each of them—"looking for a meal."

If only I could get her into my car, he thought, searching the parking lot, looking to see if anyone else was around and watching. *I could get her to do what I wanted.*

He followed Bennett. She walked out of the B&I parking lot and wandered over to a nearby restaurant. He watched as she tried the door, then cupped a hand over her eyes to look inside, before realizing the place was closed.

"I don't have enough money on me to take you out to a restaurant," Jesperson told Bennett, sneaking up behind her. "But you come with me to my house and I'll get some more money."

It was a premeditated plan, he later admitted. Stalking Bennett in the parking lot, he considered: *How can I convince her to get into my car?* He then found a vulnerability—she was hungry—and made a ploy to exploit it. It was no different from the man with the candy offering it to the child walking down the street alone.

"You remember me?" he said. "You hugged me earlier."

He could tell Bennett thought about what he'd said.

"I do."

The sun had set. The air was thin, crisp, and cold. Jesperson used this to his advantage, mentioning how warm it was inside his vehicle, thinking, *I cannot force her into my car—there are too many potential hazards in doing that.*

Bennett failed to bite.

"Listen, we'll go eat and then go somewhere else and play pool," Jesperson told her, figuring she wanted to continue partying.

Without another word, Bennett then hopped into the passenger seat.

People in the neighborhood where Jesperson lived were "nosy and watched what was going on." He thought about this as he drove to the house.

I need to walk her into the front door without a struggle.

"Something told me to invite her into my house. That it was all

I had to do. I was being deviant, Phelps—my motive was to get her inside and hopefully be able to have sex."

Jesperson parked in the driveway. Turned off the car. "Why don't you come in for a moment until I find my money?"

He could tell Bennett was suspicious about the request and sensed a problem.

She looked at the house. Then back at Jesperson.

"She really didn't want to go in," he said.

6

ROOTLESS TREE

"It is wise to direct your anger towards problems—not
people; to focus your energies on answers—not excuses."
—William Arthur Ward

JIM McINTYRE WAS FRANK WHEN I SPOKE TO HIM ABOUT PROSECUTING
the wrong people for a murder neither had anything to do with;
he admitted his mistakes. The Bennett case and subsequent
wrongful prosecution for her murder was not a part of his career
McIntyre liked going back to after all these years. But as we talked,
the prosecutor opened up, mentioning a theory regarding why
Jesperson has become so obsessed with the idea of attributing the
blame for the wrongful arrests and convictions of Sosnovske and
Pavlinac to corruption and a choreographed conspiracy. Jesperson felt slighted, McIntyre explained, and did not get the attention he thought he deserved, especially from that *Los Angeles
Times* piece.

"It wasn't about *him*. That pissed him off."

Jesperson, on the other hand, responded, "When I got those
two people out of prison, McIntyre went to the L.A. *Times* and got
a story made, pretty much trying to make excuses for why they
were arrested in the first place."

That's unfair, actually. The *Times* reported a side of the story
not generally covered in headline-grabbing, serial killer tales
major media sometimes likes to perpetuate into salacious fodder.

"A Question of Guilt" went into great detail regarding how McIntyre was at fault. Moreover, it showed that McIntyre was a fallible human being and was going through a sticky divorce involving three young kids at the time he prosecuted Laverne Pavlinac and John Sosnovske. Those aren't excuses, the prosecutor pointed out. Just facts. Pavlinac's attorney, Wendell Birkland, was one of Oregon's most revered and feared defense attorneys. If you look at the trial and study what happened, it becomes clear McIntyre believed he was doing the best job, seeking proper justice, for his county. He led the prosecution against Pavlinac, determined to put away a woman who had *confessed* to a murder.

Jesperson said McIntyre and his investigators knew Laverne was a liar after talking to John's probation officer; she "couldn't be trusted and had a three-year history of crying wolf" about other crimes.

I began to sense that Jesperson was reaching on all of this, and I was wasting my time.

"They had to know she was lying because John never drove a car," Jesperson said. "McIntyre's whole prosecution and how he handled it is why we're here now. . . ."

I asked Jesperson if he was being paranoid again. Was he making McIntyre out to be the big, bad wolf? Was he trying to say the investigators involved made mistakes they did not want to admit—that it was ego-driven? I mean, serial killer (bad guy) and cop (good guy). It's inherent they should hate each other and point fingers, right?

"But it *wasn't* a mistake," Jesperson insisted. "They *built* a story based on speculation that *this* is what happened."

At times, Jesperson sounded like one of those killers representing himself in court. Desperate. Unable to articulate his story clearly—or, rather, a serial killer who wound up without full credit for his first kill and was now anxious to reclaim it. The fact of the matter is: Jim McIntyre prosecuted the wrong people. They were convicted by a jury based on the evidence. Jesperson came forward years later and was able to get them both released from prison, after four years, and exonerated. No one can change what happened. Thus, for Jesperson, the argument has to harken back to the way in which the investigation was conducted. It's his only recourse.

All of Jesperson's opinions, whether he will agree, are built on a foundation of speculation. For example, in a forty-seven-page letter outlining the problems he has with the *Times* article, Jesperson claimed the Bennett story was in the news after John and Laverne's arrests—which is true, obviously. He said John and Laverne could have read reports in the media about the murder and used that information to confess. True again. But he also says Laverne "would have been schooled by friends to expect visits from police and prosecutors seeking a solution to the problem" of their stories later falling apart. He claims when "guilty people get caught in the same type of crime . . . their answer" to law enforcement's question of "what happened?" is always "I don't know." Whereas Laverne and John had every detail sketched out for police when they came knocking.

Pure speculation. In the scope of the case, what Jesperson contends doesn't mean anything.

The first indication of John Sosnovske killing Bennett came in the form of two anonymous calls to the police, both of which claimed the caller had overheard him "bragging about killing Taunja Bennett." Sosnovske's name was then put into the system by police. He was on probation. He'd committed violent crimes in the past. On paper, he was a solid suspect. And once that first domino fell—albeit set in motion by Pavlinac—the rest followed.

Jesperson believes law enforcement took Laverne out to where he dumped Bennett's body and showed her the location. Yet, Laverne had a reasonable explanation for how she knew where to point when law enforcement drove just past the Vista House historical monument on the Historic Columbia River Highway in Corbett, Oregon, and asked if she knew where John had placed Bennett's body.

Bennett's body was found in a ravine along the Columbia River Gorge, about seven miles from where Jesperson lived with Pamela.

From Portland, you drive past the Lewis and Clark State Park on I-84, head south into the mountainous terrain in Corbett, then drive due east toward Rooster Rock State Park, where you come to the Vista House monument, a popular tourist observatory at Crown Point. The Vista House became a common, tired subject Jesperson always went back to. Pavlinac had told law enforcement she'd assisted Sosnovske in raping and strangling Bennett (with a ligature) on the steps leading up to the Vista observatory. The news had reported only that Bennett was found "about 1.5 miles from the Vista House, before Latourell Falls."

Pavlinac, while sitting in back of the cruiser as they drove near the area where Bennett had been found, stared at the odometer of the vehicle and counted the 1.5 miles after driving by the Vista House. "Right there," she said, pointing. So they stopped the vehicle. Along the roadside were spray-painted markings made by detectives indicating the approximate dump site.

It all seemed to fit.

"Look," Jesperson explained, "when I went out there with them later, *I* had trouble finding the spot myself—and I was the son of a bitch who put her there. What's more, think about this—they killed Bennett on the steps of the Vista House? How could cops believe this? That place has constant traffic, tourists, in and out, no matter what time or day or month of the year."

WHEN JESPERSON AND BENNETT arrived at Pamela's mother's house, Jesperson decided he was going to have sex with her. Not rape Bennett, mind you. That was never his intention, he said.

Timid about going into the house with a stranger, Bennett said, "I'm leaving my Walkman and purse here." She placed her Walkman on the seat, purse on the floor.

Jesperson said his "plan B," had Bennett insisted on waiting in the car, was to get her drunker than she was already at a local bar and take advantage of her after that. As he explained this, he mentioned his true fantasy was to wake up next to "a woman" the following morning. Any deviation from that perfect picture of a man and woman nestled together, spooning and snuggling, was grounds for his anger to appear.

Bennett got out of the car. They walked inside.

Jesperson went into his bedroom under the ruse of getting more money. She walked into the kitchen/dining room.

"My penis was telling me to try and bed her now while she is behind closed doors."

From his bedroom, Jesperson stepped into "the darkness of the hallway." He stood alone, in silence, for a brief moment, "watching her move around the [other] room. Her warm body available to my touch. All I had to do was reach out."

He decided to make a move and see what happened. His rationale? "She had made the first move on me at the B and I." Here he was back to that hug—a simple friendly gesture of affection by a mentally challenged, drunk girl in a bar.

"Now it was my turn to hold on to her."

As she stared at a "portrait of Jesus Christ on the wall" while standing in the kitchen, Jesperson snuck up behind Bennett and wrapped his arms around her midsection, as if they were two teens in love.

"My hard-on pressed against her back."

This was precipitated by a compulsive, patent sexual need he could not contain. Jesperson believed Bennett could "feel me, all of me." The scene as it now played out fit the fantasy: as she turned and (perhaps tried to wiggle away), he took her reaction as an invite to kiss her.

Bennett recoiled. She wouldn't kiss him back.

"I guess sex is out of the question, then, too?" he asked Bennett. She walked toward the door.

"No meant no," Jesperson explained to me. "I was, in my mind, in line to get sex with her to hopefully provide enough foreplay so she would be a willing sex partner. It was a gamble, Phelps. But I did not look at it *not* working."

He described what happened next, using the analogy of her being "a fly and I . . . a spider." Any hope he had of a "great experience" turned into "wishful thinking."

Still, this was not what made him angry.

He walked over to Bennett, who was now standing by the door. He then "led her over to my bed in the middle of the living room and pulled her down onto the mattress, kissing her, even though she didn't kiss me back."

Bennett stared at him. He could tell, from the look in her eyes, that "she was not in the 'having sex' mood. If I was to have sex, I'd have to take it from her."

Bennett must have known she could not stop a three-hundred-pound man from taking what he wanted. So she begrudgingly obliged, according to him, but not before saying, "Hurry up and get it over with."

In these words, Jesperson heard his wife: *Go stick it in a key-hole.* Overcome by intense and overwhelming feelings of shame, humiliation, and, of course, anger, a "cue"—he called it—had turned on inside him.

Was this a "trigger," that common term used when talking about serial killers, a reaction to life's stressors turning an evil switch, setting the psychopath on a course of which he cannot turn back from? Some experts claim a serial's "trigger" begins with the choice of victim: Jeffrey Dahmer, for example, and the "young muscular men" he murdered; Wayne Williams and the "poor, young black boys"; Ed Gein and "heavy, middle-aged women who resembled his mother." In Jesperson's case, however, one of his triggers centered on what a female in his presence said to him. Her race, what she looked like, color of her hair, age, size, eyes, none of that mattered.

He told me he knew in that moment that having sex with Bennett—if he had gone through with it—would have been rape, adding, "Often, sex with my wife Rose was like that. Not in the mood, she'd spread her legs and tell me to hurry up and get it over with." What's more, his life situation made him even "angrier." Mainly, "Pamela not being there to have great sex with." In Jesperson's world, the women are always to blame.

He straddled Bennett. Stared down at her.

"I had never struck a woman before."

The longer he looked into Bennett's eyes, "the angrier" he became "over the situation." He decided that letting her go at that point would turn out bad for him. He'd held her against her will. That alone, he said, would "land me in prison."

"How hard could it be?" he asked himself during this pivotal moment when he first contemplated murder as an option to resolve an emotional, social, and psychological conflict.

"How hard could *what* be?" I asked.

"To slug her in the face and knock her out, carry her to the car, and leave her someplace."

7

THE SPACE BETWEEN

"Why'd they all have to come to me to get killed?
Why couldn't they kill themselves?"
—Jim Thompson, *The Killer Inside Me*

*T*ALKING TO A SERIAL KILLER, INVOLVING YOURSELF IN THE MADNESS inside his head on a regular basis, is research I needed to view as a clinical experience, or convince myself that it was, anyway. I'm no forensic therapist or psychologist. I'm a journalist. Generally, my goal is to interview murderers, get their stories, and move on. Speaking for five years to a man who had murdered eight women in such an intimate, violent manner was never part of what I'd signed up for when I got involved with writing true crime back in 1997. But here I was intimately gripped by the Devil's talons.

As the months passed and we entered into a more structured, interviewer-interviewee relationship, Jesperson became comfortable with telling me his secrets. Some of what he said troubled me. He wrote me a long letter in 2012, for example, not for any particular reason other than to spout off about a fellow serial killer, Tommy Lynn Sells. Sells was executed in 2014 and claimed to be behind "dozens of murders," linked by law enforcement to seventeen, many of them children. Sells was the bogeyman. He once said: "I am hatred. . . . I don't know what love is."

Jesperson had written to Sells, trying to "organize" a "network" of incarcerated serial killers to trade information about people who write to them. Jesperson wanted to create a database of "good" and "bad" pen pals, those "who help" inmates and those "who are full of shit."

A serial killer union? I thought while reading this letter. *A directory? What in the name of hell?*

In corresponding with Sells, not realizing he was looking into a mirror, Jesperson found an arrogant, self-centered, narcissistic, ego-driven, "angry" man, "who felt the need to act tough" toward him.

"I laughed at his arrogance," Jesperson said of Sells. "If he was put near me, I think he would hide."

This letter, like many, was beyond the scope of what I'd ever planned to do with Jesperson. It was great water-cooler talk, but not the research I was interested in. Still, what I learned by talking to Jesperson about other serial killers was that in every Jesperson rant or diatribe another layer of who he is peels away without his real-ization. In this same letter about Sells, he said, "I don't think too much of him as a person. He claimed more deaths than he did."

One serial talking about the other: *I don't think too much of him as a person.*

In-fucking-credible. You sit back and think about this remark and it makes you realize you're dealing with someone, a true psychopath, who thinks in a totally different manner than most human beings, which is something the general public overlooks when consider-ing the mind of the serial killer. Unusual and irrational thoughts plague serial killers, as they have no capacity for gratitude or con-cern. Most people will see a bird with a broken wing and find it within himself to help; the sociopath walks by without consider-ing that the bird is hurt and likely sees himself kicking it out of his way. What's more, the public can easily get caught up in taking a lot of this for granted while watching serial killer films and dra-mas on television, along with so-called unscripted true-crime tele-vision, *Dark Minds* included, ultimately becoming desensitized to actual crime victims and their true stories.

Most letters and conversations with Jesperson often began with him talking about someone or something besides himself—Tommy Sells in this case—but then quickly coming back around to focus on him. In the Sells letter, Jesperson went on to talk about "stages of death to us killers." There were different levels, he explained, referring to his life as a serial killer: "Inside our [heads] we make up our minds on people we meet. Give a life span to those who cross our paths—even if we haven't physically killed them, our minds are convinced they are dead already. Any good feelings we have are gone. Since we have decided they are already dead to us, to physically kill them isn't too much of a step up to complete with no real emotion to carry it forward."

He's describing the process of detachment.

What concerned me morally as we continued was that allowing a serial killer the opportunity to talk about murder was, in itself, a form of stimulation, beyond him reliving his crimes in the silence of his own head. I feared that bringing Jesperson back to those moments when he took a life, which made him, at times, giggle with a schoolboy's adolescent jubilation, was catering to his stimuli, cravings, and psychopathy. It was unnerving to hear him laugh while explaining a murder in the most horrifically graphic terms, or when he repeatedly blamed his victims. He'd use the same line—"I put her out of her damn misery"—to explain each murder, not out of habit or lack of explanation, but because he truly felt this way about each of them. My insides twisted every time he said it. I could feel anxiety throbbing through my veins. My hands tightened. My muscles tensed. I gritted my teeth, forcing my temples to pulse. It was after these conversations when I'd notice myself becoming impatient with people. Short. Lashing out for no reason. Our so-called friendship was beginning to affect me, not only emotionally, but physically, mentally, socially.

I worried about feeding or fueling his ego. He took pride and pleasure in talking about his crimes. He'd accepted who he was. He relished the celebrity that those murders and becoming Happy Face had provided him. Was I adding to it? Was I revictimizing his victims?

The answer to all is yes. On film, as long as I kept him anonymous, I felt we were not glorifying him or his crimes. Throughout the two seasons of *Dark Minds* that Jesperson appeared, I needed to keep him as my villain. A violent thug and bully. Someone who pushed his way through life, trying to get people to do things for him he's too damn afraid or scared of doing himself. I have a resilient and honorable moral instinct. I consider myself a man who strives to do the honest thing all the time, as well as the best I can. I'm relentless and determined when I want something. I stand by my victims' advocacy work and the fact that in all of my books I strive to put the victim of murder front and center. Whenever I identified with Jesperson on a subject—say film, art, fishing, vacation destinations, television, literature, whatever—or we agreed and held the same opinions about politics or a news item, I'd hang up (or put the letter down), stare out my office window, and question my sense of self. How could I reconcile identifying with a psychopath/serial killer? Going in, I would have argued we had nothing in common. All serial killers are scumbags, cowards, and cannot speak intellectually about anything worth my time. But the more we spoke, it became clear we did. And this frightened me.

He'd ask about my family. I'd ignore the question, instead replying, "Let's keep it professional." Or, after not speaking for a few weeks, he'd wonder where I was and, perhaps in a moment of letting my guard down, I'd say my daughter had a series of volleyball games, or my wife's mother was ill, or I was traveling, researching a project. He'd catch me sometimes after I went to weekday morning Mass and I'd let him know where I'd been. In my emotionally stronger moments, I'd say: "Look, don't ask me about my personal life—that's my life *beyond* what we are doing and you don't *deserve* to be a part of it. Do you understand me?"

These tiny snippets of my life I allowed him access to would come up later. He'd work them into a conversation: "Well, you know what it's like, Phelps, you have a daughter playing high-school sports."

Any mention of my personal life was confounding; it infuriated me. Understanding a serial killer, what makes him who he is, what motivates the urge inside him to kill repeatedly, requires one to keep a certain amount of distance from the subject, particularly where emotion is concerned. I kept returning to John Kelly's advice: "Don't let your guard down . . . he'll get inside your head."

As we continued to talk and I felt an unusual comfortableness begin to settle on me whenever speaking to Jesperson, I thought, *Maybe he's already occupying that space.*

IT WAS QUIET IN the living room. No television. No radio. Just the sound of two people breathing. One heavier than the other. The rhythm of life and death. Outside, night had settled on Portland, and with it a batch of arctic air, crisp, sharp, mountain fresh, blowing in from the north. The moon was about a third visible, a sliver of a reflection magnified by the windowpanes onto the waxy wood floor beneath that mattress where Jesperson had Taunja Bennett restrained.

He straddled Bennett. Then, making a fist, he cocked his arm back and punched her as hard as he could on the side of her face. This one, crushing blow spattered blood everywhere: on his face and clothes, the mattress, the floor, the walls, a few droplets on the television screen.

"Could feel my fist strike . . . the target," he said matter-of-factly. "So I hit her again . . . then again."

A frenzy of blows, each one more ferocious than the next, followed. After each strike, Jesperson stopped to check, but "she would not go out."

"Of course, all Bennett had to do was say the wrong thing and I just exploded on her—that's where my anger was . . . I had no control over myself."

Because she was still alive after the initial blows, Jesperson beat Bennett with both his fists. One solid strike after the next. As he continued, he heard Bennett scream: "Mama . . . Mama, please make him stop hitting me."

Before long, Jesperson entered into a blackout rage. It came on like a hot flash; and by the time it let up and he looked down, he saw nothing but blood. Bennett was unrecognizable. He had no idea how many times he had struck her.

He claimed that no matter how many blows he landed, she would not succumb. So he continued punching and thrashing her face until, finally, she stopped moving.

"Killing someone was not like I had seen it on television," he recalled.

Stopping once again, he looked down and, now back for a brief moment from that place he'd gone off to, Jesperson saw a "broken face," adding, "Not only had I failed in getting sex from her, I also nearly beat her to death in my living room."

In a moment of pure sexual confusion and depravity, he decided "to remind myself why she was there. Sliding down, I unbuttoned her jeans and looked at her pubic hair and vagina."

He stared for a few moments.

"Looking at her all beaten up," while she continued to breathe and still squirm, "I knew I had to put an end to her life. No way would I allow her to live after what I had put her through."

He strangled Bennett with his hands, squeezing "with all" his "might for what seemed like an eternity."

Two minutes, at least, he assumed. He watched as his hands turned white from squeezing so hard for so long. It got to the point where he could not hold her neck any longer due to fatigue.

After releasing his grip: "I could hear her body suck in air to live. She came back. She was not dead."

He searched for what he called "a solution."

Making a fist, he buried it into her throat and, with all of his body weight, pushed down hard as he could. Holding this position, his elbow locked in place, Jesperson stared "at her vagina." He didn't do this for a sexual thrill, he later claimed; instead, he "waited for a sign of death to come." It took four minutes, but Bennett then "let go a stream of urine . . . and soaked my carpet."

8

DEATH BECOMES HIM

"Psychopaths: people who know the differences between
right and wrong, but don't give a shit. . . ."
—Elmore Leonard

*P*SYCHOPATHY—WHERE THE POPULAR AND PERHAPS OVERUSED TERM
psychopath is born—was derived from the German word psychopathischen. First use is credited near 1888 to German psychiatrist J. L. A.
Koch. Translated literally, psychopathischen means "suffering soul."
Interacting personally with a psychopath for as long as I have, you
begin to get a sense that when Robert Hare's PCL-R psychopathy
checklist—with items such as "superficial charm," a "need for
stimulation," "parasitic lifestyle," "promiscuous sexual behavior," "impulsivity"—is mentioned within the context of someone
such as Keith Hunter Jesperson, you clearly recognize how the
psychopath can hide behind "a perfect mimicry of normal emotion." Jesperson is a master at concealing the killer he was and the
psychopath he is. I've experienced his anger on a few occasions,
knowing in those instances he'd unleashed only a fraction of its
full force. Each time it put me in a position of understanding, for
one brief moment, on a much, much smaller scale, what his victims might have witnessed.

Dr. Kent Kiehl, neuroscientist and author of *The Psychopath
Whisperer,* a man who's dedicated his life's work to clinical brain
imaging in order to understand mental illness, especially criminal
psychopathy, says, 'The best current estimate is that just less than

one percent of all noninstitutionalized males age eighteen and over are psychopaths."

Although a psychopath is said to be born every forty-seven seconds (as compared to 250 births per minute of every day), luckily for the general public they are a rare breed. To speak with one for an extended period of time, however, in order to try and understand what goes on inside his mind, how he views the world, and discuss his innermost thoughts, I needed to allow him to talk at length about a subject not many of us like to confront.

Death.

In what has become a classic American essay, "The Storyteller," Walter Benjamin argues at one point all narrative is, partly, built on a foundation of, and always traveling toward, death. True or not, I can say that in the dozens of books I've written, death is at the center. Death is on our minds daily, not quite often as sex, but a close second. We do things to escape death. We do things to postpone and expedite death. All without having serious conversations about it.

I've always thought of a murder in a family as a stone tossed into the water, everything that happens to that family afterward the ripple effect, reverberating generation after generation forever. I've seen it in my own family with the murder of my sister-in-law. Though I do not share this feeling any longer, there was a time when I thought I'd had a penchant for understanding or maybe sensing death. Not that I am obsessed with death. Yes, I once volunteered at my local Catholic parish as the altar server for funerals. And my days are consumed with death in all forms. But my need stems from wanting to understand it. There's far too much we don't know about death. Most of us want to exist in a world where death is not the final curtain call, for there is life afterward.

In talking with Jesperson, death was a common topic of our conversations, whether openly or in context.

"Death is final," he said. "I don't see it in a religious context." For Jesperson, death is "the end." You die and become, in his words, "worm food."

As he talked through this thought, he mentioned how, when a

man dies, all of his accomplishments die with him, and cease to move forward any longer.

"So a legacy is important to you, then?" I asked.

"It is to a degree. . . . I don't see it as anything other than a remembrance of who the person was."

Jesperson asked me about intuition once. If I thought some people had the capability to feel the presence of death approaching. I changed the subject. I didn't want to hear his asinine philosophy about clairvoyance because he'd doled out death at will. His opinions about it didn't matter to me. Yet, I've always believed that if one was to put his ear close enough to his soul and listen, he *could* hear death coming

AS SHE GASPED FOR her last breath, the sounds Taunja Bennett made while dying shook Jesperson out of his element. He could hear her choking on her own blood, spittle popping like bacon grease from her mouth, her breaths shorter, quicker, with extended spaces in between—until finally there were none at all. Just the humming of the refrigerator motor in the kitchen nearby.

Jesperson had never killed anyone before Bennett. But as she lay on his mattress, "massive amounts of blood everywhere," and he watched her take those final breaths, her body stiff and motionless, in his mind he went back to a time when he'd killed a full-grown cat, thinking how it "peed and shit all over me when it died" and how Bennett did the same thing.

The myth of Keith Jesperson capturing and killing birds, cats, and dogs, in addition to strangling helpless kittens, would become renowned in the spectacle of his Happy Face persona. Anytime a serial killer can be linked to hurting, torturing, maiming, or killing animals, it feeds the stereotype and ups his popularity. Indeed, many serials have a history of animal cruelty. But many more don't. This indelible image of the diabolical serial murderer Keith "Happy Face" Jesperson killing animals was further expedited by Jesperson's daughter, Melissa Moore, in a book she wrote about him, along with several subsequent television and print appearances Mrs. Moore took part in afterward.

In the first chapter of that book, which Melissa dates "August 1984," Melissa writes about being five years old when her father hanged several kittens from a clothesline, pinned by their tails with clothespins, and watched as they clawed one another to death. The book says that she, her father, her mother, and her siblings lived then in a "quiet farming" community in Toppenish, Washington. She describes—in colorful detail—the yard, the alfalfa fields surrounding it, a "huge peach tree," her "baby sister" and "little brother" playing on the lawn, the "faint rustlings" of her mother, Rose, inside the house, keeping it "immaculately clean." Melissa recalls the smell of the basement being akin to "luscious flowers," and describes how a "stray farm cat" found its way onto the property and into the basement to give birth to four kittens Melissa soon adopted as her own.

It is a dramatic, detailed story of a child, drinking tea in the basement of a farmhouse, an almost dreamlike state to the scene. Melissa paints a picture of putting one kitten in her dress, the feline licking her face as she sang "lullabies." She writes of "grasshoppers" and a warm "breeze" and "blades of grass" swaying in the wind. Then, after setting what seems to be a scene from *Little House on the Prairie,* Melissa recalls a desperate need to keep the kittens hidden from "him." She speaks of how intimidated she was by the mere sound of her father's voice. It's almost as if Jesperson enters Melissa's memory as a wolf creeping through a fairy tale, in search of his Little Red Riding Hood, ready to pounce on her and punish the girl for her transgressions. There's a dark feeling to it all.

"The only thing about this that is true," Jesperson claimed, "is that Melissa was five in the year 1984. Nothing else."

"Fiction," Thomas Phelan told me as I sat in front of him in Vancouver, Washington, and watched him shake his head. "That whole thing has been a joke. What she says *never* lines up with anything he says."

They were not living in Toppenish at the time, Jesperson claimed; in August 1984, he, Rose, and the kids resided in Yakima, Washington.

"All the records available prove this—school, and my brother being an accountant, my taxes. In 1983, I moved back from Canada to Yakima, Washington, and we were living at Rose's aunt's home. In the spring of 1984, we purchased a mobile home . . . in Selah, Washington. We stayed there until early 1987."

In her book, Melissa claims that as she held them to her chest and cried, she "begged" her father not to hurt the kittens. She talks about being all too familiar with the look he gave her that afternoon, same as the tone of voice he used, both of which meant big trouble, just like, she writes, his "sinister half smile."

From there, she describes how her father pinned each kitten on the clothesline next to one another as they "began frantically scratching at each other." Then she goes on to tell a story of how her father had tracked down a stray cat before this incident and strangled it in front of her and her brother.

According to Jesperson, none of this happened. The truth was that someone in the Jesperson family had routinely told a story of "tying two cats together by the tail and hurling them over a clothesline" to see which one would win the fight and survive. This family tale went around and around and the kids must have heard it at a BBQ or family gathering.

"That is the only way I can see Melissa coming up with this."

Regarding his daughter's story of him "strangling a cat in front of her, and it scratching my arms and me tossing it in the woods," Jesperson added: "That story is born out of a kernel of truth. I was plumbing one day inside a home my father rented [to tenants]. I wasn't married. I was under a sink working on a plumbing problem and this cat came up inside the cabinet and dug its claws into my arm and just started going berserk. It drew lots of blood. I stood, grabbed the thing, and wrung its neck. As it died, it pissed and shit on me and I tossed it. It was a reaction to defending myself."

Jesperson's father, Les, from that day on, would often jokingly shout during family gatherings, or when they all sat around telling stories, "You need a cat killed, bring it to Keith."

"I know that's how she exaggerated those stories into being about me. I mean, just look at the detail a five-year-old recalls in those pages of her book. Come on. Please. It's simply not true. I am a serial killer, yes, but I *did* not kill kittens in front of my children."

AS BENNETT'S BODY RELEASED a stream of urine, Jesperson took himself back to the moment of being huddled under that sink, a cat digging its claws into him. Based on that prior experience, he believed Bennett was dead. She was not moving. He had beat her so violently, her face was pushed-in, a bloody mess of tissue and torn muscle.

"To be completely sure, I felt the need to make certain she *stayed* dead."

He got up and went into the garage. Found a length of nylon rope. Went back into the living room. Tied it around Bennett's neck.

"Using a knife from the kitchen, I severed the ends of the rope to keep it a short knot."

Then a thought occurred to him: *I touched her jeans. I put my fingerprints on the button of her jeans to unsnap and pull them down . . . shit.*

He took the knife and cut out the area of the button fly he'd touched, before placing the playing card–sized piece of fabric in his pocket.

"When I killed her, time seemed to drag on. Her death came slowly."

What am I going to do?

Jesperson sat on the couch and stared at Bennett. His mind raced: What had he done and how was he going to deal with a dead body in his living room, blood all over his clothes, the floor, the mattress, the walls, his hands, underneath his fingernails?

While considering his next move, a ringing telephone startled Jesperson.

9

KILLER INSTINCT

"If you would be a real seeker after truth, it is necessary
that at least once in your life you doubt, as far as possible,
all things."
—René Descartes

REGULARLY SPEAKING WITH A SERIAL MURDERER, A DESPICABLE human being who killed eight women, began to trouble me as the years passed. Quite alarming, I became comfortable talking to Jesperson. If one is to read my essays, editorials, or books, a feminist melody, however subtle, serenades in the background. I support women's rights. Certainly no feminist, I stand by women in any capacity I can, especially where abuse of any sort is involved. What was I doing, I asked myself, befriending a man who hated everything about women? Allowing him a venue to speak his most disgusting and disturbing thoughts?

The pains in my digestive tract grew intense, as if my insides constricted and I couldn't do anything to stop it from happening, but wait it out. After hanging up with Jesperson one morning in November 2013, I felt nauseous. A cold sweat beaded up all over my body. A sense of vertigo turned into dizziness. So as not to pass out, I doubled over the bathroom sink, splashed cold water on my face, stripped off my clothes, and fought it off on the floor. The privacy of the bathroom was the best place to keep these "episodes," as my doctor would soon refer to them, hidden. My blood pressure was low, then high. My system was breaking down. I kept much of it to myself, not wanting anyone to know the extent of what was happening. I needed to continue with Jesperson; I didn't want anyone telling me to stop.

"Stress," my doctor said after I explained. "Keep an eye on it."

He ordered a series of tests.

To use a serial killer in the pursuit of other serial killers for the sake of television was the hook that sold my series. *Dark Minds* was pitched as *Silence of the Lambs* meets *Catch Me If You Can*. Cold cases, reintroduced to the public in the fashion of *America's Most Wanted,* dramatized for entertainment purposes, became an irresistible concept for TV execs at the dawn of the true-crime television boom. The goal was to shed much-needed attention on cold cases collecting dust in records rooms, with the hope of generating new information. Although I was criticized by some (Internet trolls) for not solving a case during the span of the series, my aim was never to play cop on television. I desired to bring awareness to stagnant cases by imploring viewers to contact law enforcement if they had information and wanted to help. Many of the featured twenty-one cases are active once again; three of those are closer now to being solved than they ever were; every episode generated a multitude of tips. A task force was created (specifically) after I reignited an investigation into several missing girls in Connecticut I had a personal connection to. I'm proud of the work we did and the accomplishments we celebrated.

Regardless how I feel about him, I could never deny that Keith Jesperson played a role in the show's success. As I worked toward my goals and the show aired, if there was some stomach pain involved, a couple of "episodes" to contend with, so be it. I'd learn to manage. It wasn't every day I was sick, and I considered it the cost of doing business with the Devil.

I live in a small town. Woods surround my property on three sides. My black Lab sits on the floor by my side as I write, research, conduct interviews via Skype and telephone. We take walks together. I try to make daily Mass three times a week (to balance the dark with light). I have a garden and cook my suburban version of gourmet for relaxation. In winter, I chop and burn wood, snow-blow my driveway. In the summer, I cut my own lawn. On the whole, my life is as peaceful and introverted as one might expect a full-time writer's life to be, though investigative journalism and writing books is hard work that requires tenacity, self-discipline, guts, and long hours.

I've always been alone with my thoughts. But after two years of talking to Jesperson about cold cases and what was going on inside the mind of the serial killers I was hunting, this dark, destructive figure became a relentless component within all of that. Same as a flu virus, Jesperson was there one day like a tickle in the back of my throat, but soon it was overwhelming me, taking over my life, saddling me. At one time, Jesperson called my office every day, at hour intervals. He called me "buddy" and "friend" and asked how my day was, looking for any opportunity to know me more personally. I'd force myself to forget about him from time to time, but there I was accepting his calls again, listening to him spew his venomous paranoia over why I hadn't picked up the phone or answered a letter in weeks. It was taxing, emotionally and psychically, but like so many other toxic situations we find ourselves in, I got used to it.

Beyond the health problems I now experienced, how was I going to manage all of the information coming in and the inevitable brush-off one day? *Dark Minds* would end. All television series are canceled. Would I cut him off entirely? The rapport, from the start, wasn't like most writer/source relationships. I generally interview people for stories and books several times, at the most for a few weeks, and then they're out of my life. This was a long-term commitment—with someone, mind you, who talked about the most disturbing behaviors imaginable.

"I have to ask," I said one day while we discussed a victim he was said to have dragged for twelve miles, "was she alive when you strapped her to the bottom of your truck?" I was in a bad place. The macabre and violent aspects of his crimes gnawed at me. I couldn't stop thinking about the depravity and torture he had perpetrated upon his victims, knowing that he was probably sharing about 50 percent of what he had actually done to them.

"What kind of person do you think I am?" he said, that flippant, baritone laugh behind the comment.

"You're a serial killer! You're a disgusting human being who killed people at will, without any regard for humanity. *That's* who you are."

"I heard you were straightforward, Phelps."

"*Was* she or not?"

"It would be a better story if she was alive, I know, but no, she was dead—at least I *think* so."

He laughed again.

This was the story of my life.

AT TIMES IT BECAME difficult to move forward and find a rhythm when speaking to Jesperson. But once I connected with the right space for him to occupy in my head, I went for it, presuming I could handle whatever he dished out, along with whatever he had planned. What he had to say was all at once compelling, fascinating, vulgar, inhumane, incredible, revolting, honest, and deceitful.

There has always been a dialogue in this country about why we are so obsessed with and engrossed in all things true crime, especially the most heinous acts of violence humans can do to one another. What is it that drives record numbers of people tuning into true-crime television, reading the books, and lining up to see the violent movies? I was living within the context of those questions. The insight I had access to felt unprecedented. I'd read serial killer books written by forensic psychiatrists, accounts of clinical interviews done with infamous serial killers in a contained setting over a period of weeks or even months (some on death row, some not), scoured the Internet for academic serial killer research, all while thinking: *What I am doing with Jesperson is beyond the scope of that work.*

I could ask Jesperson anything and he'd answer. No subject, he made clear, was off limits. He respected my work. He'd read every book I'd written and, to my alarm, sent them to me afterward, with his "notes" in the margins: scribbled gibberish on page after page, explaining what I got right and wrong, pointing out errors, with random thoughts sprinkled throughout. He knew what I was capable of, once I decided to dig into a story, write about it, and he praised my investigative skills.

As Jesperson collected murder victims after killing Bennett (attacking another woman months later, but letting her go—a mistake he vowed never to make again), he settled into a routine. He was a long-haul trucker by the end of 1990, traveling the country: a murder machine passing through state after state, running into potential victims everywhere he went.

"I could have killed *hundreds* if I wanted to, before anyone would have caught on," he told me one afternoon.

He was right.

Serial killers trust in the comfort zones they've chosen. The FBI specifies a comfort zone to be "defined by an anchor point—a place of residence, employment, or a residence of a relative." Most serial murderers kill within what the FBI calls "very defined geographic areas of operation"—i.e., comfort zones—and rarely deviate from that space once they feel it is working.

"My comfort zone was in a small area about the size my prison cell is today," Jesperson explained, referring to the inside of his truck. "I am alone with this person and I have total control over what is going to happen—but not sure it's a *control* thing. It's like a moral thing. When killers kill, it's because something does not sit well with them. . . . The control thing isn't automatic. It's not something you think about, Phelps. You already *know* you have it. That's why it gets easier, because you understand and have them there with you without thinking about it."

He used a spider and its web as a metaphor to describe how he went about making sure each victim post-Bennett wound up in his comfort zone: "[The spider] *knows* that's his kill zone. Basically, a killer instinct is based upon your comfort zone. My comfort zone is a tool to use in murder. It's like my victim fell into a hole and here I have [her] all to myself. There's an automatic knowledge that it could happen either way—she can live or die. It's based on the moral implications of how we *look* at our victims."

"Part of that must be rooted in the way in which the victim responds to you, once you have her in your comfort zone," I suggested. "Seems to me that if she did what you wanted, she'd live—longer, anyway. But any deviation from the fantasy you'd calculated meant she would meet face-to-face with your rage."

"Yeah, I guess. Take my seventh, Angela Subrize. Everything was going good." At times, when he started talking about a victim and forced himself to go back to those moments, he grew manic and overstimulated. He'd bounce slightly in his chair, or, if we were on the phone, I'd sense him talking too fast, stumbling over words, almost as if he was dopey. "I was giving her a ride to her dad's house . . . but then . . . well, well, well, she, she said something I did not like. For several years *after* Bennett, I never anticipated murder again. Then all of a sudden, it just happened . . . and it was like a switch turned on and I was doing it again and again."

AFTER TYING A ROPE around Bennett's neck and snipping the ends, while sitting on the couch with his thoughts, Jesperson was startled by that ringing telephone, his girlfriend, Pamela Madison, now on the other end of the line, calling collect.

"Where the hell are you?" Jesperson asked. "Where are you *right* now, Pamela?"

He was afraid she might be at a pay phone downtown, calling to see if he was around because she was on her way home.

"I would have had to deal with Pamela, had she walked in and saw this," he said.

A terrible thought occurred to me as we discussed this window of time following Bennett's murder and the subsequent cleanup. If the entire night out for Keith Jesperson was based on an obsession with finding a woman to please him sexually, did he have sex with Bennett's corpse? Necrophilia is not common serial killer behavior, contrary to popular thinking. However, several have been known to keep bodies around or revisit them at dump sites in order to have postmortem sexual intercourse.

"No," he said, insisting that once he hit Bennett, any sexual urge inside him diminished.

As he spoke with Pamela, Jesperson stood over Bennett, who was "stiffening up," as he put it. "Knoxville," Pamela told him.

A sense of relief washed over Jesperson. She wasn't down the street.

"I love you," Jesperson said.

"I want to come home. I want to be with you," Pamela said.

A dead woman at his feet, blood everywhere, and Jesperson's next thought became: *The makeup sex when Pamela returns is going to be great.*

As the conversation relaxed him, Jesperson looked around the room: at his clothes, the walls, the floor, the furniture, and the mattress. According to him, noticing the blood for the first time "pulled" him out of a panicked state and into a place of awareness, revealing to him the totality of what he'd done for the first time that night.

My God, I did all this? All this happened?

"I wasn't aware of it until I started talking to Pamela."

He continued the conversation while stripping his clothes and tossing them into the washing machine. After turning it on, he went back to his bedroom and got dressed.

What am I going to do? I have to set up an alibi. I have to make sure the bartender saw me leave that bar alone.

"For the first time, things slowed down for me as Pamela kept talking. I became rational."

Again, Pamela said, "I love you," and explained she was on her way home. She had hoped he could forgive her. It would be a few days, but she was coming back to him.

Jesperson said he was happy to forget and forgive.

They hung up.

As he stood in his living room, understanding that he was

going to have to clean the house to hide any evidence of this murder, the instincts to begin the process of concealing what he had done were there, Jesperson explained, because his father, Les Jesperson, had instilled them in him.

"My father had admitted to me that he once killed someone and had gotten away with it. So there was this thought process that *I* could get away with it, too."

10

"NOODLES"

"The Devil is always at our door."
—Pope Francis

*K*EITH JESPERSON'S IDEA OF RELIGION, SPIRITUALITY, AND/OR GOD is "karma," the universe. His father had told him religion and God were there for him if he wanted to take that path later in life. However, it was not something Les condoned or approved of for his young family. A strong work ethic, making money, never showing anybody who you truly were on the inside, and keeping the family image and reputation intact were gods inside the Jesperson house, according to a man who equates what happens in his world with there being some sort of celestial plan flung into action by the cosmos. Everything for Jesperson happens by chance, though that unintended consequence can sometimes be expedited by what is *supposed* to take place in the grand scope of the solar system, Jesperson said—and nobody can change its course once it has been set in motion.

A fundamental excuse authored by a serial killer to explain away the evil he's perpetrated, without having to take responsibility for it.

"If I was still out there, I might be dead now," Jesperson said one day as we got to talking about his philosophy of karma, and how his life had turned out. At this stage of our correspondence, Jesperson was trying to impress me. The way I'd played my hand during our early interviews, while selling him on the idea of helping me on *Dark Minds* (which wasn't hard), was that he was one of several serial killers I was communicating with and I was going to make a decision based on which one I felt most comfortable talking to.

"Maybe coming to prison saved my life," he added. "Had I continued on the road I was on, I could be dead."

He wanted the show to focus on him, his crimes, his life in prison, and his legend, Happy Face. This became his quest early on.

"No way," I told him up front. "Not a chance."

"Why can't you name me? Why can't I step out from behind the curtain and speak as Happy Face?"

He didn't get it. I was never going to allow a serial killer a starring role on a television series I was involved in, at least not in a capacity where he was glorified. He knew it was anonymous or nothing.

With the self-absorbed psychopath suffering from narcissistic personality disorder, everything is about him. Not once did Jesperson ever begin or end a conversation with remorse for what he had done. Here he was telling me that had he continued to kill, *he* might be dead. He had turned the tables on his victims and made stalking and charming and abducting each of them, along with their murders, about him. No matter what we talked about, all roads led back to Keith Jesperson.

"I could have gotten into a truck wreck next trip out," he continued, ruminating on destiny. "Who knows? When you start thinking about intervention . . . and all the things that happen in the world, and people start questioning why this happened, why that happened, maybe it *was* by Divine Intervention"—he laughed—"that I turned myself in—to keep myself off the road."

We discussed prison life. It was not a subject I was all that interested in. He had adapted well to this world. He was where he belonged. He fit into the correctional system as if it had been designed for him. He butted heads with authority once in a while, but they always put him in his place. He has a few friends he hangs out with, keeps to himself, receives scores of letters from people all over the world, media requests, money, and understands that in prison he is among men who are not only like him, but many of whom can end his life at any time. His nickname in the joint is "Happy."

"I like my life too much right now," he told me after I asked about the death penalty and why he was so adamant about *not* helping investigators in those states where he'd killed women who are still known as unidentified Jane Does.

"Why not help them? Why not give their families some answers? You killed these women. You can identify them."

Part of me believed then that he knew who they were, their full names, and was keeping that information to himself. All serials hold back evidence about their crimes to use later as a bargaining chip. They also take delight in and get an emotional high and twisted kick from the fact that only they know certain facts about their cases. Many will hold on to where a victim is buried so they can take pleasure in being the only person knowing the information.

"Because, let's suppose I identify a victim of mine and help cops," he said, explaining why he didn't want to help in the Jane Doe cases. "These are cases I have already 'settled.' But now you have a family who has put a face to the person who killed their loved one and they want revenge. They go to the courts and make a stink. The prosecutor takes another look. All of a sudden, I am staring at perhaps facing trial and now the death penalty."

As he carried on, listing more reasons for not helping, I considered that most serial killers, when you come down to it, are cowards. They're full of fear. Still, I set the topic aside, knowing we would revisit it at a later time. Part of my strategy, especially post-*Dark Minds,* was to convince Jesperson to help identify all of his Jane Does. I was beginning to enjoy the prospect of going to law enforcement in those states behind his back and outlining the close relationship I had with him, offering to act as a liaison in order to convince him to admit he knew who these women were, and maybe hid identifying markers somewhere. There needed to be some sort of redemptive plan on my part besides his television work. I needed, for my own reasons, to make our relationship pay off for his victims' families. It was one of the motivations for putting up with all the phone calls and letters, all the idiotic spew coming from his mouth, on top of all the space he occupied in my life. I needed to tell myself that some good could come from it all. It was the only way I could continue.

"So you would *never* help?" I asked. "Is that what you are telling me?"

"Why, Phelps? Is it important to you?"

"You know it is."

"If they agree to take the death penalty off the table, I might reconsider."

There was that power. It reminded me that what we cannot control annihilates our trust and we begin to fear the worst. This is the perpetual state of the serial killer.

As a BOY LIVING in Chilliwack, Canada, a farming community over the United States–Canadian border, northeast of Peaceful Valley, Washington, Jesperson came of age on a large spread of land, with a sister, Sharon, the oldest; an older brother, Bruce (born on the same day as Keith, April 6, two years prior); a younger brother, Brad; and the youngest, Jill. Within the pages of a detailed 603-page manifesto he wrote for me, Jesperson explained that on the farm one day he found "an injured raven, its wing broken." He put the bird in a box and, over the course of several days, "nursed it back to health." He was shocked, however, to come home from school one afternoon and find the box and bird gone. Neighbors had been involved with someone else close to him in the theft. They had taken the bird and pinned it to a tree, according to Jesperson, and tossed knives at it until it died.

Deciding on a "code name" for my anonymous serial killer was an important part of preproduction before I hit the road to begin shooting season two, when Jesperson came aboard. I explained this to him, talking about the process we were going through in selecting a stage name for him. My first choice was "Dante," the implication being that I was entering hell and interacting with the Devil. Time would prove this name to be spot-on.

He liked it.

The name didn't go over well with network execs, however. Yet, as the network, my producers, and I began debating various names, like anything I mentioned to Jesperson involving him, he went off to his cell and scratched ten pages of screed with his thoughts on names, his philosophy behind why we choose anonymous names for people, along with page after page of additional drivel that made sense, I'm guessing, only to him.

Jesperson's suggestion for a stage name was "Noodles." He told me a story about Noodles being the nickname of a kid he knew in school, who had been given the name "because his dick was a 'limp noodle.'" Another theory was "because he didn't have much smarts in his 'noodle.'"

Was this all some sort of a joke? This type of letter and suggestion disgusted me. It told me he enjoyed the attention being paid to him, and made me sick thinking I was the one giving him this pleasure. Anxiety grew as I thought about his letter, manifesting so severely in my gut, I once again found myself doubled over in the bathroom, a cold sweat coming on, fighting off passing out. The pain was as profound as anything I'd ever felt.

What am I doing? Why would I ever sign up for this?

"Listen, man, I am not calling you Noodles, so get that shit out of your mind," I said the next time we spoke. "And you are *not* involved in choosing the name. Understand that you are an anonymous voice on the phone. Nothing else! I gotta go. I'll let you know your name when I find out."

After I hung up, restlessness came on. I paced. I could picture him hanging up, walking around the prison with a ballooned head, his ego stoked, once again enjoying the limelight as Happy Face, even though we were never going to tell the public his identity while the series was on air.

Finally we heard Raven was going to be Jesperson's on-screen name. When he called, I explained that the president of Investigation Discovery, Henry Schleiff, had come up with Raven. We all liked it. It seemed dramatic, metaphoric, television-friendly, and easy to associate with a serial killer.

"Interesting," Jesperson said.

A few weeks later, he began signing all of his letters—and most of the paintings he sent me—as Raven.

AS WE CONTINUED TALKING about Taunja Bennett and the thought process Jesperson went through in order to dispose of her body, he interrupted the conversation. There was something on his mind. It was important to him, he said. We couldn't continue without discussing it.

Here was the give-and-take part of our relationship. He could control our conversations by withholding information I asked for until he got what *he* wanted.

"Why true crime?" he asked.

"What does it matter?"

"Because I *need* to know," he said, explaining how he wanted to understand what had inspired me down the path of my professional writing career. He was curious about my background, guessing in a previous life I was a cop, lawyer, or involved in law enforcement on some level. This was his way of learning what he could about me to better gauge how much he could trust me.

"I fell into it," I said. "My passion was writing and I wrote a true-crime story. It was successful and here we are."

This was somewhat true.

"It had nothing to do with the murder in your family?"

I knew then that someone on the outside was doing research about my life and feeding it to him behind bars. Because I'd not told him about my sister-in-law's murder. Not yet, anyway.

"I'm not sure that had a lot—or anything, really—to do with it," I told him.

Like Jesperson, most have assumed the murder of my brother's "wife" in 1996 started me on a path into true crime. I considered that myself. Perhaps symbolically or subliminally, yes, that is true. Her murder has revealed to me, from a front-row seat, how a murder affects the family dynamic and resonates through many lives. Inside of that unique space, I can speak with authority and empathy about victims of murder and talk to murder victims' family members with a certain sincerity. We can relate on some levels.

After Jesperson asked, however, I considered the question, the most common among my readers, viewers, and people who attend my lectures and signings. *What was it?* I asked myself. I took walks and thought about this. When I drove long distances, I allowed the question to fester. What had brought me to a place where I was able to speak with a serial killer, week after week? Besides an irritating and recurring digestive condition, the subjects we discussed didn't bother me as much as they might others. Why had I been so comfortable with writing about serial murderers and violence all these years? How could I look at thousands of graphic crime-scene photos without being sickened and made cynical by what a small portion of humanity does to one another? How was I able to walk into a prison, hug a woman who had killed five of her kids, sit down with her, and laugh and talk about her life as though she was a long-lost aunt? It's not courage. Certainly. Where had I developed this indifference and desensitization to all things crime-related?

Driving one afternoon through a neighboring town, I came to an intersection with stop signs on all four corners. On my right was a water tower, rusty and faded blue. Beyond it, the grimy concrete walls and greasy barbed wire of Osborn Correctional Institution, at one time Connecticut's supermax. To my left was Robinson Correctional Institution, a level-three prison. In front of me, up atop a rolling hill several hundred yards long, pastures of waist-high wild grass, the American and Connecticut state flags flapping against a breeze I recall always having blown up there, was a place I knew as CCIE, the Connecticut Correctional Institution of Enfield, a level-two prison. As I stared up the hill, memories flooded.

I drove through the intersection and pulled over.

Even all these years later, with the sun reflecting in jagged Harry Potter bolts off the circular razor wire surrounding the red-brick building on the hill, as I sat in my vehicle, I could smell the ammonia steaming in invisible, sterile waves from the yellow bucket on wheels the cons passing me in the corridors used to mop the waxed floors. I could hear the echo of guards' voices over the loudspeakers calling everyone to the "chow hall" for dinner. I could see the steel locks on the doors keeping people out and inmates in. I could envision the same women, week after week, screaming kids with runny noses in tow, waiting to see their men doing fifteen, twenty, even thirty large.

And I knew, right then, as my car idled on the side of the road and people drove by staring at me, gazing up at this past life, the answer to what had eluded me all these years: my journey into true crime began the first night I spent inside that prison.

11

THE "REALITY" OF TRUE CRIME

"Cage an eagle and it will bite at the wires, be they of iron
or of gold."
—Henrik Ibsen, *The Vikings of Helgeland*

AFTER HANGING UP WITH PAMELA, JESPERSON FACED THE STARK REalization that he needed to cover up his movements for the night, in addition to the disposing of Bennett's body. He stood over his victim, staring down at her. She would have to stay behind, right where she was, in the living room. First things first: Jesperson needed to go out and do something he viewed as vital to getting away with this murder.

He locked the house. Jumped into his vehicle. Drove back to the B&I Tavern.

Approaching the bar, making sure patrons saw him, Jesperson yelled for the barmaid, "Hey? Can I get a beer over here?"

She looked at him. "Yeah, course."

When she brought the beer and set it down on a coaster, Jesperson made a point to speak with her. "I needed to make this impression so she knew that I was there by myself."

As he drank the beer, Jesperson thought about where he was "going to put" Bennett. He'd later promote the notion that the serial killer is most vulnerable just after he commits murder, when he has the body in his possession.

"This is the thing that goes on in our heads: the hardest part is not murder itself, it's getting rid of the body without being seen . . .

The sooner you can put distance between yourself and your victims, the safer you'll be. We don't hang around our crimes like [serial killers do] in the movies."

At the bar, he thought about the Columbia River Gorge near the Vista House monument in Corbett. Jesperson knew the area to be secluded, steep, and with dense forest. He'd spent time hiking there. Knew the layout well. Jagged hills, cliffs, rock ledge. Thickly settled woods all around, winding roads that people rarely, if ever, pulled over on.

Taking one last pull from his beer, he yelled for the bartender.

"Another round?" she asked.

"No. Just wanted to say good night."

"Yeah . . . sure, man. Take it easy."

Back inside his vehicle, Jesperson drove toward Troutdale, east of Portland, past Gresham on I-84, beyond the Lewis and Clark State Park. Crossing the Sandy River, heading south on secondary back roads toward the Vista House, he pulled into the monument parking lot. It was packed with cars. Kids, mainly. "Lovers' lane type of thing."

If I can get past here, away from those cars, I can drive down to the ravine, and there's where I'll put her.

He parked on the side of the road about 1.5 miles past the Vista House.

"All I saw was darkness."

Perfect.

Leaving the area, backtracking fifteen miles to fetch Bennett's body in Portland, he stopped at an open-all-night mini-mart along the way to gas up and check to make sure all of the outside lights on the vehicle worked. Last thing he needed was to get stopped by the police for a broken taillight.

As he started the vehicle, a thought occurred to Jesperson. So he reached up and pulled the dome light out of the housing inside the car. Whenever he opened the doors of the vehicle, now the inside lights didn't go on.

He backed up to the front porch of the house on NE Everett

Street. He opened the passenger-side door and went inside to get Bennett's body.

Before picking her up, Jesperson stood behind the living-room curtains and looked out to "make sure nobody in the neighborhood was watching what I was doing or walking their dog." It was 12:30 A.M.

"Initially I grabbed her by the arms and began dragging her toward the front door," he explained. "And that's when her pants went right down to her ankles."

He'd cut off the button-fly snap. There was nothing holding up her pants.

After pulling up Bennett's pants, he "carried her" in both arms—Frankenstein and his bride—"and set her in the front passenger-side seat in an upright position . . . shut the door, and she leaned into the door like she had fallen asleep."

Certain nobody had seen him, Jesperson drove back to the Vista House, past the monument, and down into the area he'd chosen earlier.

With no one around, he parked on the side of the road, got out, and checked to see if he could find a spot deep enough into the woods, far enough away from the road and secluded, so that nobody would stumble upon her. It was pitch-black. He could not make out his hands in front of himself.

Jesperson opened the door and dragged Bennett by her arms from the car to the edge of the woods, heading deep in. It wasn't as hard as he'd imagined. The forest was covered with a carpet of "greasy, slimy, dead leaves" that led down into a ravine, making it easy to pull Bennett's body along.

There was a tree, "or big bush," about thirty feet in, which poked him in the face as he dragged her by. Crawling underneath the branches, with Bennett's body in tow, unable to see where he was going, Jesperson slipped on some wet leaves and fell down a steep embankment, an eighty-five-foot drop, Bennett's body bumping and sliding, headfirst, behind him.

This was the place. He had no choice. He could not carry Bennett's body back up the cliff. Plus, he considered it to be far enough away from the road, deep enough into the forest, where nobody would ever find her.

Jesperson started to cover Bennett's body with leaves. As he reached down to pick up a pile of branches and debris, however, a pair of headlights hit him in the eyes.

Shit . . .

But the worst news wasn't the car driving by—there was no way the driver could see him—it was where he and Bennett had landed after sliding down the embankment. The headlights had shone on an area of the ravine cut in by a dirt road.

"I had placed her body in the middle of a switchback," he told me.

There she was: one arm over the top of her head (facing south), her pants down around her ankles, leaves and dirt and rubble all over her body, a rope around her neck, her face beaten into a distorted, decomposing pulp.

HE HAD A THICK shock of dark black hair, parted on one side, shaved tightly around the ears, slicked over (probably with patchouli oil). He sat on the edge of the couch. His son stared at him from a chair nearby. He'd made the boy sit and watch the display he was about to put on.

In front of him on the floor was a pail, one of those old-school mop buckets with a handle and wooden rollers to wring the long hairs of the cotton mop. On the table was a fifth of rye, half of which he'd consumed. In his hand a pair of pliers. It was 1945. Summertime. My father, that child sitting, looking on, was eight years old.

"Watch me, boy," the man said. "And learn."

My grandfather had a decaying tooth. He explained to his son that this was how the Phelpses dealt with these types of setbacks in life: You man up and take care of the problem yourself. You get good and trashed and you pull that problem out with whatever tool can get the job done, bleed into a bucket, finish that damn rye, and continue on with your day. The world did not owe anyone an easy life.

Hearing this horrific story, I realized that we don't choose our lives; our lives choose us and we decide how to respond. My paternal grandfather, Harold Phelps Sr., a man I've never met, died at "thirty-nine or in his early forties," my father told me, "I don't know. Your grandmother kicked him out of the house long before." Harold drank himself to death. Dad was a witness to the sickness of his alcoholism. This tooth-and-bucket story was one of several my dad shared—shielding us, of course, from the more violent and abusive tales. Another favorite was how my grandfather used to turn the gas stove on in their Hartford apartment and leave it running without lighting the burner. My dad never knew whether he did it intentionally, or passed out while trying to cook something to eat. Either way, those experiences of living with an alcoholic were enough to send my father running in the opposite direction, never having touched a drink himself.

My oldest brother, Mark, and I, however, inherited the addiction gene, which was what put me in CCIE, that prison on the hill, every Monday night for five years of my life. I've never gone to prison as an inmate. I'd step into CCIE on Mondays and speak to hundreds of men serving time, many of their crimes a by-product of alcoholism and/or drug addiction. I was part of a group on the outside supporting the in-house drug and alcohol abuse programs. This is why I believe having had that experience drove me toward wanting to understand the criminal mind later on in my professional life—my motivation for focusing on true crime.

I could relate to these men. Standing in front of hundreds of convicted criminals, incarcerated for a variety of serious crimes—murder to manslaughter, DUI to theft, battery to violent assault and rape—and having each one of them stare back at you, expecting something profound to come out of your mouth every Monday night, is a humbling experience. It instills the absolute belief that we take the most basic gifts of life—a sunset, the smell of a flower, the sight of a boy and his dad walking in a park—for granted.

"You need to do it," I was told by a friend the first night, terrified to step into a prison and tell my "story" through a microphone, pacing, delivering a monologue about my drunken history like a stand-up comic in front of hundreds of men I'd never met. It was 1995. I had been sober six months. Yet, those men taught me more about making judgments than I could have ever figured out on my own, regardless of how many times this guilt-saddled Catholic had heard otherwise. Before going up to the prison, I'd condemned and prejudged them. I'd made up my mind that men in prison were all bad—and deserved to be where they were. My brother Mark had done hard time. We often visited him. It was awful and sad. Before CCIE, I'd written men in prison off as the dregs of society who merited no empathy from me.

One of the many challenges I faced with Jesperson was putting my judgments aside, as well as culture's judgments regarding vicious, bloodthirsty serial killers. I had to talk to him under the pretext of wanting to understand what he wanted to say, while grasping what criticisms and problems he had with society, allowing him the opportunity to speak freely and talk about why he committed his crimes. But as we entered our third year, what worried me most was: If I accomplished that, would I feel the slightest hint of a human being talking back to me? Would I find a person who once wasn't a killer, but a simple workingman, married with children?

The meetings I attended at CCIE took place in the cafeteria, which smelled of a revolting combination of stale, institutionalized foods, bleach, and body odor. Standing in front of men who had ripped and ran on the meanest streets, with the worst society produced, men who had grown up without guidance and discipline, feeling all that bottled-up energy radiating back at me, made me realize I was on the same page as far as trying to stay sober. Week after week, this meeting filled me with a real-world judiciousness I could not have gotten anywhere else. I never looked into their eyes and saw their crimes. Addiction, desperation, a self-effacement (at least in those men who were serious about sobriety) stared back. I went to prison to stay out of prison. For years, I stood and bared my soul to these men, sharing my secrets and arduous journey into and out of active alcoholism.

By the time I began speaking with Jesperson, I'd been away

from that atmosphere for eleven years, sober for sixteen. Yet, as I thought about it, I could never forget the emotional influence and permanence behind the stories I told and heard. I hadn't stumbled into true crime, after all, as I had told Jesperson, and maybe even convinced myself. Nor had I chased some hidden understanding within my sister-in-law's murder. True crime was, it turned out, where I felt most comfortable.

12

WOUNDED BIRD

"There are some wounds that one can heal only by
deepening them and making them worse."
—Villiers de L'Isle-Adam

GETTING AWAY WITH MURDER IS ALL ABOUT LUCK," JESPERSON SAID.
He was explaining how he dumped Taunja Bennett's body on
that cold January early morning in 1990. "Timing—and the *luck*
of good timing—is key."

As he scurried up the steep hill, slipping and sliding, grabbing
at branches and tree stumps, pulling his large frame up and onto
flat land, his one thought was to get the hell out of there. A car
had driven by. The only people out at that time of night, Jesperson's growing paranoia convinced him, were cops and killers.

Jesperson had put on a "different pair of shoes" before he left
the house. "A pair of Cannondale bicycle shoes." It was the reason
why he had slipped down the hill, he said. "There was no flex in
the shoes."

Back inside his vehicle, he spun the tires and took off.

"At the corner of that switchback, our cars came into view of
each other. My headlights hit the side of a Multnomah County
Sheriff's cruiser."

It had been a cop whose lights flashed across his face.

There was little concern on the sheriff's part; Jesperson was
one more car out in the middle of the night. Still, as they drove
away from each other, what-ifs careened inside Jesperson's head. It
had been a close call. He knew where Bennett's body had landed

would make it vulnerable to being found sooner rather than later. There was nothing he could do about that, however. As he drove away, the feeling he struggled with the most was that this goofy, overgrown kid from Canada, a divorced father, was now a killer, a part of himself Jesperson claimed to have not known existed before that night.

As our friendship developed, Jesperson now trusting me with his secrets more and more, he said something about this murder and the ones that followed I thought I'd never hear.

"She didn't deserve it. No one did."

"Your victims?"

"Yes."

"I had wanted to make love to a woman," he claimed, recalling that night he met Bennett. "Not kill her. Looking back . . . I tried to justify her death. Had put myself into the situation. Didn't look past the end of my penis. Sex had been my motive to follow her from the bar. To pick her up and take her home. It just didn't go as planned. She said I could have it—to take it and let her go ASAP. Not the sexual encounter I saw in my head taking place."

Was this the serial killer simply telling me what he believed I wanted to hear? Was Jesperson trying to show me he was capable of empathy? He had told me by then I was all he had left. Family had written him off. His kids never contacted him. No one that meant anything to him on the outside had written or visited in years. Nobody would accept his calls.

"*You* answer my calls," he said. "At least right now."

Thinking about this call later, I considered there had to be a wounded mess somewhere inside of me in order for me to speak with a psychopath for years and, during that time, begin to search for the good in him. I told myself this many times. Maybe to feel better. Maybe so I could continue. Maybe to help convince my gut to calm down so I could control those intestinal episodes. Either way, I began to think that to overly demonize someone—anyone—must be wrong.

My job, in going into and continuing a conversation with a serial killer, was not to stare at him under a condemnatory microscope focused on what he had done. It was an opportunity to unravel the emotional state—body, mind, and soul—of men like Jesperson. If my only purpose in what I was doing was to see him as a madman and evil incarnate, which he certainly is, then I would never allow myself the opportunity to understand anything else about him, those like him, or their malicious behaviors and crimes. We get nowhere thinking this way. I needed to concentrate on what makes us uncomfortable about them within ourselves.

A question that arose near this time became: Do serial killers want to be who they are? Did Jesperson wake up one day and become that killer he is? Or, perhaps, did an evil seed germinate and evolve, and then he embraced it?

As would be the case, time after time over the course of our relationship, as I began to ponder these ideas—whenever I thought I had the right questions—information that I had been searching for, for years, would arrive and radically change my feelings and goals.

13

HIGH HORSES

"If you do not tell the truth about yourself you cannot tell
it about other people."
—Virginia Woolf

S HE WAS OUT "FOR A SPIN" ON THE SCENIC HIGHWAY ALONG THE
snaking roads of the Columbia River Gorge. It was early morning,
January 22, 1990. A Mt. Hood Community College student, the
young woman on her bicycle was thinking about class later that
day when she looked into the woods and saw what appeared to be
an arm sticking up out of the brush. Scared and startled by the
sight, she hit the brakes on her bike, parked it on its kickstand,
and walked down the embankment. Realizing what she'd stumbled upon, she rode ten minutes up the road to a café and called
police.

Bennett's head was grotesquely distended because of that length
of rope Jesperson had tied around her neck, which effectively
acted like a knot on the bottom of a balloon. Postmortem decomposition fluids caused her brain and tissue to swell and bloat. Her
jaw and teeth were caved in and pushed down into her throat.
What the college kid had seen of her face was covered with dried
blood, dirt, leaves, and bruises. Her pants were down around her
ankles, her panties intact, untouched, her bra stretched above her
breasts, exposing them. Jesperson could later play the naïve card
of novice killer with me, unaware of what he was doing when
dumping Bennett's body, but this crime scene, once the location

had been chosen for him by that slip down into the switchback, had been staged for dramatic effect.

No doubt about it.

As the Oregon State Police arrived and word spread of the gruesome discovery, none of the details privy to only Bennett's murderer—the cutaway portion of her jeans, rope around her neck, the extent of her injuries, how she was found, exactly where her body had been recovered—were publicly shared. The *Oregonian* newspaper reported a few identifying markers:

> . . . *unidentified woman, between the ages of 18 and 25, with dark brown hair and brown eyes, 5 feet 5 inches tall . . . found below an embankment of East Crown Point Highway, about a mile and a half east of Vista House.*

It wasn't until a week later when Bennett's mother, Loretta, saw a sketch of her daughter released by police and called that Taunja's brothers made a positive identification. In speaking with family members, police learned Bennett hung out at the B&I Tavern. After interviewing the daytime bartender, Detective Al Corson reported Bennett arriving at the bar "sometime around noon to one P.M. . . . alone. . . . [She] appeared to be in a happy mood, and she purchased a beer at the bar, paying for it with small change . . . [before] talking to . . . two men who were playing pool. . . . At approximately four to four thirty P.M., Taunja walked over to the bar and asked [the bartender] if she wanted to go out disco dancing. . . . [The bartender] told Taunja she should not go with these two men because Taunja did not know them and it was not a safe thing to do. Taunja replied she would be okay and returned to where the men were playing pool."

A second bartender recalled arriving for work at 5:00 P.M. She watched Bennett, whom she knew to be a regular, "hang around with two guys who were playing pool on a table at the east end of the tavern. . . . One of the men [was] about thirty years old, about six-two, with short blond hair." All the bartender could remember about "the second one was that he was somewhat shorter."

None of this information pointed in any way to Jesperson.

Once Laverne Pavlinac absorbed enough of the news accounts about the murder, crime scene, and, most important, Bennett's life (from an *Oregonian* interview with Bennett's mother), she initiated a plan to frame her live-in paramour, John Sosnovske, a man Pavlinac claimed routinely beat her. First, she phoned in anonymously. But when that call failed to yield his arrest, she called again with a new version, implicating herself in the abduction and murder, giving cops a story of her and Sosnovske's bringing Bennett to the Vista House, where she helped John commit rape and murder. She then produced a purse and a cutoff fly portion from a pair of jeans (both later proven not to be Bennett's).

The Oregon State Police interviewed Pavlinac and Sosnovske and built a case based on her admissions and knowledge of details never made public. A jury deliberated for three days before convicting Laverne Pavlinac on three counts of aggravated murder. Scared of facing the death penalty, John Sosnovske pleaded guilty not long after.

In many of his long-winded diatribes written and spoken to me about the Bennett case, Jesperson maintained that Laverne could not have known as much as she did about Bennett, the crime scene, and the murder if those details had not been "given to her" by police. Hearing this from Jesperson year after year became nauseating. I felt as if I were speaking to a child at times; at others, talking to someone who could not accept (or was in denial of) facts. For example, in our discussions about the so-called frame-up, Jesperson never mentioned that Laverne Pavlinac and Taunja Bennett knew each other. I found out later that Laverne was a former psychiatric aide at Dammasch State Hospital, where Bennett had been admitted several times because of her mental state. If I'm a cop investigating this murder, that piece of information alone, put together with an admission, becomes almost a smoking gun.

"Look," I told him one day, "did cops maybe put blinders on once Laverne and John came into the picture? Maybe. Did they give Laverne details without realizing it? Perhaps. But the one thing you've overlooked is that they had two people admitting to a murder, sharing intimate details about the crime that had never been made public. Once that occurs in any investigation, everything seems to line up unless it's blatantly obvious the suspects are lying."[2]

AFTER DUMPING BENNETT'S BODY, Jesperson spent the night at the Burns Brothers Truck Stop on I-84 heading back to Portland. Not having control over the actual location of where he placed Bennett's body began to bother him. He knew she would be found sooner rather than later. Yet what could he do?

Jesperson collected his thoughts and figured he'd have to deal with the consequences.

After watching the sunrise, having breakfast, several cups of coffee, even stopping by a table to have a short chat with three Oregon State Police troopers, near 8:00 A.M., Jesperson walked out to his car. Looking to see if there was any evidence of Bennett inside the vehicle, he discovered her purse underneath the passenger seat.

"So I pulled it out and rifled through it."

She had $2.11 "to her name. Blood money. I kept it."

He'd already found her Sony Walkman inside the car and threw it out the window "on the Sandy River Bridge, right before Troutdale." But now he had her purse, which included an ID card. As paranoia set in, Jesperson thought of where he could get rid of the purse and ID card. Those Cannondale bicycle shoes he had worn had to go, too.

Continuing on I-84, he tossed one shoe out the window and watched it fly down an embankment. A mile later, he hurled the other shoe.

Her purse? Shit.

The purse went out the window. But her wallet needed a spe-

[2]Laverne Pavlinac gave two very detailed admissions, both of which are available with some searching online. John Sosnovske, moreover, backed her up and admitted to the murder, giving details only the killer could have known.

cial place. No one could find it. Also, he needed to put it somewhere he could recall. So he drove past the town of Troutdale,
parked off the road close to the Sandy River, got out of the car,
walked up a path "where nobody could see me [and] found a
wide spot up the hill a ways." He looked around to make sure no
one was around. There were bushes "about forty feet off the
road." He tossed the wallet.

As we talked through the Bennett case, Jesperson asked if I had
spoken to Jim McIntyre, the prosecutor, who had convinced a
jury to convict Laverne and John.

"I'm going to," I said.

Four days later. "Well, what did he say?" Jesperson asked. I
could tell the anticipation of this call had eaten him up during
the interim.

"I'll go through this *one* more time, and that's it. The idea that
a 'cover-up' or conspiracy took place to 'frame' John and Laverne, as you have obsessively upheld, is not something I have
found. Not even close."

He ignored the comment. Instead, saying, "One thing I want to
clear up. I haven't lost sight of the idea that the guy who's made
the mistake here is me. . . . I'm not trying to take the high horse,
trying to say that I didn't do anything wrong. I want to let you
know that I have not lost track of why we're here doing this."

"That's encouraging."

"The only guy who did the really bad thing is me."

There were days when I thought, while speaking to him, he was
telling me what he believed I wanted to hear. At times, I could
sense no feeling in what he said, no direct link between his words
and emotion. He was a man prone to eruptions of bilious misog-
yny. He'd hurl a fusillade of insults about his victims while in a
constant state of turmoil with his past, the present, and his future.
The only part of life that was absolute for Keith Jesperson was
where he woke up every morning and went to bed every night.
Denuded of basic human rights, though some would argue access
to cable TV and other amenities is hardly a man stripped of luxu-
ries, he complained about *everything*.

As we talked about my interview with McIntyre, the first words out of Jesperson's mouth, that reckless arrogance he could not control exuding from each breath, was: "I bet he regrets doing the L.A. *Times* story."

"No," I said. "Not at all."

In speaking with McIntyre, I explained, I found a humble man who admitted his mistakes. He'd moved on from this mess many years ago. I didn't tell Jesperson, but I felt a bit embarrassed calling McIntyre about this case.

"What is it that [Jesperson] wants me to *admit* to? He wouldn't know the truth if it was a train that ran him over," McIntyre told me. "Not [only] did all of the evidence point to [Laverne and John], but Laverne *confessed* to her own daughter *after* she knew she was being charged."

I told Jesperson he needed to move on. When talking Bennett, however, he has an unyielding doggedness pushing him to come up with an answer for every possible scenario that doesn't fit into his paranoid theory.

"That makes sense," he said, referring to McIntyre's comment about Laverne convincing her daughter. "The reason why it makes sense is *she* wants to convince her daughter that she is telling the truth to get John put away."

"So what?"

"Have you followed *any* of this?" he asked. He grew impatient, angry.

The next comment I shared from McIntyre riled him even more: "*He's* saying that law enforcement framed [John and Laverne]?" McIntyre asked rhetorically. "We did think we had a rock-solid case, because that's why we tried Laverne to a jury. All the manufacturing of the evidence was Laverne being shrewd enough to spot 'the tells' in the detectives indicating to her . . . what she should say. I'm convinced she's one of the most premier borderline personalities I've ever met."

Jesperson wouldn't buy this. "That's absurd," he said. "Laverne has a history of going to law enforcement to get [John] incarcerated."

This was true. But again, so what?

He had no answer. He was back to the cut-out button-fly section of jeans, wondering how Laverne could have possibly known this fact about the crime scene.

I reiterated that McIntyre said Laverne was an expert at pulling information out of detectives to support her story. She was a woman on a mission.

"The only person framed was John, by Laverne," McIntyre said.

Was it possible that Laverne somehow got hold of a file while being questioned? Maybe they left it on the table for her? The fact is, she sold detectives a hell of a story and they (along with a jury) bought it and convicted her.

"Look, there's no way to prove they told her about the evidence—unless they admit it. Get over it," I told Jesperson. "You *need* to let this go. Move on!"

"I know Keith Jesperson for what he is," McIntyre told me. "He is not even worth my time anymore. There's a double tragedy in the Bennett case. Laverne was able to convince us and be convicted at trial"—which closed the Bennett case. "So nobody continued to investigate, as we should have, which might have led to Jesperson. And Jesperson [later] gets up on his bullshit high horse and begins to confess, but how many others were killed between Taunja Bennett and the time he confessed. . . . What's documented? Four? Five?"

I corrected the prosecutor, "Seven."

There was silence on the phone for a brief moment.

McIntyre told me he believed Jesperson added a few more bodies to his total to make himself appear more notorious. Because Jesperson relished becoming Happy Face, he bolstered the number and lied about other details surrounding the murders to make himself appear to be more like Bundy or the Green River Killer. Whenever he talked about other well-known serials, Jesperson played down their notoriety and how smart they came across. Anytime I mentioned a case I was looking into, how calculating or crafty a particular serial killer had been at avoiding capture, he'd distill the comment down to, "He's not smart, Phelps—just lucky." Jesperson was envious and jealous of other serial killers.

Jesperson laughed when I relayed the McIntyre information to him: "I've taken polygraph tests and passed every one."

"Did he skip over the part where he recanted his confession?" McIntyre asked, referring to interviews with Happy Face in Bend, Oregon, conducted after his arrest. "He told them some wild story about killing some woman and that he lied about everything in the Bennett case?"

"I've lied about a lot," Jesperson responded.

McIntyre believes Jesperson made up the story of dragging Angela Subrize's body underneath his truck for twelve miles to make himself appear more diabolical, adding that shredded body parts would have been splayed over the road, but law enforcement found no such thing.

"That scenario was completely a lie," McIntyre told me. "The body would have shown wear signs of being ground on the road itself."

Jesperson said a "coroner would confirm that's what it was. Body parts? I don't know! I mean, I wasn't behind the truck watching."

"You *have* to come clean here with me," I told him. "If you made that up, you *have* to be honest with me. Please. Let's set the record straight. If you perpetrated a lie to build yourself up, I want you to admit it—that's big."

He grew angry. I felt had we been in a different situation, maybe alone and outside the prison, I would have seen that volcanic rage I knew was inside him.

"I. Don't. Care. I did drag the body. . . . I described the case as it is and I'm not going to deviate. I don't give a *shit* about *big*. I want truth."

"He has a strong moral compass, you didn't know that?" McIntyre commented in jest, adding how he once asked Jesperson in court about drinking and driving. "I looked at him and, talking about that night with Bennett at the B and I, asked, 'You were in a bar, had you been drinking before you drove home?' He then sat bolt upright in the chair, like I had shot his dog, looked at me, and said, 'I *never* drink and drive.' He was righteously offended that I had made the assumption. That was his morality—the women he killed didn't matter, but the drinking and driving, *that* was a big deal."

"It *was* a big deal for me," Jesperson responded. "I never wanted to be a drunk driver like my father. . . . I didn't want to be anything like that man."

I told McIntyre that Jesperson was adamant about never having raped any of his victims.

"Oh, that's a lie! In his first interview with us, he admitted that she [Bennett] said something to him about the size of his penis and he punched her in the face—and it all went downhill from there. She laughed at him and he punched her, and that's when he started choking her out."

"No," Jesperson's lawyer, Thomas Phelan, told me, laughing in response to McIntyre's comment about Jesperson's penis. "I've never heard that." What set Jesperson off, Phelan insisted, "was Bennett's lack of being enamored with him. Her lack of *wanting* him."

Further, when I asked Phelan if the Multnomah County Sheriff's Office (MCSO) ever went to Jesperson after his arrest and asked him to "take other cases" they wanted to close, as Jesperson maintained to me, Phelan said, "No, there was *never* a conversation between me and McIntyre or anyone else in the Multnomah County Sheriff's Office about other cases they wanted to close."

IN A LETTER ANONYMOUSLY sent in May 1994 to the *Oregonian*, the publication that dubbed him the "Happy Face Killer," Jesperson admitted binding and raping several of his victims "again and again." In that same letter, Jesperson doodled a "Happy Face at the top of the first page, two tiny circles for eyes, an upturned sliver of a moon for a mouth," along with the note: "Have a nice daaay." That one scribble was enough to tag him with the infamous nickname.

In the letter, Jesperson explained how he took "Sonja [sic] Bennett home . . . [and] raped her and beat her real bad . . . ," before saying it "turned me on. I got high." Jesperson sent this letter to the paper, he claimed, because he was upset that two people had taken credit for his first murder. He had killed five in total by then. "I want the world to know that it [Bennett] was my crime. So I tied a half-inch soft white rope around her neck. I drove her to a switchback on the scenic road . . . dragged her downhill. Her pants were around her knees because I had cut her buttons off." These were details only the killer could have known. Thus, the letter, along with a call from Thomas Phelan, sparked an inquiry into reevaluating Laverne Pavlinac and John Sosnovske's convictions.

Jesperson, no doubt wanting more credit, described additional victims:

> She [Bennett] was my first and I thought I would not do it again. But I was wrong. I went to truck driving school and learned to drive. While driving I learned a lot and heard of people that have gotten away with such a crime because of our nomad way of life. . . . About November 92 I picked up a girl named Claudia in California. On the way out of L.A. my mind went wild with the thought of a sex slave, and when I stopped at a rest area I took her. I taped her up and raped her again and again. I kept her for 4 days alive then I killed her and dumped her body about 7 miles north of Blythe on 95. . . . This triggered something in me. It was getting easy! Real easy! A week or two later . . . I stopped in Turlock, CA, rest area. A hooker became my next victim. This time I just strangled her right there without sex. She was in my truck only five minutes. . . . I dropped her body off behind the Blueberry Hill Cafe 10 miles south on 99. I placed her body in the dirt and stepped on her throat to make sure she was dead.
>
> My next victim was a hooker I had used three weeks earlier. I summoned her on the C.B. She had a raincoat on. We went through the Normal procedure. . . . I felt so much power. I then told her she was going to die and slowly strangled her and dropped her off behind GI Joe's in Salem. I put her against the fence under the blackberry vines and covered her with leaves.

He referred to his fifth victim as "a street person" he'd charmed into his truck while passing through Corning, California. "I stopped at a rest area near Williams and had her. I put her body on or near a pile of rocks about fifty yards north of Highway 152 west-bound, about twenty miles from Santa Nella."

Armed with these details, law enforcement went to work and soon uncovered that, beyond having two people in prison un-likely to have committed Bennett's murder, they had a serial killer roaming through the country in an eighteen-wheeler, murdering women, now sending letters to a newspaper and including infor-mation backed by facts from cases only law enforcement knew of at the time.

As we discussed this period of his life, I figured we were done with the Bennett case. We'd talked about Bennett for years al-ready. One morning, I explained that I needed to move on. I'd done all I could. Fulfilled an early promise I'd made, explaining how he'd felt all these years about the wrongful convictions. On some days, after we hung up, a complete emptiness washed over me. It was as though what we'd discussed was meaningless and what I might accomplish didn't matter. He was a killer. I couldn't get through to him. Our opinions would never coalesce.

"Did you speak with Al Corson and . . . ," he started to ask me after I'd told him I was finished talking about Bennett.

"Ah, ah, ah . . . ," I said. "Enough about Bennett! No more. Shit, man. Give it a rest."

A few weeks went by. A source introduced me to Bennett's brother, Dave Rowe. So I called him. Dave had gone to the morgue with Bennett's other brother to identify her after their mother called police. Dave couldn't bring himself to go into the autopsy suite, however, and left it up to his older brother. As we chatted, Dave said he'd wanted to talk about "what really happened" for a long time.

"What do you mean, 'what really happened'?" I asked.

"That Jesperson committed the murder *with* John and La-verne."

"Wait a minute. What did you say?"

"Jesperson killed my sister *with* John and Laverne. They should have stayed in prison."

I'd never heard this.

Then Dave told me he once met Jesperson.

"He came to our house about three months before he killed my sister to pick her up and bring her to Seattle, where he was living. I shook his hand on my front porch."

Seemed no matter what I did, how hard I tried, I couldn't move on from this case.

14

LONG, LONG WAY

"Survivors look back and see omens, messages
they missed."
—Joan Didion

*T*HREE MONTHS AFTER JESPERSON MURDERED TAUNJA BENNETT, ON
April 14, 1990, twenty-one-year-old Daun Slagle, a new mother
with inviting blue-green eyes, sandy-blond hair past her shoulders, left her house in Mt. Shasta, California, having had an argument with her husband. Slagle was not in a good place. She was
upset and crying, hurrying away from home with her baby in her
arms. Mt. Shasta is about 3.5 hours north of Sacramento, one
hour south of the Oregon border. It is a small town of about three
thousand, with an elevation of 3,600 feet above sea level. If you
are driving on the I-5, the gorgeous snowcapped mountains and
dart-shaped evergreens of Mount Shasta creep up and into the
skyline.

It was close to 10:30 P.M. as Slagle wandered into downtown. As
she walked with her baby, the only "well-lit" place Slagle could
think of was the Mt. Shasta Shopping Center, with a drug and retail store, bank, cinema, a few local shops. As she made her way
into the parking lot, Slagle spotted two cement planters, about
three feet tall: pillars, so to speak, welcoming shoppers as they
walked in through the outdoor area entrance. She decided to sit
down on one of the planters and take a moment to figure out
what to do. Married just three weeks, Slagle had left the house to

avoid a heated confrontation. There was a sense of an end, she later told me. Within three weeks of this night, she and her husband would separate and initiate divorce proceedings. Making matters more complicated, Slagle was in the very early stages of pregnancy with her fourth child. She'd dropped her two girls off at their grandmother's earlier that day.

Slagle passed a couple of vehicles in the parking lot on her way toward those planters. There was nobody around she could see. It was late. The mall itself was closed. Jerry's Restaurant, situated in front of the parking lot on West Lake Street, was open twenty-four hours. Maybe she could settle there and have some coffee and think things through.

As she contemplated where to go, she said later, she "could feel eyes" on her. "I just kept thinking I was being watched."

Looking around, she didn't see anyone.

After fiddling with the baby, who was swaddled inside a blanket and zipped up inside her coat, she looked up again to see a large man standing in front of her, leaning against the hood of a bronze-colored, late-1970s Chevy Nova. He had his arms folded in front of himself.

Oh, God, please don't come over here and talk to me, she thought.

Slagle had no idea how long he had been watching her.

Go away, go away.

Before she knew it, the man was standing in front of her.

After an introduction, Jesperson mentioned how he'd had trouble with his wife, had separated from her, and was in the process of getting divorced. "I miss my kids," he said, according to Slagle.

At some point, after the two of them talked, she told Jesperson she had to use the bathroom and asked if maybe he could drive her.

"Sure," he said, pointing to his car. "Get in."

In a second scenario she later laid out, Slagle claimed Jesperson invited her into his car to "warm up." And once inside, he suggested they "drive around" for a while.

Either way, along with her baby, Daun Slagle had just stepped into Keith Jesperson's comfort zone.

* * *

THE NOTION OF A serial killer enticing a potential victim into his comfort zone was a topic I was interested in. This was one area within my work with Jesperson that could benefit women. If would-be victims knew what to look out for, maybe a situation could be avoided. In this respect, Jesperson could help.

I asked him how a woman might avoid a predator and, if she does find herself in his comfort zone, is there anything she can say or do that might convince him to let her go? I've always told women (and children) to fight to the death at the first location if they sense an abduction is taking place. Meaning, never allow an abductor to take you to the second location. Let's say you're jogging and an attacker rolls up on you. Fight to the death there. Because you will die—and likely be tortured and raped for hours—at the second location he takes you to after the abduction, regardless of what he promises. The idea is to not allow a predator to get you into his comfort zone. When confronted with resistance (i.e., throwing them off their game) and a determined person fighting back, most predators will run away. They won't risk getting caught.

Jesperson thought about my question, but didn't immediately answer. My experience told me he either took it seriously or was trying to come up with a response he thought the public wanted to hear.

"You know, that's an open-book question," he began. "I mean, there are so many variables. The person, the killer, must also want to *be* a killer at that time. You're not a killer *all* the time." He laughed. "If people were killers all the time, there'd be a lot more dead bodies out there. There is a choosing of when it is convenient to kill and when it is proper to kill. And each [serial killer] has [his] own set agenda, or trigger, so to speak. Now, if someone is in our clutches, well, let's say this, if the person stayed honest . . . ," he said, but then stopped.

"What is it? 'If the person,' you were saying?"

"If you were . . . ," he tried to continue, but stumbled. He did not know how to answer.

"So you *don't* know?"

Whenever I confronted him with a question he had trouble facing, Jesperson couldn't admit defeat. He'd talk his way through it. He now collected his bearings and continued: "Some killers catch and [the victims] know right away they're caught. Other killers sit back and decide at a later time whether that person is going to die or not."

He further explained how a victim might not even know she is in the midst of a killer's fantasy. In that sense, he said, none of *his* victims knew. He wooed and charmed them, convincing each they needed something from him: a ride, booze, cigarettes, food. And then he *decided* to kill them.

JESPERSON DROVE DAUN SLAGLE to a rural section of town, all under her direction, he later told me, adding, "How could *I* have known where to drive?"

There were houses along winding roads. He said Slagle pointed him toward a dead end, a cul-de-sac with no houses, thickly settled woods nearby. He claimed she wanted to use nature's bathroom. He also said she was drinking and had asked him to stop at a store so she could buy more alcohol, which he did.

They'd talked along the way. Mostly about the predicament she found herself in on that night. She explained she was waiting to go back home to her husband, who she'd hoped would be in bed sleeping when she walked in.

"I'm just returning from Washington," Jesperson explained. "I had a birthday party I went to. . . ." Traveling through California, having murdered Bennett months before, Jesperson understood he had within him the potential to kill. His emotions were volatile. If it happened again, he might not be so lucky in getting away with it. At this time, he claimed, he was not a serial killer. He had killed Bennett. But in picking up Daun Slagle, he was not only attracted to her sexually, but from his view, she had come on to him.

"Name's Keith," he told her. "I'm from Portland. I'm heading to Sacramento to start a trucking job."

Two scenarios played out here: Either Jesperson planned on

not doing anything to her, other than giving her a ride, or he knew in that moment she'd wind up dead by the end of the night and her knowing identifying information about him wouldn't matter.

"I did not plan on doing anything to her," Jesperson told me. "She said she wanted to party. That narrative she gives you of us meeting, her feeling 'eyes on her,' all lies. She was sitting, breast-feeding her kid. When I rolled up, she showed me her tits. She asked for a ride. She had me stop at the store. She bought us beer."

"Specifically, before the attack started," Slagle claimed, "he asked me about blow jobs. He asked me if I was the kind of girl that did that for my husband." She told Jesperson it was none of his business.

"She told me," Jesperson countered, "that she gave the best blow jobs in Shasta County and that was how we got started on the subject."

"I'm not going to lie to you," Slagle told me, "you are the only person that I ever told this to. I told him that at one time one of my boyfriends had told me that I was the best blow job. . . . But I did not say it in the context that he is saying it, like I was 'trying to entice him.'"

"There I was talking sex with her," Jesperson explained, "expecting to get the best blow job in Shasta County and then didn't get it. Why talk about it if we were *not* going there? Even Daun will have to admit to how anyone could be confused over her intentions."

Slagle had her baby with her. She needed to use the bathroom. She was in distress over a fight with her husband. She asked a stranger for a ride. They talked. She says one thing; he says another. Jesperson insisted that after she bought beer, she asked him to take her to park somewhere in the woods so they could drink and she could go to the bathroom.

"I took it as a come-on," he said.

"None of that happened," she claimed. According to her, before she got out of the car to urinate in the woods, Jesperson talked about how "pissed off at his wife" he was that "she never would do [oral sex]."

When she came back to the car, Jesperson got out and walked into the woods without an explanation. Slagle assumed he was going to the bathroom himself.

"I didn't see him for what felt like a long time," she said.

"That's not true," Jesperson said. "Never happened that way." (A police report backed up Jesperson's version.)

Slagle was puzzled, she said. They'd left the shopping mall parking lot and talked about where he worked, his kids, his wife; then out of nowhere, he broke into a rant about never having gotten oral sex from Rose. The conversation, for the most part, revolved around sex. That was all Jesperson wanted to talk about.

"I don't even know where [the sex talk] came from," she recalled.

"We drank the beer," Jesperson said. "We talked. She wanted to have sex with me."

When Jesperson returned to the vehicle, Slagle claimed, she sensed something wrong. She said Jesperson looked different. Walked different. Sat down in the car different. A look on his face unlike anything she had seen. Something had come over him.

Without speaking, instead of backing the car out of the woods, where he was parked on the edge of the street and grass, Jesperson pulled forward, deeper into the woods, so as to be out of eyesight to anyone around (according to Slagle's version).

"I knew I was in trouble," Daun Slagle said.

15

TRANSFORMATION

"Change the way you look at things, and the things you
look at change."
—Dr. Wayne W. Dyer

*B*EFORE I MADE CONTACT WITH DAUN SLAGLE, I'D BEEN CHUGGING
along with Keith Jesperson, feeling as though I'd made progress,
especially in understanding the mind of the psychopath. My intentions and emotional state were another thing. I suffered bouts
of anxiety and felt, on some days, I could not continue and needed
to end our friendship. Murder, my day job, was enough. Adding
the obsessions, rants, and constant drivel from a serial killer became overwhelming. I'd quit smoking three years before I met
Jesperson, but I was thinking about picking it up again.

As I went over what I'd learned thus far, putting my health—
mind and body—to the side, it occurred to me that I'd proven to
myself what clinical research had contended, but society and the
media had not been too interested in. There is, essentially, no
specific serial killer typology. For one, there are far too many versions of him, with far too many variables at play. The common
myth that all serial killers are diabolical and like to play cat-and-
mouse games with cops, want to be caught, are solitary figures, is
entirely grounded in Hollywood mythology. I'd crushed this common belief with my Jesperson interviews.

The one constant with Jesperson throughout my research was
that the fantasy he gravitated to most was sexually motivated and

paired with trying to find a willing partner, or, as an alternative, a prostitute. When met, the fantasy was emotionally and physiologically rewarding and stimulating. When not met, rage arose and he needed to release it. He would harness his anger into an asset later when he became proficient as a killer, but in 1990, as he was getting started, he had little control over his thoughts or temper.

Back talking on a regular basis as 2014 began, I wondered if Jesperson, with almost two decades now behind bars to think about his crimes, focused on his victims within the fantasy that held such a grip on him while he was killing. He'd told me once he did not like to "go there"—that place where his victims resided in his memory. It was one thing to repress certain aspects of his kills he did not want to face, talk openly about graphic details of his crimes, but quite another to deal with recurring flashbacks or recollections he couldn't control or stop. Did he still view his victims as sexual "things" within the context of his past obsessions? Were the women he murdered still fixed figures in his mind? One of the narratives many serial killers claim is the illusion that they can effortlessly detach from their crimes, let go of their victims and erase them—and the violence—from memory. I wanted to know if this was true for Happy Face.

"I think about them at different times throughout my days of being incarcerated," he explained, his answer surprising me. I was under the impression that the psychopath/sociopath[3] could not care less about the people he'd hurt or harmed; writing off the women he'd murdered and forgetting about them were part of that. Psychopaths, particularly, are generally unable to form emotional attachments.

He said it wasn't *how* he murdered them, or their actual deaths, he chose to revisit; it was how they met, what they might have talked about, and how they interacted.

---

[3]There are marked distinctions between the two. For more information, please see Dr. Scott Bonn's excellent article on the subject in *Psychology Today*: https://www.psychologytoday.com/blog/wicked-deeds/201401/how-tell-sociopath-psychopath.

"I think about that a lot. I go back and maybe in a dreamscape try to change the outcome. Hoping that I wake up, let's say, and I open my eyes, and I'm not in prison."

No matter how hard he tried, or how much he wanted to make me believe he's "not a bad guy," his narcissism was impossible for him to suppress. The killer is who he is, part of his ego and id. His answer proved as much. He views life, not just his kills, through a prism of self. The world does not exist for any other purpose besides what he deems important and what he can take from it.

After he killed Bennett, a change occurred inside Jesperson. Once the anxiety of being caught left, he embraced and "enjoyed how he was becoming somebody he wasn't normally." Now there were two versions of himself—and he liked how it made him feel.

Staring out my office window through the slits of my blinds one afternoon, watching the sky turn from bright Caribbean blue to a dull gray, thinking about what he'd said, I considered that the answers I sought from this man were complex. A second question I'd been thinking about nagged: Is there a difference between, say, a worldwide hated psychopathic creature such as Hitler and a serial killer like Jesperson? Can evil and a level of disregard for human life some human beings harbor be weighed on a scale from eight to eight million victims? Is it even fair to ask this question? How can we judge one psychopath's behavior as more significant or violent or hurtful than the other? Whether the killing of millions of innocent men, women, and children was done for ideological purposes or out of a sexual obsession, can we classify one as more evil than the other? I could call a forensic psychiatrist friend and ask, but the simple textbook answer was not of any interest to me.

"The lighter side of this was that after each murder they got easier and easier," Jesperson continued. "The heavier side was that I was out of control. I was not in control of myself any longer. I had lost control of who I was. I was actually somebody else, like I was looking at somebody else doing this."

During our conversations throughout the years, Jesperson had (without trying) exposed several different versions of himself. Every survivor of extreme violence I've interviewed—if what she says is true, Daun Slagle included—shared some part of the same narrative regarding the person they met and the psychopath that person became in their presence: At some point during their time together, a drastic change came over the perpetrator. Generally, the perp disappeared for a moment: to the bathroom or into a store, maybe a bedroom. Walking away one person, he returned another. He looked and spoke different, if he spoke at all. In talking with Jesperson, I sensed various personas on the phone, sometimes saw two different faces during our personal visits, and heard two different people comment on the cold cases I looked into on *Dark Minds*. Not different personalities. At times, Jesperson could be—and I realize this might be hard for some to grasp (it was difficult for me to come to terms with)—just another member of society I interacted with throughout my day. We could talk like two old friends who knew each other from high school. Those conversations, it's important to note, were still centered around his feelings, but it was as though I was speaking to someone who liked talking about himself. We all know these types. Yet, at other times, Jesperson could come across cold, dark, unfeeling. He could change his demeanor in the course of a sentence, even a word. I'd sometimes forget about the killer he is and then be jarringly reminded that person had been (hiding) there the entire time.

Once realized, this revelation opened a chasm. I became aware that somewhere deep inside the mind of this psychopath was the faint rustling of a human being. There had to be. In the beginning, I despised the killer Jesperson is and those like him. A journalist is supposed to remain objective, neutral, part of a tacit and invisible team out in the world, there to report news to the public, personalities and opinions aside. But that is impossible when writing books of this nature. One cannot stand idle, lips zipped, and not express feelings. It goes against human nature not to be offended and horrified by what you hear and see and feel. I stepped into this relationship with a serial killer with no interest in digging into his psyche for an extended period of time. I was, as I have said, under the impression there were people in the world born evil and then bred, throughout their lives, to embrace an inherited darkness and make a choice to become violent and murderous. Some serial killers have admitted this about themselves: they do not care about anyone and cannot love.

As our relationship progressed, however, something in me changed. I found myself, same as passing a terrible wreck on the freeway, unable to turn away. Jesperson badgered me incessantly about the Bennett case, how he needed to get the truth according to him out into the public lexicon. I would find myself doubled over with stress pains one day, but then asking him for more details the next, knowing how hard it is for the general public to accept what a serial killer actually has to say.

"People don't *want* to understand who I am," he said one morning. "They want to look at me and see only the murders I committed. Some of these [murders] happened so quick, I didn't even have time to think about what I was doing. I knew I was killing," he added, at this point nearly out of breath, a mania I'd witnessed many times pouring out of him as he struggled to connect words and construct sentences. "But I wasn't in a conscious thought of how it affected my life. I just did it, to do it. I had the opportunity and went with it."

I asked about the "other" person inside him.

"I became someone I didn't like. I'm not a split-personality character. I am who I am, but then there's this *other* side of me. There's this voice on one shoulder telling me it's okay, go ahead and do this. It's like pushing; it's got a prod and pretty soon you are the one acting out on it. I'm the one doing it, but *they* are the one actually *doing* it for me."

He knew how I felt: the serial killer he is "repulses me."

"I know. I cannot do anything about that, Phelps."

I hesitated. Then: "But you can now. You can help identify your Jane Does. You know who they are. Don't screw with me on that."

"Do what I said. Get the death penalty off the table."

I was working on that, but also debating whether to lie and tell him I'd gotten it done. He'd never ask me for written proof. He trusted my word enough by now.

"You understand that my sister-in-law was murdered, I'm a victims' advocate, what you've done to people, I hate you for that." Continuing, I explained that over the years we'd spoken, "I've become . . ." I stopped. Took a deep breath. "A friend, I guess, to this other person I speak to at times, and I don't look at you as a serial killer in that moment—and *that* concerns me."

Exactly what John Kelly had warned me about: letting my guard down.

"There is a—" he said, before taking the conversation, as he sometimes would, in another direction: "I am a nice guy. I see myself as a nice guy. But by the same token, I know this other person inside me exists. There's this other side of me that, well, I accept death as okay."

Weeks went by. I got into a spell where I stopped answering his calls. A feeling of understanding what was happening inside me grew into one of concern. I was baffled by my tolerance for what he could say, how vile and offensive his thoughts were to most, how much he'd opened up to me. At times, I felt as though he didn't care what anybody thought, and wasn't thinking about the public consequence or reaction to what he said. He was, instead, telling me what was going on inside him, uncensored. Something of which I'd strived to get out of him from the beginning.

In between our conversations, be it a day, week, or longer, I pondered what had been said. I'd reevaluate where he and I were coming from. It was strange. The world between us, so small and compact, confined to that telephone line and words on paper, became a place entirely closed off to what was going on around me. I live in a small farming community. Cornfields surround our homes. When the farmers fertilize, watch out, you go outside and the smell is pungent and vile, hitting your sinuses like a busted sewer main. But then I'd hang up from a conversation in which I believed a human being actually existed within him, step outside into the reality of my life, now forced to face a sobering thought:

He's a serial killer doing life. He's not a nice guy, no matter how much he can manipulate me. He killed eight women. That's what he does. He lies and he charms and he kills. What the hell am I doing?

Was I softening up? Had I lost my sense of what I did for a living? Or was I like so many others: a human being with feelings, going through a process for which there was no precedence? How many writers—or people, for that matter—spent years of their lives talking to a serial killer about every subject imaginable?

There was one writer I knew of and had read about, Jason Moss. He wrote a memoir about his "exploration into the minds of incarcerated serial killers." But that situation did not end well for Mr. Moss: he committed suicide on June 6, 2006—or 6/6/06.

JESPERSON BEGAN SENDING PIECES of art he'd sketched specifically for me. Donkeys. Sunrises. Parrots and parakeets. Elephants. Tropical landscapes. All of them boldly colorful. Over the years, the drawings became darker and more in line with the subject matter we focused on—cartoonish, strange sketches, mostly done in reds and blacks and blues: Ted Bundy, Freddy Krueger, the shower scene from the Hitchcock film *Psycho*, Hannibal Lecter, and Charles Manson, a bleeding swastika tattooed on his forehead. He signed all of them as Raven. I could sense that during the twenty years he'd spent behind bars, he'd learned how to express his feelings with colored pencils and charcoal and a modicum of talent. Some of the art he'd sent to pen pals and others had sold on the Internet for hundreds of dollars because of his Happy Face legacy. These early pieces he mailed me sent shivers down the spines of anybody I showed them to. I wanted to frame an Oregon duck (the local college football team's mascot) and hang it in my office. My family shared an opinion that there was no way I was going to be allowed to do this. "Creepy" was the unified opinion at the household dinner table. Everyone around me saw his art— regardless of the subject—as the essence of evil, scribed by the psychotic hand and mind of a madman.

Indeed, it is. Yet, without telling anyone, I felt the paintings— even the most disturbing among them—to be nothing more than a gift from a friend. It scared me that I was not offended by them. I had changed, somehow, without realizing it.

As he broke into a soliloquy about his "nice guy" status one morning, I countered by saying nobody gives a shit how he views himself or the world. "You are a serial killer. No one cares about your feelings, how I feel about you, what you think caused this malicious need in you to kill those women, or the notion that you want to right some wrong in the Bennett case. On top of that, you are paranoid. There's no proof of your accusations. It's all specula-tion bouncing around inside your manic mind. Pure supposition. You want someone to go down with you—that's all this Bennett thing is about. And that *someone* happens to be a couple of cops and a prosecutor. Big fucking surprise there. Twenty years after the fact and you are *still* trying to keep attention focused on *you*."

"I need to go to work," he said, hanging up. I'd pissed him off.

At one time, Jesperson was employed in prison as one of those annoying telemarketers calling your house while you're eating dinner, trying to sell you windows, solar panels, cheaper electric-ity, maybe asking for a donation to the policeman's union, or any number of other products/services. He loved this job. There was triumph in his voice whenever he talked about it, as though he'd beaten the system somehow.

"I spoke to someone in Vernon today," he said one day. "Isn't that where you live?"

Then he called to say he got fired. My assumption was that a victim's family member found out the serial killer who had mur-dered his loved one was calling unsuspecting homes to try to sell them a free vacation to Mexico.

What became an oscillation of hatred and friendship pushed back and forth: I sympathized with a serial killer on some days, wondering how in the hell I could possibly feel this way; on other days, I wanted to end what we were doing because I felt I needed to honor his victims' memories by not giving him what he wanted: more media space and notoriety. It went on for years, really, me leaning more toward tossing in my inhibitions and questions and listening to him for as long as I could emotionally handle it. Then, I didn't know why, but I started to feel sorry for him.

I told no one.

Working on *Dark Minds* and writing the types of books I do, getting through it without crumbling from all the darkness and pain, and curling into a fetal ball in the corner of my office, I tried to take myself out of it as much as I could and focus on the writing and work, not the consequences or results of the violence. That space between collapsing and allowing the pain to take total control of my days is a flimsy wire I walk every day that I sit down at my desk or head out on the road.

Speaking with Daun Slagle about her ordeal with Jesperson became an anomaly within all of this. Slagle claimed to have lived with a monkey of guilt on her back weighing her down after she ran across Jesperson. For many years, she believed that had she stopped Jesperson after she interacted with him, seven women would be alive. This comment spun me around to face the true commitment I'd made to this project when I began in 2011: to expose this man for who he truly is.

16

SPECTATOR

"I am solitary as grass. What is it I miss? Shall I ever find it,
whatever it is?"
—Sylvia Plath

*K*EITH JESPERSON WAS ON HIS WAY TO DUNSMUIR, CALIFORNIA, IN
April 1990, on the night he met Daun Slagle. The story he gave
her regarding why he was in town was true. Dunsmuir is about fifteen miles south of Mt. Shasta. Jesperson was on his way to meet
Pamela in Weed, California, when he took a detour into the town
of Mt. Shasta, he said, "to get a bite to eat." The plan was to pick
Pamela up at a local Weed truck stop that night and drive to Dunsmuir, where Pamela's brother lived. But Jesperson had gotten
into town early. Making matters more complicated for him, he
said, was that Rose's new husband grew up and lived in Dunsmuir.

"Our sex life was great," Jesperson said of his and Pamela's relationship before she took off to Tennessee and he killed Bennett. That fabulous sex life came to a screeching halt, however,
after Pamela returned home from her fling and wound up with
custody of her kids. Jesperson said he hated being "Mr. Mom." It
cramped every part of his lifestyle.

"I missed *my* kids. The situation just made me want to leave it
all behind."

His plan was to start a new job in Sacramento and walk away
from what he called "the haunted house," which he still shared
with Pamela (and now her kids) in Portland. Being inside the same

house where he'd murdered Bennett, interacting with Pamela and the kids, was a constant reminder of what he'd done. And so he made up his mind he was going back to Portland to pack and leave, without telling Pamela.

Before heading into Mt. Shasta and meeting Slagle, Jesperson stopped by an old girlfriend's house along the way. Previously published reports claimed Jesperson "wanted sex" and was going to rape and kill his ex if she wouldn't give it up. "The closer I got to her house, the harder my penis got," Jesperson was quoted as saying in 2002.

"I wasn't thinking of killing her," he told me. "But [a previous writer] seemed to imply I could have. That's ridiculous."

He didn't have to worry about losing control, because after finding nobody home at his ex's, Jesperson heard she'd been raped and murdered by two men in the weeks before he arrived.

"Having killed Bennett and hearing about [my ex-girlfriend], I really wasn't in the mood, or there wasn't the *idea* of murder on my part. I didn't want to engage in a date. Daun was persistent. And so I just followed along. She showed me her tits. Bought us beer. She was drinking a bottle of Jack Daniel's when I met her. I took it all as an invitation to sex."

Like a lot of facts from that night Jesperson laid claim to, Slagle denied that she was breast-feeding her child in the parking lot of the strip mall when she met him, or drinking, or that she ever mentioned partying and asked him to stop so she could buy beer.

DAUN SLAGLE WAS WARY of me when we first spoke, and I did not understand why. But as we got to talking, it made sense. "The flashlight," she said. "Raven, on your show, explained in an episode how he had left a flashlight at one of his crime scenes and I knew *then* that Raven is Jesperson."

Slagle wasn't the only viewer to pick up on that slipup. I'd gotten a few e-mails and had seen comments on social media alluding to the fact that, as much as we tried to cover up who Jesperson was, this clue (and maybe others) had gotten by us.

According to Slagle, after Jesperson walked into the woods, uri-nated, sat back down in the car, and drove deeper into the woods, she looked over at him and sensed something was off. She claimed that after Jesperson parked the car a second time, without warning, he grabbed her by the back of the head and smashed her against the dashboard.

"Never happened," Jesperson claimed.

"And then he started trying to break my neck," she insisted. She said her baby was on her lap and soon fell onto the floor-board by her feet.

"I don't recall doing any of that," Jesperson said. "The baby was on the backseat on a blanket, not in the front."

"What did you do while you were in the woods?" I asked him. During this call, I made a point to confront Jesperson with all of the inconsistencies I'd heard from Slagle. "Daun claims you were gone quite awhile and when you came back you were 'different.' Did you go out there to masturbate? Dredge up the courage to rape her? Think about killing her?"

"No, no, I never left the car. She left the car to urinate. That's why we went out there to begin with. I later showed police where she pissed and the alcohol bottles left behind."

"She said you changed—and she wouldn't be the first one to say this about a serial killer."

He grew subdued. Withdrawn. I could feel him wince. He spoke in a low monotone. I knew the voice. He was angry with me for persisting. He was fighting off, best he could, that rage. "I *wasn't* a serial killer at that time," he said, frustrated.

"But look, man, you *were* a killer."

"Right." He paused. It was difficult to hear him because he spoke in such a delicate whisper. "We're one in the same."

"This metamorphosis in the woods—do you recall that hap-pening?" I asked.

"I don't remember. That's all I can say."

"She says you began to smash her head against the dashboard."

"No, I didn't smash her face against the dashboard. That's not true at all. I had my arm, well, I don't know *what* happened. I remember it one way. I had my arm around her."

The police report from the incident tells another variation. Concisely written, it speaks of how Daun Slagle got into the car and Keith Jesperson drove around, parked, and then "pulled his dick out and said, 'Suck my dick.'" She refused, so Jesperson "grabbed [her] around the neck and tried to force her." Within that "struggle," the report continued, her baby wound up on the floor.

Slagle said later that Jesperson stomped on her boy at some point.

Jesperson denied this, saying there was no way he would have hurt the child. The police report backed up Jesperson, indicating "the baby was not injured."

Slagle believed Jesperson was "trying to break my neck," as opposed to trying to strangle her. She felt pressure being applied to her neck bones so harshly, "a little more and I knew it was going to break."

This "struggle" lasted a few minutes. As Jesperson squeezed, trying to get a handle on her neck, according to Slagle, she leaned into his grip, hoping to thwart any leverage he might have over her.

"What the hell do you think you are doing?" she claimed she screamed. "I'll do anything you want! Just don't hurt my baby. Stop, stop, stop!"

Jesperson continued. She knew she needed to find a way to "get him off of his game and confuse him for a second."

As she contemplated what to do next, he stopped.

She grabbed her baby, held him close to her chest.

Jesperson came back from whatever place he had gone off to, Slagle claimed; that "change" gripping him was gone.

Jesperson sat. Didn't say much.

"This metamorphosis was over," she said. "He started the car."

She had no idea what he was planning, where he was going.

The car ride was silent. Jesperson drove out of the woods, got onto the main road, headed toward the I-5. As he approached the entrance ramp heading northbound, he pulled over.

Slagle didn't speak.

He looked at her. According to Slagle, he pushed the frame of his glasses up the bridge of his nose, then said: "Don't ever get into the car with someone you don't know again—it might be the last thing you ever do."

She held her baby tight to her chest and got out.

Jesperson took off onto the I-5.

"Now *that* is funny," Jesperson told me. "None of it is true. Remember, I do not know this town one bit. I have no idea where I'm driving. Because of that, she is giving me directions. 'Turn here, go there, park over there.' She asked me to pull over by the side of the ramp. Then she got out without any fanfare or words. As far as I was concerned, we'd had a go of it and she wound up not wanting to do anything. I got a little angry. I don't believe I hurt her."

The Mt. Shasta Police Department (MSPD) was five blocks from where Slagle stood on the side of the road watching her "attacker," as she called him, drive away. She walked in and explained what happened. She described the vehicle. Gave them a description of Jesperson and his name. Said he was on his way to Sacramento.

A Be-On-the-Lookout (BOLO) was sent out to all local police.

The cop who took the report drove her home. It was 1:17 A.M. when they walked in and woke her husband.

"He blamed me," she claimed. "It was my fault for taking off alone."

By 3:40 A.M., Corning Police, one hundred miles south of Mt. Shasta, pulled Jesperson over and took him into custody. (He told me later, "I turned myself in.") After contacting the MSPD, Corning allowed Jesperson to drive back to Mt. Shasta "on his own agreement to return [there] and clear this matter up." He got into his car and drove himself back to Mt. Shasta.

At home, Daun Slagle was ready to press charges against Keith

Jesperson for sexual assault and battery, maybe forced imprison-
ment, kidnapping, whatever fit. She wanted justice. In her view
(later), she'd been attacked and her child was nearly killed. Jesperson needed to be prosecuted.

"Just let it go," Slagle claimed her husband told her. "Forget
about it."

"Discuss this between the two of you," a police officer suggested. "But don't take too much time." The impression was: file
a report as soon as possible.

Slagle and her husband were at odds, still arguing. She wanted
to press charges. She claimed her husband kept insisting no, she
shouldn't. So she left the house and walked to a phone booth,
called, and told the MSPD she wanted to move forward with
charges.

By now, the sun had come up and it was late morning.

"Well, it's too late for that," she said the cop told her. "We've already let him go."

JESPERSON SEIZED ON THE idea that if Daun Slagle had pressed
charges against him and saw the case through, seven women might
still be alive. "I think about what might have happened, had they
charged me and put me in jail. I seriously considered heading
back to Canada, where I had lived a good portion of my life," Jesperson said, "just to run from what I believed was a case they could still
make."

Tragedy and trauma seemed to follow Daun Slagle. She had
been pregnant when she met Jesperson. According to Slagle, that
baby would be killed in 1991, at four months old, by her second
husband, who spent five years in prison for involuntary
manslaughter.

Quite incredibly, in 2014, Slagle claimed to be attacked again.
In July of that year, she said a man with a weapon grabbed and
cornered her in an alley in back of her house just after sunset.
She said he had a weapon and forced her to masturbate him (his
semen was later found on her).

Slagle claimed to have gotten out of this situation in a similar manner she used on Jesperson: "I'm on my period, please don't touch me there," she said. "Sorry, that's not part of my religion."

According to Slagle, "I was constantly just throwing a wrench in there. You have to counteract it from a physical sense and bring the situation into a mental battle."

The man, thirty-year-old Claudio Sanches, was arrested a few blocks away from the incident after she phoned police. After claiming that she had actually come on to him and asked him to pull his pants down, Sanches was charged with assault and battery. One trial ended in a mistrial. In December 2015, after a second trial, Sanches was found guilty.

In a startling turn of events, in March 2016, Daun Slagle was charged with stabbing her boyfriend in the ribs, along with a host of other crimes, including leading police on a high-speed chase, putting her credibility into question. Claudio Sanches's attorney, Stephana Femino, had filed a motion for a new trial before the stabbing incident—and, in April 2016, a judge agreed. As of this writing, Sanches awaits his third day—mistrial, conviction, and now new trial—in court on this matter.[4]

"My client vehemently denies Slagle's allegations and maintains the sexual contact was consensual," Femino told me, adding how her "client passed a lie detector test." In the judge's ruling overturning the conviction, thus granting a new trial, he pointed out there was "no physical evidence presented" to suggest the contact between Slagle and Sanches was "anything but consensual, which is why Slagle's credibility (or lack thereof) is an essential part of the case," Femino said. "A prime example of this is she claimed she was violently attacked and dragged by her hair down a gravel and cement alley, yet she did not have one scratch or

[4]Daun Slagle is a paradox: I don't know what to believe anymore. I want to embrace her Jesperson story because she is a victim; on the other hand, I find a lot of holes. If interested in a longer version of her story, Google her name. Read the available *court* documents, not the rhetoric posted on the Internet masquerading as "facts."

bruise. She also claimed my client dragged her down the alley by her hair to get to a place where he could continue the attack in private, yet for some reason, according to her, he gave up in the middle of the alley. . . . Keep in mind, this happened during the broad daylight. Just as in Jesperson's case, Daun's story in my client's case changes each time she tells it."

17

TRUSTY AND TRUE

"Much unhappiness has come into the world because of
bewilderment and things left unsaid."
—Fyodor Dostoyevsky

SOME HAVE ASKED IF KEITH JESPERSON SCARES ME. NO. HE DOES NOT
scare me. Despite headlines such as TEN GRIM FACTS ABOUT SERIAL
KILLERS YOU WISH YOU NEVER KNEW and all the insipid serial killer
lists compiled on the Internet, spelling out alleged "facts" we
should know about them, all of which is meant to instill fear, serial killers in general don't frighten me and shouldn't frighten the
general public. Being murdered by a serial killer is a rare crime.
According to the FBI's most recent statistics, serial homicide accounts for about 1 percent of all homicides committed in the
United States, while homicide rates themselves have dropped 50
percent since the 1990s.

In speaking with Taunja Bennett's brother, Dave Rowe, checking into what he'd said, I am convinced he never met Jesperson
on the front porch of his home during those months before his
sister was murdered. Dave is traumatized and devastated by the
loss of his sister. My heart goes out to the guy. I understand that
pain as one I've seen on the faces of my nephews, niece, and
other family members. What's clear to me is that Jesperson was in
Tualatin, Oregon, outside Portland, and Eugene, staying near the
University of Oregon, at the time Dave claimed to have met Jesperson before he picked up Bennett and drove her to Seattle.

Likely, Jesperson never met Bennett before the night he killed her. I don't see any reason why he would lie about this now. Furthermore, the one piece of evidence proving Jesperson acted alone, despite rumors and reports of him conspiring with Laverne Pavlinac and John Sosnovske to kill Bennett, including what Dave Rowe added to that speculative narrative, was uncovered on October 14, 1995.

Jesperson was in custody, having been arrested after mailing a letter to one of his brothers and turning himself in. After Thomas Phelan secured a deal and convinced Jim McIntyre and his troops that Jesperson had killed Bennett, sparking a storm of controversy and legal battles to get Pavlinac and Sosnovske out of prison, while speaking with detectives, seeing there had been so much talk about Sosnovske and Pavlinac playing a role in Bennett's murder, Jesperson told them he was the only one who could point to where Bennett's wallet and ID card were located.

"Wouldn't that prove I acted alone?"

They agreed it would.

Phelan had actually gone into a meeting with everyone and mentioned his client wanted to confess to killing Bennett and they nearly laughed at him.

"That's fine," Phelan said. "But what if you're wrong? You do not want to be wrong about this."

McIntyre went to see his boss, returned to the meeting, and decided to hear them out.

It took some time, but after a group of Explorer Scouts set out in that area forty feet off the road by the Sandy River, where Jesperson had tossed Bennett's wallet, just underneath a blackberry bush, which searchers had chopped down during an unproductive search a week prior, stuck in a muddy patch of debris, there was Taunja Bennett's wallet and ID. No one but her killer could have known where that evidence was hidden.

18

THE WORLD ACCORDING TO RAVEN

"I'm guilty of giving people more chances than they
deserve, but when I'm done, I'm done."
—Turcois Ominek

*T*HROUGHOUT THE SUMMER OF 2014, THE SOUND OF THE RINGING
phone in my office as I stared at the prison Telmate number on
the LCD screen, pausing a moment, picturing Jesperson, the
phone receiver up to his ear, smiling, waiting for me to accept his
call, became like the chirp of a smoke alarm going off inside my
head. Every day, as the number popped up and I contemplated
ignoring it, an emotional ulcer grew inside me. My stomach had
that perpetual feeling one gets when he knows he needs to end a
long-term relationship but puts it off because he doesn't want to
hurt the other person. A pit. A thousand fluttering butterflies.

When *Dark Minds* was canceled after three seasons in 2014, I
faced a dilemma: Jesperson was sucking the life out of me. I was
depressed. Emotionally empty. On top of all the calls, whether I
answered or not, there were all of those letters, maps of dump
sites he'd drawn on scraps of cardboard, photographs of him and
his "cellies" (additional lowlifes who'd committed savage acts of
violence), newspaper clippings, birthday and Christmas cards,
artwork, his continuous obsession with the Bennett case. All of
this drove me once again to question my ethics. Here was a person the rest of the world viewed as an *enfant terrible*, a monster—a
twisted psychopath who uses, abuses, and discards people. Yet to

Jesperson, his incorrigibly manipulative and psychotic ways were nothing more than social imperfections: *This is who I am. Deal with it.*

Well, I grew tired of it all. Enough was enough.

"Doesn't it bother you that everyone you've killed has been someone other people have loved?" I asked one day, fed up, in a mood to cut him off. "You took their loved one away from them forever. If someone—"

He interrupted. "I understand what you're saying. . . ."

"Wait, wait, wait. Let. Me. Finish. This doesn't *bother* you at all?"

"No," he said, his voice firm, serious. He meant what he said. Right then, a faint rustling of optimism I'd had of maybe dredging the bottom of some scummy pond, hoping to find a film of empathy, or perhaps getting him to see what he'd done in the framework of morality and being human, dissolved. A nauseous feeling—right before you know you're going to throw up—came over me. I knew in that moment there was likely no good in this person. I'd been kidding myself believing maybe there was and I could find it.

"What if someone *you* cared about was murdered? How would that make you feel?"

"Well, I would care about my loved one being killed. I would be upset about it, yes, because I care about my loved ones. But I didn't know these people I . . . I dealt with. These people are not in my lifestyle . . . my . . . my . . . my world. They don't exist in *my* world. They are in *their* world. They are not in *my* world. I don't know who these people are, so therefore I have no feelings for these people. I know there is a loss here, Phelps. I know there is a loss and I should feel there is a loss. That I should feel sorry for them. I feel for their loss. However, I don't *know* who they are"—he sounded like a child unable to say what he wanted—"and so it is hard for me to have an emotional commitment to these people without knowing who they really are."

The fact that he referred to eight human beings as *these people* said it all. He couldn't even dignify their lives or memories by calling them *victims*.

During another call, I asked about his logbooks. Being a trucker, he kept a record of all his movements during the time he killed. These records would help me figure out other victims he could have killed and also answer questions about his known victims. I had been trying to get my hands on the logbooks for three years.

"You need to get those," he said. I sensed a patronizing tone to his voice. "Good luck with that." He laughed.

Because his cases had never gone to trial, he knew the records were almost impossible to come by. In a way, he could hide behind them: act as though he wanted me to obtain them, under the personal belief I never would.

Hearing this, I made it a priority to find them.

While figuring out my next move, I'd accept his calls, listen to him rant about prison officials, a woman who self-published what was an unreadable book about him and how she had let him down, pen pals who had abandoned him, how they messed "with my mail in here all the time," among all sorts of other complaints. I'd hang up hating him with vigor. Then he'd call and say something that piqued my interest about a potential crime he might have committed, which, in turn, fueled an urge in me to keep digging.

I had this desire to crack him. I figured he was admitting to about 75 percent of the crimes he'd committed and roughly the same in terms of what he'd told law enforcement. I felt several Jane Does he was on the books for were women he *could* identify, if he chose. Plus, there had loomed the outside chance he'd murdered more women than he had self-confessed and would one day come clean and explain to me where authorities could find additional bodies. Internet reports accused him of murdering as many as 166. That was impossible, I knew, and he told me it was a lie he once told cops during a period when he was playing with them. Still, after the years I'd put in, I deserved truth—and demanded it from him.

Some time went by and I stopped answering his calls altogether. I needed the space to heal, think, and work on television projects and other books, without the interruption of a raging serial killer, mad at the world, writing me so many letters every week I didn't have time to read.

He called and called and called: six, seven, ten times a day. *Relentless* was the word that came to mind most often. I had a Trac-Fone I used on *Dark Minds* that he could call me on when I was out of my office and on the road. He blew that thing up with calls, figuring I was traveling.

He became a fly in my head I could not swat.

One day, I picked up and told him to stop calling. I hadn't yet shared with him that *Dark Minds* wasn't coming back for a fourth season. He was itching for me to send him material on new cases we were going to profile on the show, so he could prepare. I kept telling him we hadn't chosen the cases, but I would send the material soon. If I told him the series was over, he'd fear I didn't need him anymore and, feeling sorry for himself, badger me about cutting the cord and walking away. I was still on the fence about whether I was going to continue interviewing him.

"Okay," he said. "How long should I wait? When are you scheduled to start filming?"

"Not sure. Give me some time. I'll be in touch. I'm sure *you* will be."

When dealing with Jesperson, I understood he functioned best when he had assigned tasks. A serial killer's mind runs at hyperspeed. I needed him to utilize that energy toward a project that could benefit me. What that project had now morphed into, I wasn't sure. I would figure it out soon enough. I'd been pressured by many to reveal Raven's identity, along with the nagging impulse to scream at all the naysayers and Internet trolls claiming Raven was an actor and did not exist. Seeing that the series was over, I began working up a proposal for a three-part documentary about Jesperson's life, our "friendship," and his role as Raven on *Dark Minds*. That kept me busy for a while.

I wasn't sure what—if anything—to tell him about the documentary, because once I did, that'd be his only focus.

"What can I do?" he asked, looking for direction.

"I don't know, man. I *just* don't know. I need time away from you. You need to confront who you are, I suppose. You still haven't done that. You make excuses. You blame your victims. You blame your dad. You know how I feel about the way in which you talk about your victims. I've held back. I've stuffed my feelings of the scourge I believe you are and I find myself feeling sorry for another part of you I've gotten to know. It's confusing and . . . well, challenging and overwhelming. You are probably lying to me and laughing at me when we hang up."

"No, no, no," he tried to say, but I cut him off and demanded to be heard.

"I have to reevaluate. Doesn't mean we're done. Also, I have other serial killers I am speaking to and thinking about using on *Dark Minds* and other television projects I'm developing. You're not my only source."

He went quiet. The mere mention of competition made him seethe with contempt. "Sometimes I think I'm your only game," he continued with a pathetic, somber tone, "but you have a life beyond me, I know that. And you also have your work that I know very little about and have nothing to do with. I know you are talking to other killers."

Imagine: he was jealous.

Contemplating whether to tell him *Dark Minds* was over and I was considering a feature-length documentary, I got a letter from him explaining how we could now set up Video Visits.

Skype with a serial killer? He had to be confused.

So I went online, logged into my Telmate account, and, to my surprise, he was right. In late 2014, OSP initiated a program called Video Visits, basically a Skype system for inmates and those on their visiting lists. I set up an account so Jesperson and I could utilize the technology and communicate on a far more personal level. It included being able to e-mail each other as often as we wanted. Within a few weeks of the program being installed at the prison, incredibly, there was Happy Face—a ghost I could not expel, a demon I could not exorcise—staring back at me as I sat at my desk three thousand miles away.

I decided to record each Video Visit on a GoPro, with the

thought I'd use the footage in my documentary. My office is inside my home. Though it is not part of an active area of living space, I made sure to schedule the visits when no one was around. It was bad enough that whenever Jesperson called my office, the Telmate number popped up on television screens throughout the house, reminding everyone who was calling. Here now, though, was a man who hated women, a psychopath who had killed eight females, inside my professional and personal space. Three thousand miles separated us, but he had managed, somehow, to infiltrate every facet of my life.

After recording hours of Video Visits, we got back to talking on the phone. "Listen," I told him, "why don't you take some time and write about your father, your childhood, and let's try to find out exactly how you were made and where you might have begun to unravel?"

I expected resistance.

"Okay. Yes. I can do that."

"I still need some time. Let's not talk for a while."

What came in the mail about a month after my request, us not interacting much throughout that period, as my emotional burns healed and I felt strong enough to step back into the fire, once again ripped to shreds any preconceived notions I had about serial killers.

PART TWO

FAMILY

19

SELECTIVE MADNESS

"Who we are takes generations to create and doesn't
end with death."
—Stanley Siegel

*T*HEY CALLED HIM "CRAZY CHARLIE." HE OWNED A PATCH OF PRO-
ductive farmland outside Chilliwack, British Columbia, Canada,
allegedly worth what would be considered millions by today's
standards. It was the early 1930s. Some in the Jesperson family
wanted a piece of Charlie's pie. Whenever one of the clan stopped
by, sniffed around, asked questions, old Charlie barked at them.
He was hostile and ferocious. He could sense certain family members were hoping one day to bask in the glory of his wealth.

"You want what I have, work your ass off for it like I did," Charlie said.

Keith Jesperson, a teenage kid the size of an NFL lineman, who
by then had become known within the family as "Igor," a nickname one of his brothers had given him based on the character's
abnormal looks, had heard the "Crazy Charlie" stories. Charlie
had built a fortune blacksmithing and buying up land around
Chilliwack. No one in the immediate Jesperson family liked him.
He kept to himself and was considered a bitter, antisocial miser.

"They're all out to get me," Charlie claimed. "They want to take
my land from me."

According to Keith, the one member of the family leading the cause to get his hands on what old Charlie had worked a lifetime for was Les Jesperson, Igor's dad, the root cause, according to Keith, of all his childhood suffering. Les would adopt Charlie's Scrooge-like ways later, Keith said, by doing the same thing to him. After making his mark in the machining business, Les bought land and made Keith work the land, but he never once shared its prosperity with him. "He gave it all to my brothers and sisters, nothing to me," Jesperson told me.

After not making much headway convincing Charlie to share, as the Jesperson legend goes, the family got together and sent a doctor to see Charlie. He was acting strange, family members claimed. One report included Charlie publicly displaying "incessant masturbation" and also making "death threats" against people, family, friends, and neighbors. He was said to have not made much sense when he spoke, while threatening trespassers by waving the barrel of his shotgun at them.

"They wanted to commit him," Keith said. "Talk around town was that Charlie was crazy. Why? Because the Jespersons *said* he was." Where we lived then, Keith added, was "like a chicken coop, all wanting to peck at someone."

Charlie stood at his door, his wife by his side, demanding to know what the doctor wanted.

The psychiatrist explained.

"Well, you can take your ass off my property right now," Charlie responded. "All this amounts to is another way for them to steal my land."

As he got older, after having experienced the same treatment from his father, Keith realized that Charlie wasn't stupid or mind sick. It was the Jesperson way: take what you wanted, implications aside, by lying, cheating, and stealing.

Charlie threatened the doctor with bodily harm if he didn't hit the bricks.

The doctor left "rattled," Keith heard. So much so, he called the local Royal Canadian Mounted Police (RCMP) constable, who then took Charlie into custody, as the doctor insisted Charlie was suffering from what he determined to be a hereditary disease of the psyche: dementia praecox, or "precocious madness," a psychotic disorder passed somewhere down the genetic Scandinavian line of Jesperson DNA. Medical records claimed Charlie was diagnosed as delusional and paranoid.

Committed to the local mental facility, Charlie was beside himself. The family had managed to initiate a plan to pinch his land out from underneath him and get rid of him in the process. He was doomed to a rubber room, tiny paper cups filled with colorful pills, his slippers sandpapering down the hallway to his seat in front of a window.

After losing all hope of ever convincing the facility he was sane, Charlie surrendered. Medical records indicate he managed to get hold of a three-and-a-half-inch spike and hammer. Alone one night, he placed the spike into his eye socket and used the hammer to bang the sharp piece of ragged metal through his head, a half-inch piece sticking out of his eye socket.

He survived the night. It wasn't until an orderly pulled the spike out the next afternoon that an infection set in, swelled Charlie's brain, and killed him.

Les Jesperson would forever make the claim that his homicidal son and Keith's certified "crazy"/suicidal great-uncle shared the same psychotic bloodline: "That's where crazy Keith got his antics—Charlie."

As Jesperson told me many times, however, details from the tale might be true, or might not be. However, it was Les, making his son the butt of all the family jokes and his savage "belt punishments" and alcoholic madness, that turned what was an eccentric, awkwardly large, hardworking, shy boy, living on a farm in Canada, into a hardened, violent man who learned how to kill from the same man who had given him life.

"There are real times we all wish we could go back to change, especially the force of the blows with our belts or spoons," Jesperson told me, speaking of his father's punishments. "But we would rather say, it didn't happen like that. We, as children, remember it differently. We remember pain."

Les didn't recall raising Keith in this way. In everything he later said about raising his serial killer son, Les denied being an alcoholic and an abuser.

"Selective amnesia," Jesperson said of his father's memories. "That's Les Jesperson."

20

DEATH—AS A PERFORMANCE

"The most loving parents . . . commit murder with smiles
on their faces. They force us to destroy the person we
really are: a subtle kind of murder."
—Jim Morrison

*T*HE TOWN WHERE I LIVE TODAY IS A SUBURBAN PASTORAL; ROLLING
green hills and meadows amid thousands of acres of cow corn;
maple, birch, willow and white oak trees, poison ivy snaking around
their trunks in candy cane–like swirls, canopies of branches tower-
ing over the immediate skyline. Geese fly in flocks above like the
Blue Angels. There's a peaceful, community, New England charm
emanating outside my door: red barns, John Deere tractors,
rolled-up bales of hay in the shape of cinnamon rolls, men wearing blue jean coveralls and ball caps while working the land, signs
denoting "fresh farm eggs." A gazebo dots the center town green,
the antiquated façade of the library just west of that, a marble
stone war memorial monument at the foot of our flagpole, a
greasy spoon called The Chuck Wagon we all love to eat at, Siv's
Scandinavian Gift and Food Shop, with the orange-and-blue
Swedish horse sign out front, two churches (Congregational and
Catholic), their spires like swordfish pointing into the clouds, a
small hardware store across from the grammar school on Main
Street.

At times I leave my driveway and find myself in back of a tractor
with wheels higher than my car, its yellow hazard lights blinking,

towing tons of cow manure piled in throwers. Welcomingly, this slows life down for a few moments and allows me to focus on what's important and how fortunate, blessed and grateful I am for the opportunity to live amid such serenity and grace.

From my home office it's a thirty-minute drive to PO Box 3215, in Vernon, Connecticut. That's the town where I came of age (twelve to twenty-nine years old) and lived. I check my box once a week so mail doesn't pile up. With Jesperson writing to me, however, it became a twice-a-week job. Heading there one afternoon, passing an old Quality Inn nearby, I started to think about Jesperson once mentioning in a letter that he wanted to help with my sister-in-law's unsolved 1996 homicide. My brother and Diane once lived at the same Quality Inn. Funny how the mind works: smells, songs, a photograph, a building, they take you right back.

Staring at the hotel, I rolled my eyes. Jesperson's gesture felt insulting. How the hell could a serial killer three thousand miles away, who knew nothing about this crime, nothing about my brother or his wife, help? Why would Jesperson even go there? Her murder was a family matter, I'd expressed to him many times. He understood I shared as little as possible about my personal life and he needed to respect that space.

"Anytime you want me to delve into her case, let me know," he said, ending it there for the time being.

Stepping out of my car, shaking my head at his arrogance, opening my PO box, there were a few letters from fans, a series of nonsensical, waste-of-paper solicitations, and a yellow card, which meant I had a package they couldn't fit into my box. After retrieving a vanilla, spongy, plastic-bubbled envelope the size of a small couch pillow, sitting inside my vehicle, I thought: *What the hell is he sending now?* I'd forgotten the task I'd set before him—to write about his childhood—that last time we chatted.

When I say Jesperson is a prolific writer, I mean it with every ounce of jazz the word conjures. Inside the package were three black-and-white Norcom Composition books grammar school teachers hand out to their fifth-grade writing classes on the first day of school. Six hundred pages of writing—a manifesto detailing the Jesperson family saga, the first volume titled: "Life of Keith Jesperson—Family History, 1800s to August 1975."

I opened the cover of volume one. The first entry: "Denmark 1800s."

You've got to be kidding me. Denmark? Seriously?

What could a literary stroll down the Jesperson Danish heritage of ancestors do for me or my research?

Volume two: "Keith Jesperson's Life for Phelps: August 2, 1975," where volume one left off, "to basically 1990." Volume three: "1990 to 1995 ('96 to 2013) Stories Nonfiction and Fiction, Keith Jesperson."

The embodiment of pathological sat on my lap in front of me. The overstated and lurid visions stirring in Jesperson's brain, fused by a narrative brimming with what he perceives as great moments of *deus ex machina,* were nothing more than woven-together anecdotes from the disturbed and knotted memory of a psychopath. I sat, contemplating: *Am I kidding myself in what has become a futile quest to uncover a drop of compassion inside the mind of a man who's looking to do nothing more than to keep himself occupied and in the spotlight while serving several life terms? What a pathetic creature.*

The theme that arose out of volume one included Les Jesperson being the manufacturer behind the public having to live with the violence and horror of Happy Face. Here was 201 pages of handwritten text in blue pen, single-spaced. Keith Jesperson had mentioned his mother only twice, in passing. Les, on the other hand, was a presence on nearly every page. Reading this, I knew, if nothing else, Jesperson had put a bull's-eye on his father's back for a reason.

Going through volume one, taking notes, searching for an answer as to why he turned into one of the nation's most notorious, violent, sexual serial killers, actually helped me to focus on and face what had happened in my own life—to take a look back when my brother and his "wife" were two of the most hated individuals in my family. Our familial history shapes us; it is the only part of our development we can look to for the answers we seek later in life. Sometimes we embrace what we find. Other times, we sink deeper into the abyss. I'd already been swallowed, so why not try to perform a bit of alchemy while there and possibly move on?

I decided to pick Jesperson's brain and find out what he was thinking at the time he killed. This might give me an indication into the thought process behind the man who had killed the mother of my niece and nephews, kids who had sometimes looked to me for answers. I had none. We'd always assumed a serial killer working the streets of Hartford at the time of her homicide had taken Diane's life, as well as close to a dozen other women. But we, and the early news coverage, were wrong about that: strange as it might sound, Diane's murder was far more complicated.

"What's going through your mind at the time you decide to murder a human being?" I asked Jesperson one morning as we got back into our weekly calls. This was something I'd tried to emphasize within the overall narrative arc of my television show. It was a question, answered honestly, that could put us a step closer to how serial killers evolve and develop into the murderous fiends they become.

I wanted images. What, precisely, was going on inside that boundless portion of Jesperson's brain, the spot where, similarly, we all go to judge ourselves? Not the anger, the emotional toil of pulling the trigger, so to speak, or the decision to commit the murder. But after the fact: when murder has been decided and the act itself has commenced. Has a wellspring broken open and, maybe like a heroin addict, a rush that can be compared to none other has been unleashed? Euphoria? A dreamlike state? Did the same tape play over and over inside Jesperson's head during every murder? Or was each murder different? Each feeling varied?

"Tell me," I said. "Be brutally honest. I need—and deserve—that from you."

"When I kill, I decide at *that* time it is going to happen. The thought process is, basically, I have committed myself to this. It's not a . . . I don't dwell on maybe other things around me. I have decided that she is going to die. It's basic instinct. I don't dwell on past events."

He insisted that his upbringing and nurturing had something

to do with his later behavior. So I wondered if he was killing those memories with each victim. "Are you in a happy place, you know, at the ocean, in that moment? Or enjoying the suffering of this person?"

"My mind-set is probably more of that I *am* in the moment. I know at that time this person is going to die and I'm just going through the motions of performing the death. It's not a . . . a . . . going off into la-la land somewhere, into euphoria. It's about taking care of business. It's basically just doing the task. That's the easy part. Once the death is over with, the hard part is actually just getting away from the body without being detected."

I began to wonder what he did between the time he killed Taunja Bennett and allegedly assaulted Daun Slagle. This was an important period of his life. According to Jesperson, at one point he walked a fine line of being a one-off killer and becoming a serial killer. As he started to work as a short-haul truck driver, Jesperson didn't have time to do much of anything else, he said. He went on short runs, from Portland to Salem, Salem to Spokane, Seattle to Portland. But once he stepped into a long-haul trucking career, the "time to think" became available, explaining it this way: "Driving time, sleeping time, screwing-around time, killing time."

From January 1990, when he killed Bennett, until 1992, when he took his next victim, Jesperson obsessed over murder. He had done it once, gotten away with it—and two people were doing life for that crime. He would look at people he passed throughout his day: *I could kill you.* Murder itself became part of the sexual fantasies he'd had since two years before divorcing Rose.

"It's almost like you dwell on this idea of death. I've done it. But do I *want* to do it again? I don't need to do this, I can move on. I got away with it. Someone else is in prison for it. I don't have to play that game. I can stay focused on my life and do what is right for *me*."

Then, in November 1992, he pulled into the Burns Brothers Truck Stop in Wilsonville, California, and Laurie Anne Pentland walked into his life. She was twenty-six, lean, pretty. She approached and asked if he wanted a date. He invited her into his truck. She said something after they had sex that he didn't like and her murder happened in the spur of a moment. One minute they were arguing, the next he had his hands around her throat and she was dead.

"How did that feel?" I wondered.

"It was like the stars were all aligned."

It was her time, in other words. He was there. She was, too. She needed to die. He needed to kill her.

"Karma."

Before he took Pentland's life, Jesperson said, "I wasn't a serial killer. I killed someone and I moved on." Killing Pentland made Jesperson a serial killer. In his view, once he crossed that line, he gave in to this "other side" of himself. "Everyone thinks I was a serial killer the moment I killed, but that's not true." This was important to him.

In between Bennett, Slagle (1990), and Pentland (1992), Jesperson played the role of dad as best he could when with his children. He spent Christmas and other holidays with them. He picked them up and gave them rides in his truck. Bought them toys. Took them to the park.

"Pamela was with me again throughout that period, we were riding together." He worked in Spokane and spent one Christmas there. "I got a motel. I grabbed the kids. They went swimming. We all ate pizza. I took them shopping. I even bought my ex-wife something."

He adored his kids and had no trouble showing them love. "That relationship was as normal as it could be, with me being a truck driver and divorced."

Jesperson's worst fear was for his kids to find out he was a killer. And, he said, contrary with what his daughter Melissa Moore would later write about him in her book, he was able to hide who he was from them. "I never wanted to put that on my kids."

The possibility they'd find out was something that scared him. He was embarrassed to stand before them as a known killer.

After listening to a man describe killing another human being with the same affect he'd use to describe a football game he'd watched with his cellies, I'd hang up and feel anxious, a need to unwind and get the stink off myself somehow. I couldn't just immerse back into my life as a writer, father, husband, son, Christian, friend, community member. I needed some sort of buffer zone between the Devil and me. Reading helped. As I've mentioned, taking strolls with my dog and just sitting, petting her, calmed me down. I'd take a walk or sit out on my back porch with a cup of coffee and think about what he'd said.

It occurred to me during one of these downtimes that a certain trepidation I'd picked up on in his voice early on wasn't there anymore. Not because he was watching himself and what he said, or even what he wanted to say but couldn't quite articulate. It was desperation, I now understood. He was trying to provide an explanation that covered him. Every time I felt this way, it provoked in me a greater and clearer acceptance that he was a pathological liar, a master charmer with a disregard for social mores, the rights of others, who felt no remorse, and I should be aware at all times. I could not allow him ever to think he owned me; it would exacerbate and stimulate the disease he had become in my life, aggravating my health issues.

21

I REMEMBER

"A family without a black sheep is not a typical family."
—Heinrich Böll

ON FEBRUARY 14, 1993, DIANE FERRIS, MY BROTHER'S THEN–THIRTY-one-year-old common-law "wife," met a guy at the Windsor Court Hotel & Conference Center bar. It was a locale where she and my brother were holed up in one of those weekly, prorated rooms that transients frequent. Thomas Myers was a thirty-seven-year-old Windsor Locks native, a heating and air-conditioning installer, who hung out at what was a neighborhood gin mill to him. He was described as "quiet," "pleasant," someone who grew up in town and kept to himself. He lived a mile down the road from the bar.

Thomas and Diane sat together and had cocktails. My guess is Diane watched him stroll in after a hard day's work, smiled at him, and charmed the local blue-collar guy into buying her drinks. She and my brother were heavy drinkers and drug users by then, deep in the throes of their addictions. I loved them both, but could not stand to be a part of their lives, hear from them, or be taken in by whatever drama—criminal or financial—that had befallen them. I'd just turned twenty-six. Facing demons of my own, I was trying to raise not only my two kids, but my then-wife and I were also foster parents to two of Mark and Diane's children, my nephews. I had four young boys, ranging in ages from four to eight, running wild in my house.

Diane had done a stint in jail the previous year for possession of narcotics. She and my brother had a long history of arrests for drug-related crimes, which juxtaposed with trying to support habits. I remember as far back as my early teens the two of them being pinched for everything from stuffing meats up the shirts of their kids and trying to get out of the grocery store to stealing clothing from the TJ Maxx they'd try to return for cash, writing bad checks, scamming credit card companies, or using the Social Security numbers of their children to access credit. At one time, my brother was trying to prove he had Mashantucket Pequot blood in him so he could get a yearly stipend Foxwoods Casino was offering to anyone who could prove Native American tribal lineage. Diane and Mark were on a hamster wheel: drugs, alcohol, cops; drugs, alcohol, arrest, probation, move to a new hotel or find a welfare apartment complex they hadn't burned. Looking on from afar as their lives sank deeper into despair was akin to standing on the shore of a lake, with a sick feeling of never being able to reach them, as the two of them descended into the water as if on an escalator, their hands extended.

As a child looking up to my oldest brother, Mark reminded me of a hippie you might hire to play Jesus off-Broadway: long, black hair past his shoulders, goatee and mustache, a shy smile, a lock of hair curled around one ear, cigarette tucked in the other. When we lived in East Hartford, the images that come to mind are of Mark standing in the driveway wearing a greasy wife-beater tank top, listening to the Allman Brothers Band ("Whipping Post" was his favorite ABB song). He would be working on his beloved brown Oldsmobile Cutlass 442 (he could pull the carburetor out on a Saturday morning, have it in pieces on the kitchen table Saturday night, and be driving the car Sunday morning), with a Newport dangling from his mouth, a can of Bud with the peel-off tab, sharp as a razor, on the side fender wall.

Mark was skinny, but tough. He had a reputation. Nobody messed with him. A kid could have me in a headlock down the street at the Nature Trail, a wooded area where we hung out, but if I pulled Mark's name, it alone protected me. He had a hole on the right side of his belly we'd sometimes poke a finger into. It felt squishy, like a balloon—a scar left behind from Mark having had a kidney removed as a child. These images are from about the time Mark first started dating Diane, who, at thirteen (my brother four years older), walked into our lives as if she had been part of the family all along. Diane belonged, that was the impression. I can see her stepping out of a red Volkswagen (her sister's, a girl Mark also dated in between breakups with Diane), a mound of snow piled in front of our Hollister Drive house from where the plows pushed the entire neighborhood snowpack, those sounds ringing out as I lay in bed (what could be better?): *Beep . . . beep . . . beep . . . beep,* the plow truck going in reverse, telling us neighborhood kids we had a snow day. I can still smell the dust under the stairs in that small white house of ours, where I usually slept on a cot. The punch of the purple lilac bush as you rounded the south corner in the front yard, where a neighborhood kid once tripped and gouged his eye on our chain-link fence and my parents were scared they'd be sued.

And I can see Diane sitting on our front steps, a sweltering summer afternoon, watching Mark work on his car, her long, thick, dirty blond hair, smelling of Farrah Fawcett Shampoo by Fabergé. She was obsessed with that hair, always nervously twirling a lock, legs crossed over one another, bouncing a mile a minute, laughing and smoking cigarettes. There I sat, playing with my Matchbox cars in the sand, thinking how beautiful Diane was, and how lucky Mark was to have her. She was like the sister I'd never had. I grew up in a house with three older brothers. Diane smelled like a woman should.

No matter how bad things got for them later on, she made sure she looked the best she could—always. She'd spend two hours putting on makeup and doing her hair. She loved Tom Petty and Stevie Nicks, and to me she resembled Stevie. Those memories, when I recall life being normal (whatever the hell that is), Diane singing Fleetwood Mac's "Sara" in our living room, dancing, Mark reading the sports page, watching basketball, explaining to me how point spreads worked. I think back now, what the hell happened to us? How had everything spiraled so out of control—all the death and dysfunction and drug use—in the years that followed?

ON VALENTINE'S DAY, 1993, Diane met Tom Myers at the Dugout Bar inside the Windsor Court Hotel. The two of them, for whatever reason, left. Diane drove. They wound up parked on Norwich Street, near the corner of Wyllys, at Dutch Point, downtown Hartford, in the same car she and my brother had been tooling around in. Tom sat in the passenger seat.

"Relatives [of Myers] believe he asked Ferris for a ride home—but Ferris instead drove to Dutch Point . . . where friends believe she often had gone to buy drugs," a *Hartford Courant* article claimed.

Indeed, Diane and Mark often drove into downtown, Frog Hollow, Charter Oak Terrace, Garden Street (where Diane would be murdered a little over three years later) and Barbour Street, Dutch Point, and any number of popular areas in Hartford to purchase drugs. On this night, however, something went wrong. As I heard the story, Diane left Thomas Myers in the car and went up to a familiar residence to buy drugs or collect money somebody owed her. When she returned, he was dead, a stab wound through his chest (heart, I was told). My brother, incidentally, stayed at their hotel room the entire time, in no condition by then to go anywhere, no doubt waiting for Diane to hit the bar and find him drugs.

Every ounce of my being cannot associate the notion of Diane being a killer. It just wasn't in her. I could see her robbing Thomas Myers. She'd stolen from me, my brothers, my mother, her immediate family. Could she have threatened him, gouged his eyes and arms and spit in his face, while screaming vulgar obscenities at him? I'd witnessed her do this to my mother, to my wife, and all of us had experienced Diane's volatile wrath, her temper, and her violence. But could she drive a knife through a man's chest?

No way.

"She was not a killer—she had nothing to do with it," my brother Mark's best friend, Gary Saccocia, told me. "She went up to get dope, came back, and he was dead."

Thomas Myers was said not to be involved in drugs.

"No one was ever charged with the homicide," but "Hartford Police," that *Courant* article noted, "said they don't know if Ferris was involved in Myers' death."

The next day, Diane called her daughter, my niece, Meranda VanDeventer. Meranda was fourteen and had been living with her aunt for almost a year by then. She kept in close contact with her mother and father, and visited Mark and Diane often. "Because my mom had me so young [Diane was sixteen], I kind of," Meranda told me, "became the mother in the relationship." Meranda had spent weekends at the Windsor Court Hotel, witnessing, first-hand, how deeply immersed Diane and Mark were in their addictions.

"They kept me and interrogated me for almost twenty-four hours," Diane told Meranda, explaining what happened: She and Thomas Myers drove to Dutch Point, she went up to visit a friend about something, came back down, and found him dead. "I had nothing to do with it."

Cops tried for months to get Diane to talk about that night, but she wouldn't budge. Diane knew how to handle herself around anyone (she was feared on the streets for her ability to defend herself), but she had a special way of dealing with cops.

The great irony—or maybe tragedy—of their lives was that Mark and Diane were perfectly matched as a couple, maybe too perfectly. They were inseparable. Soul mates, if such a thing exists. When they had the emotional stability and the drugs had not yet controlled who they were, where and when they ate, where they slept and shit, who they slept with, they deeply loved and cared for each other. Yet, with the drugs and booze becoming a third member of the relationship, they could never figure out how to make it work. Because of that, and the fact that they could better utilize state and city welfare services as individuals, they never got officially married.

* * *

I ANSWERED THE PHONE one morning. "Call me back in ten minutes, would you? I just walked into my office. But I *need* to talk to you."

This was, for the psychopath, the ultimate invitation: *He knew I needed* him.

The only reason I answered the call was because I had to touch base with Jesperson for logistical reasons. Development on my planned documentary was expanding. My production company and I were focused on the research and I needed a few questions answered. I'd just walked into my office after exercising and had been waiting for his call. I was winded, out of breath, sweating.

He ignored the comment: "Did I ever tell you about a marathon I once ran?" I could hear the air inflate into his head. "I was quite the runner. I would . . ."

"Dude, come on. I am out of breath. You *need* to call me back."

Every call, every letter, every moment between Keith Jesperson and me, was about him; this phone call illustrates that dynamic. The psychopath is continually focused on himself. There is no respite. He cannot view the world under any other context except for how he lives in it and what others can do for him. Jesperson does not have in him the capability to say, *Oh, I caught you at a bad time. Catch your breath and I'll call you back in ten minutes.*

This sort of narcissistic grinding, the constant churning of *me, me, me,* was never more evident than the writing within his 600-plus-page manifesto/family history I opened that day in my car. As I continued to read through Jesperson's Canadian childhood memories, it became evident that his view of that life was now being rewritten through the lens of the serial killer he'd become.

Sketching out a biography of his father, Jesperson smeared Les's reputation, something he knew the Jesperson clan had a low tolerance for. After talking about how Les, as a young man, "mastered the skills of forge and hammer," learning from his father that change was not something a man should accept without question and reason, he accused Les of taking the "easy" way through life, making others do most of his bidding, while conning his way through whatever predicament the family faced. "Shortcuts,"

Jesperson reiterated, were what Les would be "punished" for by *his* dad if he ever took another track. The one anecdote Jesperson used to explain how scheming and revenge-driven Les could be was when Les put flypaper down on several farm outhouse toilet seats, which were for use by Les's hop field pickers, after discovering outsiders using the toilets at night when no one was around. Les had even stayed up late several times to watch "people leaving the outhouses naked," afraid to put their clothes on, just to enjoy the moment.

"So your dad was a mischievous young adult," I commented. "He lived in a different time. Cut the guy some slack."

By now, I'd taken a defensive position of sarcasm and resistance. I could not allow the stress of this guy to put me back in the emergency room, where I'd ended up once, doubled over with stomach pain, having an episode. I was going to win this battle.

Ignoring me, Jesperson mentioned how Les had once told him he enjoyed "derailing a train with metal left on the tracks" and "killed chickens with carbide bombs."

Les liked to make Super 8 films of the kids, like any doting father from the 1960s and 1970s. The Jespersons traveled more than most families, heading south from Canada into the United States, to all the major tourist destinations: Yosemite, Grand Canyon, Disneyland, and Disney World. Les liked to film the kids. Later, Les turned a lot of the film into VHS, narrating certain scenes. In one particular moment, according to Happy Face, the kids were out in the woods somewhere along the road, chasing gophers out of their holes. Little Keith, just five years old, had a club in his hand, same as, he said, his siblings. He was on the hunt to whack any gopher he saw coming up out of its hole. Dad, he said, set a voice-over track to the scene later on, which, in terms of who his son became, was a chilling portend: "Here [is] my natural-born killer."

Memory, Jesperson explained, is a tenuous part of the psyche we might rely on a little too much. Although he said he can recall details about each of his murders as if he'd recently committed the crimes, he saw childhood, teen, and early-adulthood memories tarnished by the context of how we view those memories later.

"So it's safe to say a lot of my memory is of those films of us kids playing way back when we were . . . and I can only gauge life's memories by what is not on film—time lines."

"Memory is funny," I responded. "But also, for you, rooted in your father. He infiltrates just about every memory of childhood you have shared with me—do you realize that?"

Whenever his dad had a problem and wanted to know if Little Keith did something he didn't want to admit, "he would pull out the belt and beat it out of me. That was the way Dad dealt with me. Just pull the belt out and go for it. I didn't respect my dad. I *feared* him. I knew that had I gotten in trouble at school and my brothers and sister told on me, when I got home I was going to get a beating."

I wondered if he'd subconsciously thought that by killing and eventually being caught, part of it was smearing the Jesperson name Les had fought so hard to keep clean all those years. This was a major contention in Jesperson's version of his family history: Les would do anything to save the Jesperson name from tarnishing. It was the main focus of their lives, Jesperson said. Thus, within that dubious explanation, I wondered, was his need for media attention and exposure based on committing the ultimate sin against the family reputation?

"I actually believe that I killed and continued to do these crimes, and in my mind while I'm doing this, I am tearing down the Jesperson family name."

"That could be your 'cop-out' at this point—hindsight?"

He took a breath. Went quiet for a moment. Whenever he did this, I knew he was busy checking his anger, trying to come up with the most plausible answer, one that might carry me into the next topic or question.

"You live on that side of the line," he said. "I live on *this* side of the line. You look at a case from the victims' and law enforcement's point of view. You're trying to understand why a person did this based on what society has pushed down your throat. The cases are black or white. There's no color. And right or wrong may not even be part of the case."

"Killing is wrong," I said. "Putting away killers is right. That's what it comes down to for me. You knew it was wrong. You knew taking a life was wrong, morally, ethically, whatever. You knew that you'd hurt people and go to jail for it."

"I did it, anyway. Because"—and, as always, we were back to January 20, 1990—"I'd gotten away with it in the first place."

22

FEELS LIKE FIRE

"Perhaps home is not a place but simply an irrevocable
condition."
—James Baldwin, *Giovanni's Room*

*E*VEN DECADES AFTER LIVING IN AN AVERAGE-SIZED, SPLIT-TO-BACK,
ranch-style home about twelve miles northeast of Hartford, the
thought of driving down Susan Road (I still pass by it often) and
into the neighborhood where I'd spent seventeen years of my life,
beginning at the age of twelve, summoned images and memories
I did not ever want to face again. To make that trip, I knew, would
take me right back, despite how well-schooled I now was from sitting in my living-room recliner, taking in an Oprahfied version of
self-analysis and psychobabble purporting how one should confront his past if he wanted to move beyond the pain. Even so, as I
dredged up the nerve for the first time in over a decade to drive
by my old Susan Road house, located in what is a residential, typical suburban Connecticut neighborhood, complete with the
"babbling brook" running through the backyard (a comment I
will never forget our real estate agent sharing the day we trekked
from the city—East Hartford—to the "country"—Vernon—to
look at the home), it felt as though I'd entered a tunnel, dark as
the Milky Way, a million voices, like blurry stars at warp speed,
screaming words I couldn't understand, pointing out all I'd done
wrong during a period of my life that, at times, feels as though
someone else lived it.

Staring at each house leading up to ours, as I drove slowly and took it all in on that afternoon, it struck me that this was the same neighborhood where my parents decided to divorce (months after we moved in); where my first wife told me that I, too, would be divorced; where I drank my first beer, a Haffenreffer forty-ounce Private Stock (skunky as swamp water, piss warm) out of a slime-green bottle and threw up on the curb after having a McDonald's milk shake Mom had delivered to me ("Are you all right," she asked, knowing damn straight I was drunk, "you seem a bit off?"); where I first heard Sugarhill Gang's "Rapper's Delight" on vinyl as a twelve-year-old; where I locked myself in a bedroom the size of a closet one summer and learned how to play guitar; where, as a naïve young boy, after asking what the word meant, I got Dad's version of *hypocrisy* ("You see that family," himself un-religious, "they go to church on Easter and Christmas only—they're hypocrites"); where I learned to drive; where I first fell in love; where I brought up my two boys and then Mark and Diane's two boys I won custody of through probate court and raised (with the unselfish, dedicated, loving, and humbled help of my first wife); where I became an alcoholic; where (while standing on my porch after a funeral) I asked a friend how the hell our best friend could have blown his fucking brains out over a *woman* (the same road where, years later, after she told me she was leaving and wanted a divorce, I parked in the woods at the end of our cul-de-sac, a six-pack and half pint of brandy between my legs, and contemplated placing the garden hose in my hand from the tailpipe into the window and joining him); where I decided to quit high school the day I turned sixteen (and my mother said it was okay, as long as you work); the same neighborhood where I got into my first real fight (with blood—mine—involved); where I started smoking and writing; where we hung out on the corner (without mini i-Things in our pockets and talked the Doors and which member of KISS was the most feminine and what the Lynyrd Skynyrd song "That Smell" was *really* about, at the same time not worrying about yesterday or tomorrow, but only *that* moment of *that* day); where I got so high from smoking a bong as big as a lab experiment I swore off weed altogether; where my neighbor (an older kid who bought us beer) spent a summer with his stereo speakers leaning against the screen of his bedroom windows and blasted Molly Hatchet's "Flirtin' with Disaster" record (and whose sister was later stabbed to death by her husband); where I sat in my living room and unknowingly watched the birth of reality TV and true crime (as O.J. Simpson was chased down the highway in his white Ford Bronco by cops, fans, and the media); where I first heard Kurt Cobain had shot himself and Freddie Mercury had died of AIDS; where I saw green bombs explode on my TV at night in Baghdad like a video game; where I learned that burning pine in a woodstove will ignite the roof of your house and cause a scene; where I played cards with my first wife one afternoon at the kitchen table and Pearl Jam's "Better Man" played on the radio (Google those lyrics) as she sang it out loud and I had no idea until years later she was singing to me; and the same neighborhood, the same house, the same kitchen, where I explained to my brother Mark, after he'd returned from shopping one night, that the woman he loved, the mother of the three children they'd been unable to parent for years, the same woman he'd been estranged from, but still loved, and was possibly pregnant with their fourth child, had just been murdered.

This was the Memory Lane I had not wanted to drive down.

READING THROUGH JESPERSON'S MANIFESTO gave me a clear sense of how he blames everyone around him for not only the decisions he'd made, but the consequences those decisions had on his life and the lives of others. Putting his inherent, obvious narcissism aside, in the first volume Jesperson never speaks of any love or concern for his siblings, his mother, certainly not his father. It reads as though he is being attacked from all sides, by everyone, for everything, each person around him with some sort of hidden, set, secret agenda, not to mention a collective conspiracy to spoil and disrupt his life.

Ponder Jesperson's comment, if you will, after I asked about victims of murder in general: "Consider a victim an apple on a

tree," he shared. "This apple has matured all of its life and becomes ripe for the picking. And the person who wants this—a
rapist or pedophile—looks at that person as the ripe peach he is
waiting for. In the end, all *it* is, is a victim, and when he's done, he
is going to discard it because it's not going to tell him no."

Holding my contempt in check, I listened as he then broke
into a story about being rejected by his wife and only wanting, at
the time he became a killer, a fresh start. Not with Rose, but any
woman.

"We've been down that road," I told him.

"Hear me out. There's always been a disassociation toward victims," he insisted. "We do not want to associate them as human
beings. I don't see them as someone I care about. I don't know
who they are. It's really hard to have emotions for someone you
don't know."

I didn't respond. So he continued, adding how his "hatred" for
his victims was so profound he even despised the family of his victims as well, because "of what their loved one did to me."

Which was?

"They caused me to trigger and blow off and kill."

"Of *course,* it was their fault, right? Not only blame the victim—
but her family, too! Get serious, man." I was growing tired of
keeping my feelings checked, allowing him to smear the memories of his victims.

"I knew you would say that, Phelps, but you just *don't* get it,
do you?"

"I guess not."

In his manifesto, he talked about an incident when he was
three, his brother Brad Jesperson two. It was as if this one situation between Brad and Keith set up a life of disunion and rivalry.
Within the manifesto, Brad is the good son who can do no wrong
in Les's eyes. "Was told I rolled a rock down the slide and it hit
Brad in the head causing a scar."

Because of that single incident, Jesperson's paranoia later told
him he was forever viewed as the child in the family who caused
pain, the one who inflicted scars on the Jesperson dynasty. He

used the incident as a metaphor in his writing to justify the "black sheep" sentiment he felt growing up and, later, as he murdered.

"Brad and I lived in a room the size of the prison cell I live in now," he explained. "That pitted us against each other. And it never went away."

Any torture or death Jesperson had brought upon animals became someone else's (generally Dad's) doing. He claimed when they first moved to Chilliwack, into the Hickman Road house on a large spread of land, there were "thousands of garter snakes" roaming the countryside, infesting their living space. So "Dad gave us kids a chore. Kill the snakes whenever we saw them. Get rid of them." Jesperson took to the job passionately, calling it "slaughter." He used "shovels and hoes" and went about walking the land in a gridlike fashion, chopping the heads off hundreds of snakes, their headless bodies, rubbery and slithery, scattered about the property.

He wrote of scattered "memories," saying, "Life seems all mixed up . . . scrambled over." Living in Canada was "easier" for him and "made more sense." He called it a "quiet" life. It wasn't until years later when they moved to the States that he was viewed as an "oddball" by his peers and had a hard time fitting in with American kids.

It was on the Hickman Road farm in Chilliwack, as a young teenager, that Jesperson first "felt something different" brewing inside his mind. He described an almost me-against-the-world sentiment, while blaming his family, especially Brad and Les, for feeling this way. He spoke of his father coming home one day with two chocolate Labradors.

Jesperson named one Duke, a dog "who was with me every moment." Duke and Keith went fishing and hunting and took walks together. Duke slept with Keith.

It wasn't until Jesperson got to know some of the boys on Hickman Road that he understood just how mean and abusive kids could be. He said certain neighbors and others close to him were into "animal abuse," but not him.

"I witnessed [those boys] throw knives at cats and dogs they caught. Strays. They'd nail down their paws and use their bodies as targets."

He was proud of himself for never telling on any of them. By contrast, "My siblings couldn't *wait* to tell on me."

Jesperson once smashed his brother's toys when his brother made him mad. His dad walked in. Keith explained how his brother had made him angry. He was upset, and so he smashed Bruce's model plane to bits.

"Dad bought [Bruce] a new plane. I got the belt."

Several days later, he was down at a swimming pool located west of Cultus Lake, a popular hangout for area kids. He ran into a neighbor. "Hey," Jesperson said. He thought maybe they could become buddies.

The neighbor didn't say much. Instead, he grabbed Jesperson by the head and held him underwater until the lifeguard broke it up.

"I never got even with him," Jesperson said. "I just stayed away."

Growing into his teens, Jesperson was always the biggest kid; yet the way in which he outlined life then, he was the butt of all the jokes and picked on more than anyone else. They called him "Baby Huey" and "Tiny." Hazing became a daily part of his life. By then, the family had moved to Selah, Washington.

Dealing with American kids was difficult for Keith. He was a freshman in high school. A bunch of upperclassmen gathered and waited for several freshmen one day to walk by an area of the hallway. There were girls standing around, giggling, pointing, making fun of the new class of zit-faced kids coming into the school. Jesperson's older brother, Bruce, was among the upperclassmen waiting to initiate the freshmen.

"It was [something] to humiliate us," Jesperson said. "I saw it as stupid." He decided: "I'm a big kid. No one is going to tell me to, or make me, drop my pants, so they can all laugh and make jokes." All the time, Bruce and his friends were calling Jesperson by the nickname of Igor. "Enough was enough." He'd had it.

Every time he walked by a hazing platoon of kids and a senior told Jesperson to drop his pants, he responded: "Go 'f' yourself. It's not going to happen."

After a time, Jesperson found out Bruce had been told by his peers to do something about his brother. He would have to submit to initiation, same as everyone else.

Bruce and ten of his friends cornered Keith one day in the hallway.

"[Screw you], Bruce, no way." Jesperson knew what they wanted.

Soon, a flock of girls gathered. A fight broke out. Jesperson hurled blows. He tossed one kid down the stairs. He punched a few others and hit Bruce a couple of times in the face. Still, even with his size, they managed to get hold of his arms and legs and dragged him into the hallway, where everyone waited.

One of the boys pulled Jesperson's pants off while the others held him down. There he was for the entire class to see, naked from the waist down.

About twenty girls, he said, stood around and laughed at him.

Bruce went home with a black eye and told their dad that if Keith would have only allowed them to initiate, like everyone else, there would have been no trouble.

NOT LONG AFTER THAT nostalgic drive into the old neighborhood, I was doubled over on my office floor, the throbbing pain on the left side of my abdomen and two specific areas of my stomach burning like a thousand toothaches. This type of excruciating pain only had occurred once before, in 2007, during a period of grief after a friend had committed suicide. Thinking then that I was having an appendicitis attack, I called my doctor, who sent me to the ER.

Sitting outside the ER, I held my left side (come to find out, not the same side as your appendix) as gentle as I could without making the pain worse. Tender to the touch, somehow holding it made it better. I could not bend. I waited two hours before they got me in, conducted an assessment, and scheduled a litany of tests.

Suffering through this same episode again as my interviews with Jesperson became more intense, I considered how deep I'd allowed myself to become immersed in a project that was now affecting every part of my life. My writing never had such a visceral, somatic reaction on my body. People would ask how I could speak with a serial killer as often as I did, talk about the most heinous behaviors imaginable, and not be drawn into that darkness. My stock answer worked on them: "I don't think about it—I just plow through and then let it go." But the sicker I became, the more anxiety I suffered, I knew I could no longer fool myself. My friendship with Jesperson was deteriorating my health, mentally, spiritually, and physically.

On some days, not having a handle on it was all I thought about. Yet, it was easy to talk myself into continuing. When I became physically ill, I focused on the bigger picture: that Jesperson might have additional victims, and if I gained his complete trust (which I knew I was close to), he would admit to me where they were buried. This drove me to keep him talking. On top of that, I could maybe identify and bring home one of his Jane Does.

BACK WHEN I WOUND up in the ER, convinced I was having an appendicitis attack, I was sent to the CT-scan unit. The staff there had me drink two quarts of a thick, white, chalky, metallic/synthetic-tasting concoction. I gagged with each swallow. Took me about an hour to choke the stuff down. This CT scan would be the first of several, along with X-rays, colonoscopies, endoscopies, and other invasive tests.

After drinking the chalk, lying on the table, staring at the ceiling, I saw myself in surgery at some point down the road—if I wasn't on my way already.

Knowing how bad these episodes had gotten in the past, I needed to choose a path with Jesperson: Cut him loose or try to push him over the edge of coming clean. Playing psychologist and friend to a serial killer, listening and ingesting all of his issues, was not working out.

Back in 2007, the hospital had sent me home after explaining they'd send the CT-scan results to my doctor and he'd be in touch.

My doctor called and asked me to come in to see him.

Not a good sign, I knew. *He must have found something.*

He explained that I had gallstones and diverticulitis, the cause of that doubled-over pain sending me to the ER. I'd had an "episode," a flare-up (infection), of the diverticulitis in addition to a gallstone attack. The episodes might be caused by an allergy to certain foods, he said—as I pictured myself becoming one of *those* people: a gluten-free-eating, kale-chip-munching, quinoa-devouring, Dr. Oz-watching hipster.

Not in a million fucking years.

The underlying problem was stress, my doctor explained, which aggravated and enhanced my digestive issues. Stress produced an abundance of stomach acid; acid exacerbated the situation. For that, he was going to send me to a surgeon for a consultation.

"Listen," he then said—a tone that meant we were now entering into a more serious part of the conversation. "The diverticulitis and the gallstones are not what really concern me. We can easily treat those with antibiotics and get your infection, at least, under control."

My stomach twisted. *There's more?*

"It's this right here," he added, pointing to his laptop. My CT scan.

I stared at the screen. The CT scan of my colon had picked up the bottom, lower section of my right lung. On the rounded portion of that lung was what looked like a small yellow jacket nest hanging from a window shutter: *A spot on my lung?* It was as if my eyes were drawn directly to it. Clearer than anything I'd ever seen in my life.

A tumor?

"Let me get you hooked up with an oncologist. We'll see what's going on here."

He never used the *C*-word, instead opting for the *O*-word. But it was all I heard inside my head as I drove home. I'd just quit smoking that year, after inhaling a pack or more a day for twenty-seven years.

"It's probably nothing," he said, patting me on the back. "Don't worry."

To a guy suffering from anxiety, it was a fatal diagnosis—and all I thought about. Now, all these years later, with Jesperson taking over my life, that fear of being chronically ill as I lie on my office floor, doubled over, holding my side, contemplating and questing what the hell I was doing, well, that sense of dread and finality came back to me. There was going to be a price to pay for my so-called friendship with a serial killer.

23

STRANGE CONDITION

"I'm so scared of dying without ever being really seen."
—David Foster Wallace, *Infinite Jest*

*O*UTSIDE HER CAMAS, WASHINGTON, HOME, SNOOKY COLLINS watched as a dark blue Peterbilt 359 Series tractor-trailer pulled up, its air brakes letting out a loud *hiss* as it stopped and parked along the street. Just a few months old, the truck had a shine to it. As Snooky wondered who it was, her daughter, Julie Winningham, popped out of the passenger-side door and climbed down from the tall perch. Snooky hadn't seen Julie in quite some time and so she smiled as Julie and a rather tall brute of a man walked toward the front door.

"Julie," Snooky said. "Julie! Julie!"

Was there anything better than a hug from your mother?

After the embrace, pleasantries and *I-missed-you-so-much,* Julie looked up at her companion, whom she referred to as her boyfriend, and, according to several reports, introduced him as "Chris."

Snooky thought it odd that after they sat down and talked, Julie called him Keith. Which was it? The first time Julie said Keith, Jesperson looked at his girlfriend and, Julie later characterized, "reacted as if she wasn't supposed to use that name."

"That's not true," Jesperson told me. "I had met Snooky several times before this day. That story was trumped up later on, published in the papers. Just another one of those recollections of people *after* they realized I was the infamous Happy Face serial killer. It never happened that way."

By the first week of March 1995, when he stopped with Julie by her mother's house in Camas, Jesperson was a man filled with increasing inner chaos, a bloodlust pumping through his veins. He had killed seven thus far, three Jane Does among them, along with Angela Subrize, the woman he strangled and dragged underneath his Peterbilt. Paranoia drove every Jesperson emotion, thought, and decision by this point. There was not going to be a woman who crossed paths with him, made Jesperson the least bit angry, and lived to talk about it. He'd hit his stride as a killer and had little control over his rage.

"I hated myself. Every time I killed, I told myself it was the last time. I wanted it to end. I was thinking then about turning myself in, mostly just to stop it all."

He had suicide on his mind, too.

With an addiction to violence and acting on impulse governing his life, although he considered admitting to his crimes, Jesperson feared walking through any door, stepping out of his truck, or paying a dining bill at a rest stop, turning around, and finding himself in the clutches of waiting cops. His antisocial behavior was now controlling his life. The only obstacle standing in the way of Happy Face committing suicide and ending the desperation he claimed to have felt—an attribute many serial killers in this regard lack—was the guts to get the job done.

Julie Winningham came across as a pretty, wholesome forty-one-year-old housewife next door. Jesperson was attracted to this quality. She appeared clean-cut, but could fulfill most of his sexual fantasies, however dirty or twisted. Jesperson was into duct-taping his victims' mouths, securing their arms behind their back, and having his way with them. As he evolved as a pervert and killer, each murder became darker and more sadomasochistic.

Julie wore her brownish-blond hair in a bouffant, and its shiny, thick texture accentuated her tanned skin and arresting, sky-blue eyes. She'd divorced a trucker in the years leading up to meeting Jesperson. Happy Face ran into Julie in 1993 at a truck stop and began dating her on and off. Born and raised in Washougal, Clark County, Washington, Julie personified that Northwestern Pacific charm Jesperson had come to find favorable in his women. He picked up Julie from time to time while on the road whenever he traveled through the state, if only to use her as a sexual partner during the trip. He frequented prostitutes, yet loathed the notion of spending money for sex, feeling it was beneath him.

"And with Julie, I didn't have to pay her for sex, so it was perfect."

Julie had traveled with Jesperson for a week in his truck once. Scheduled to head east on a run, however, and not wanting to take her along, Jesperson found Julie a room with a friend, where she stayed, according to Jesperson, for "a few months" while he worked (and committed an additional murder).

The guy Julie roomed with was a family man. Jesperson called from the road to find out how things were going. His friend said, "Hey, man, she needs to go." Julie was too much trouble. She might have come across as the girl next door, but she was a full-fledged partier. "She's corrupting my family."

Jesperson picked Julie up and, dropping her off in Clark County, said his good-byes, telling Julie he'd see her around. By then, he was fed up with Julie and needed—"for her sake"—to put as much distance as possible between them.

"She went to Utah, Salt Lake City, I think."

One of the first points Jesperson made when we got to talking about Julie was how "hard" it had been for him in 1993, after the incident involving his friend, "to walk away from her without ending her life." She had embarrassed him. He wanted to kill her then, but he decided against it for reasons he didn't know himself.

After parting ways in 1993, it became "impossible" for Jesperson to "avoid" Julie. Every few weeks, no matter where he parked, there she was—quite a common theme whenever he described the excuse of "fate" and "karma" playing a role in his murders: *They were there. What could I do?* Julie was, same as several Happy Face victims, a piece of rotting fruit on a counter Jesperson forced himself to walk by—and she needed to be discarded. In his damaged way of viewing himself in the world, Julie magnified Jesperson's failures. As he saw it, she and the others brought out the beast within, thus everything Julie did while around him became a check in the wrong box. Sex with Julie, he told me, "always came with a price."

Knowing her for two years by the time he and Julie visited her mother in early March 1995, Jesperson said, "I'm [at her mother's] and I'm very surprised I hadn't killed her by now." He'd once wanted a relationship with Julie. Feeling it wasn't worth the effort, when "I saw her that March. I saw her out of lust. I had time to party with her. Maybe too much idle time to think too much into what she meant to me."

"What *did* she mean to you?" I asked.

"She wasn't more than a romp in the sack." He claimed Julie "gave off two sides of herself—an image to some people was not what she showed to others."

He believed Julie viewed him as a free ticket, a ride, someone with money to hang around and party with. Yet, he could have been talking about any of his victims, with the exception of Bennett. Under Jesperson's code of conduct, they were all out to use him and walk away.

By 1995, "I had become not a good person." Jesperson grew "angrier and angrier" by the day "at how things were happening." He was "mad at life in general." The silver lining, perhaps keeping him from going entirely off the rails, became his kids. "The love for my kids kept me going to try to support them. The sinking ship was about sunk, though. My murders were consuming me."

Back inside the truck after visiting her mother, Julie explained that she had a court date coming up and needed Jesperson to take care of it for her.

Jesperson had just told his boss he wanted a load to drive east and had been waiting for the trip to come in. He'd decided Julie wasn't going with him.

"I need your help," she said. "Do you not hear me?"

Jesperson looked at Julie. "I know of one way to get you out of your court date."

"Thanks."

The man who had murdered seven women turned and looked at his on-again, off-again girlfriend and smiled.

"And I knew right then that Julie would not have to worry about court."

"COME IN, SIT DOWN." His office was much smaller than I would have assumed a guy specializing in all types of cancers worked in. Clean as a sacristy, but also cramped, with lots of dark-colored, cherrywood furniture, which, same as a funeral home, gave me the creeps.

Getting called into the office of a cancer specialist back in 2007 was about as bad as it could get—under any circumstances. Why couldn't he explain things to me in the checkup room while listening to my heart or holding on to my little fellas, telling me to cough? Why his office?

During those agonizing days and nights leading up to this appointment, like any true anxiety sufferer, I Googled spots on the lung and other words related to lung cancer. Immediately I began to picture myself bald and sans eyebrows, sitting in the hallway of some antiseptic-smelling hospital, in one of those sticky leather chairs on wheels, hooked up to an IV, a tea-colored liquid poison flowing from a bag hanging on a shiny, chrome, coat hanger–like apparatus into my veins, while gawkers and hospital staff walked by feeling sorry for me. Google is to the anxiety sufferer as Keebler cookies are to the sugar addict: feels great as you open the bag, but soon you're sick to your stomach. How great a tool is the Internet that you can Google a tiny pimple, say, on your arm (probably an ingrown hair), and by the end of the morning fully convince yourself it's skin cancer.

The doctor asked me how I was feeling.

Like jumping over this fucking desk and strangling you assholes who don't *have the C.*

"Not bad," I said, "all considering."

"Let me get to that." He spun his desktop computer monitor

around and had my CT-scan image blown up. I'd gone back in since the ER visit and had both lungs scanned. This time, though, instead of making me drink two quarts of a Pepto-Bismol-like emulsified chalk, they pumped a bag of urine-colored liquid into my right tricep, which I could literally feel hit my heart and same as an ice crack on a lake, spread spiderweb-like out into my entire body, while the person behind the glass inside the little kiosk said over the scratchy speaker, "You might feel a burning sensation down *there*."

"That nodule right there, the area of concern," the doctor explained, pointing to it with a pen, "nothing to be worried about."

Nodule, they're calling it now. The N *word. How PC.*

"You're going to be fine," he added, leaning back in his chair.

"Excuse me?"

"It's a scar, the nodule. Probably from a bout of bronchitis or from smoking and coughing all those years. We measured it and, though we might keep an eye on it and measure it every five or ten years, it's really nothing to be concerned about."

I felt relieved, to say the least.

"But you do, however, have emphysema," he said.

The E *word. The dreaded old-man smoker's disease.*

But I had just turned forty. How could that be?

He pointed out a black portion of one lung that encompassed about 75 percent of what looked to be a field in California that had been consumed by wildfire.

I tell this story because for those weeks of not knowing what was wrong with me I had never experienced such intense anxiety—true breathing-into-a-paper-bag type—in my life.

Until, that is, the years of interviewing a serial killer began to add up.

BY THE TIME *I* spoke to Jesperson next, that doubled-over bout of diverticulitis I'd suffered after driving into the old neighborhood had passed. I'd seen the doctor, got a dose of antibiotics, and was feeling better: "Slow down. Take a break from whatever you're doing," he suggested. By this point, Jesperson and I were close enough where it would not have been out of the ordinary for me to have shared my ailments. I'd told him by now that *Dark Minds* wasn't going to a fourth season. He accepted the news without badmouthing the network or my production company too much. He (of course) sent me his ideas for a new series, and he encouraged me to start thinking about outing him publicly as Raven.

"You do that yourself and we're through," I said. Part of my anxiety was centered on the fact that Jesperson, the most prolific letter writer I'd ever known, could, at any time, write to a reporter or anyone else on the outside and easily prove he was Raven. He understood the consequences if he did that, but with the series over, my fear was he'd want the notoriety of everyone knowing he was my Hannibal Lecter.

"I understand," he said.

I half-trusted his answer.

Throughout the time of our correspondence, I'd shared a few personal issues with him I would have never shared with an interviewee before stepping into the role of what John Kelly called Jesperson's surrogate father. But allowing him to know about my anxiety and physical vulnerabilities and ailments was not a space I wanted to go. Plus, Jesperson was suffocating. I'd started talking to him about the difficulty I'd been having figuring out a way to write a book based on our friendship (which would include the promise I'd made about his Bennett obsession), especially the narrative flow and how I wanted to approach all the research I'd collected. Once again, after merely mentioning my dilemma, I received an outline in thirty pages, explaining how each chapter of the book should unravel, along with a detailed structure of all the content, which people I should interview, along with a concluding note: "Guaranteed bestseller."

Of course, I told Jesperson there was no way he was going to tell me how I should set up my book. I followed none of his advice.

I'd get my anxiety under control. Enjoy a spell of pleasant living. But after a few weeks of this sort of back-and-forth with him, hundreds of pages of his ramblings spread across my desk, now embedded in my mind, maps and drawings of crime scenes from him on the floor of my office, I'd feel that pain well up in my lower-left abdomen, another episode no doubt on the horizon.

24

NIGHTMARES

"Gardeners produce flowers that are delicious dreams, and
others too that are like nightmares."
—Marcel Proust, *The Captive & The Fugitive*

WHILE IMMERSED IN WRITING INVESTIGATIVE JOURNALISM, IT HAS
never been difficult for me to work all day (and sometimes well
into the night) inside my office, leave that space, sit down at the
dinner table, and then talk to my family about their day, leaving
the work behind. I could transition from my office to the living
room, turn on CNN, my favorite food/travel series (*New Scandinavian Cooking*), or, embarrassingly, a DVR'd episode of *The Bold
and the Beautiful,* a soap my daughter got me hooked on, and forget about the violence and psychopaths I'd spent the day trying to
figure out. Sure, I'd be uptight after a tough day. But, for the
most part, I was fine.

As Jesperson and I got into the specifics of his crimes and what
he thought about his victims, law enforcement, me, other prisoners, his philosophy of life, his childhood, Hollywood's depiction
of serial killers, this man and his entire presence stuck to me like
lotion. He occupied space as I went about my life outside my office doors, which I'd rarely experienced with other projects. He'd
say something and I'd be drawn deeper into his mania. Some of
the details haunted me—Angela Subrize's murder and the subsequent mutilation of her body being first and foremost. I'd wake in
the middle of the night and, there on my ceiling replacing the

sheep, was the scene Jesperson described with disturbing details he'd shared far beyond any fictionalized version of murder I'd ever read or seen in a film.

The impetus for Jesperson to mutilate Subrize's body in January 1995, several months before he and Julie Winningham sat with her mother, came about, he claimed, because he'd allowed Subrize to use Les's credit card to make a call to her father. He had become connected to her by an electronic paper trail. As he sat in a Burger King, he claimed, eating a Whopper after strangling her in a fit of rage (Jesperson usually took a nap and ate after committing murder), her stiffening corpse wrapped in a blanket inside the cab of his truck outside in the parking lot, the idea that he needed to make certain Subrize was never identified came to mind. He'd not faced this dilemma with any of the other murders, since there had been no direct connection between him and his victims.

"I'm discussing with myself my remedy," he told me. "What am I going to do? It's January. Cold out. The ground is frozen. I'm in Nebraska."

He'd come from Wyoming, via Washington. He'd hooked up with Subrize after meeting her in Spokane. She was looking for a ride into Colorado to visit her father, she said. As they got close to Laramie, a nasty blizzard kicked up.

Arriving in Laramie, Jesperson told her he could take a direct route south to Fort Collins, Colorado, from there. But they needed to wait out the storm.

"I'm really not interested in seeing my dad," she'd since decided.

"When we got into Laramie, I called her dad a second time, which did not go well," Jesperson recalled.

Subrize said she wanted to go east now.

"She was afraid I would drop her off at her dad's house and just keep going. I think all she wanted pretty much was a ride. She just wanted someone to take care of her. I thought all I would end up being was a ride."

"I cannot carry you on any farther," Jesperson told her.

"Just take me to Indianapolis, that's it," she pleaded.

The snow was blinding. Jesperson could not see the front of his rig. He was stressed. He'd already taken a corner wide and jack-knifed the trailer. "Cranky" was the way he articulated his mood. He'd seen several rigs parked, unable to go anywhere. Here it was, this young girl chewing his ear off about a ride east. What's more, he was illegally driving; his logbook had him stopped for a manda-tory rest about one hundred miles before they'd hit the storm head-on.

Abandoning the idea of Fort Collins, Jesperson headed east, Subrize by his side. He'd now made the decision to kill her.

Angela Subrize was a twenty-one-year-old, blond, fair-skinned, average-looking woman from Oklahoma City. Jesperson picked her up in a Spokane bar on January 19, 1995, and, according to him, had no trouble convincing her to spend the night having sex and drinking beer. A few days later, Subrize called the trucking company Jesperson worked for and left a message saying she wanted to talk to him. When he called her, she asked for a ride to go see her father in Fort Collins. So he picked her up. Along the way, besides becoming "demanding" and not "shutting up and letting me sleep," she shared with Jesperson a plan that she'd ini-tiated, which was something he could not allow her to follow through. According to Happy Face, she was heading to Indiana to trick a man into marrying her.

"She said he wanted to marry her," Jesperson explained. "She said she was pregnant with someone else's baby, but was telling this guy it was his. I wasn't about to let her do that to him and his family."

"So you killed her?" I asked. "You played God?"

"Yup. She was a liar and I couldn't let her destroy this guy's life."

In Nebraska, as the snow came down sideways, Jesperson pulled into a rest area. "This is it," he told her. "I'm not going any farther."

It was time to wait out the storm.

Subrize complained because truck stops had TV and conveniences, such as food and coffee. Rest stops didn't. What was she to do while he waited out the storm and slept?

"Now she wanted to dictate where I parked," he explained. This angered him. Explaining this to me over a Video Visit, Jesperson smiled. "She started to act like my wife."

There was that trigger—*Rose.*

Jesperson told her if she didn't like it, get the hell out. He turned over and fell asleep.

Twenty minutes into his nap, she pushed on him. "Get up. I'm bored. Let's get going." She stared out the window. "Look, traffic is moving again."

"Now you listen, I need to rest."

"Come on," she pressed.

"Look, you *really* don't know who you are messing with—now *quit* it."

Jesperson closed his eyes.

"She pushed on me again and I said I've had it."

Jesperson then threw her against the back of the sleeper cab.

"You told me you'd never hurt me!" she screamed.

"I'm not going to just *hurt* you, Angela," Jesperson growled. "I'm going to *kill* you."

He grabbed her by the neck, flipped her onto the mattress, pushed down on her throat.

"Then, as she gasped for air . . . I told her she would be my seventh murder victim."

Happy Face "strangled her and put her out of her *damn* misery. . . . I felt like I was being used, so I got rid of her. Pretty Angela Subrize lie dead in my bed. I rolled her up in a blanket and put the truck into gear and drove on."

After his rage settled, Jesperson realized, *Shit, I used Dad's credit card. How stupid was that?*

While eating his Whopper, after taking a four-hour nap next to her corpse inside the cab of his truck, Jesperson realized he'd have to come up with a way to be certain she was never identified.

Then, as he sat and picked his teeth after the meal, an epiphany: a film he'd just seen "dawned" on him. It was the 1983 comedy

National Lampoon's Vacation. In the film, the family dog is tied to the bumper of the Griswold family car during a pit stop. As they pile back into the vehicle after the stop, they forget the pooch. Thus, the dog is pulled down the freeway, until there is nothing left but a dangling leash.

If I do that, Jesperson thought, *I could get rid of her identification.* Without a face (teeth) and hands (fingerprints), Angela Subrize could never be easily identified.

So he made the decision to tie her body underneath his truck and drag it for as "far as needed" to "rub" those body parts off. Whatever was left over, he'd discard in the woods along the side of the highway.

Jesperson left Burger King and parked at a truck stop "near Mile Marker 198" in Nebraska. It was 3:45 A.M. There were plenty of rigs around, but everyone seemed to be sleeping. He parked his truck in the corner of the lot in order to have a clear view of anyone coming or going.

"I tied a rope around her neck and . . . I left a loop there, like a handle, so I could, like, grab it. I used another rope and I cut the rope about six to eight feet long, tied one end on one ankle and one end on the other ankle, which made another loop." He dragged her corpse out of the sleeper cab, plopped it onto the tar below, and pulled her underneath the truck. He found a cross member, a steel bar going the length of the truck from side to side. "I wanted to position the body between the duals [axles] and the back of the trailer so it could ride and nobody would be able to see it." He'd "envisioned all of this in his head" before doing it. "I taped her hands together so that positioning her facedown she'd ride facedown on the pavement, so I'd get rid of her facial features and handprints."

Certain her body was secure, he conducted a final walk around, "to see if anybody was watching."

He didn't see anyone.

Confident everything was clear after a cluster of vehicles passed by, Jesperson revved the accelerator, popped the clutch, and took off.

Merging onto the freeway, he hit the gas and, only able to get the truck up to sixty-four miles per hour because of a company-mandated speed-control governor, he got her up to speed and drove.

His only concern was that Nebraskan state cops had a habit of parking in the median at night, the middle of the freeway, and pointing their headlights out onto the road.

Strangely, he said next, "We drove for about twelve miles."

We. The way he described this scene made me shiver. He'd sometimes address his victims in disparaging ways: *It, That, The Body, Piece of Shit.* Never by their names. Now, within this gruesome situation, he opted for *We.*

Jesperson pulled over after a congestion of cars passed him, worried someone might see her bouncing underneath the vehicle. He then got on the CB radio and told any nearby truckers coming up not to be concerned if they saw him pulled over and his flashers on. All was fine. No help needed.

Pulled over, his rig still running, Happy Face jumped out, grabbed his side cutters, severed the rope tied around her neck and, with the loop he'd made around her ankles, pulled what was left of her body out from underneath the rig and dragged her thirty feet off the road shoulder. He found an area of tall grass, snow, and ice, flinging what was left of her there, where he believed nobody would find her.

"From her ears forward on her skull was missing . . . and her chest cavity was missing, and both arms were missing."

This image, a corporal nightmare in the fashion of a graphic novel scene, forcibly sketching itself inside my head, had aroused me from sleep on several nights. I'd had a difficult time getting the entire narrative out of my consciousness.

"Her jeans had actually worn down to where there was no fly area left, no internal organs there."

As we talked through Angela Subrize's murder and the disposal of her remains, a lingering thought was that perhaps he was lying about her being dead when he tied her up and dragged her underneath his vehicle. Part of an image I'd had dreams about included a woman screaming as she was forced out of a vehicle by a faceless man and then dragged to her death.

I explained to him that Angela Subrize was a victim. A woman loved by those in her life. Pregnant when Jesperson murdered her, this fact hit a personal nerve with me, I explained. Angela Subrize was not a discussion piece, a fictional character (a box of which Jesperson had sometimes placed his victims into) within the context of Happy Face's spree of murders.

"What do you want me to say, Phelps? I'm telling you how it was. You need to harden up and face the facts. I gotta go now."

Click.

25

SATAN'S WHISPER

"We are each our own devil, and we make this world
our hell."
—Oscar Wilde

JESPERSON WAS ALWAYS ASKING ME ABOUT "THE BOOK." WHEN WAS I
going to write *his* book? You know, finally tell the world about the
Taunja Bennett case and all of those corrupt law enforcement officials. This was the drum he beat—constantly.

"You're my last hope for the truth to come out."

"You mean *your* truth?" I said.

"I guess." He paused. "You're not *ever* going to write a book
about me, are you?"

"I said I would. I am a man of my word, even if that promise is
to a serial killer."

As we got to talking over the next few weeks, I opened up a bit,
explaining that, at times, despite all the horrors he'd shared with
me, I couldn't stop myself from thinking of him as another person I'd spoken to or interacted with throughout my day, not the
vicious psychopath he is, and these feelings were bothering (and
weighing on) me. I couldn't reconcile being friends with a serial
killer, liking him in the least, or thinking there was another side
to him. There was no way to explain the way I felt. I'd kept my
feelings from everyone I knew. And yet, for some reason, here I
was telling him.

"You have been a highlight to me for over three years," he said. "I look forward to our talks."

I knew this. Beyond all the groupies he'd acquired, his cellies, those in the general public who wrote to him, he depended on my friendship. I was there for him in more ways than being his storyteller. I'd never sent him money. He'd never been paid for *Dark Minds*. I would put twenty-five dollars, here and there, on his telephone account so he could call me on my cell phone. And even though he'd send those irritating subscription postcards that fall out of magazines (prompting me to buy him one), a commissary checklist of all the goodies I could purchase for him, I'd given in only one time and purchased a magazine (fishing), which I did not renew. He had plenty of money. He made, on average, sixty-five dollars a month working. A woman in Texas sent him forty a month, "just because"; a woman in Michigan was good for twenty-five to fifty every month; a woman in Australia, twenty dollars; a guy in Wisconsin one hundred dollars "every few months"; in addition to receiving random money orders from twenty to two hundred dollars periodically from all over the world. He'd check his account and find fifty here and twenty there from people he didn't know. The trimmings of being a serial killer with a household name, I reckon.

"A guy from Spokane wants to come in and see me soon. He's gay—he'll probably be good for one hundred dollars a month when he decides to be a better friend," Jesperson said. "I don't play gay. I'm straight and he knows it. Call me a whore, Phelps." He laughed.

Part of me understood those wanting to know him because he's famous. Living in the shallow, celebrity-driven culture we are currently smothered by, some people feel inadequate enough to want a piece of him in whatever capacity they can get it. But I will never understand why strangers arbitrarily send their hard-earned money to a serial killer and, likewise, why beautiful women, young as twenty, send a serial killer pictures of themselves clad only in swimsuits or panties (both of which he has shown me). It defies practical understanding.

Jesperson never looked to me as a cash cow—obviously, he didn't need to. He knew and respected that I'd never provide him with money. Still, I didn't know how to respond to the "highlight" comment he'd made, so I let it pass and, same as those days when I felt talking to him was overwhelming me, my guard weakening, said I had to go.

"Don't call me for a few weeks, okay? I need a break."

"One day, Phelps, I won't hear from you again and, like all the others, you'll be gone, too," he said, before explaining how several people had befriended him throughout the years, only to abandon him after they got whatever it was they'd wanted: his signature, a painting, a letter, a few phone calls, a personal visit. "You'll have what you need from me one day and you'll disappear. And there is nothing I can do about it."

He was right. The only plan I'd buttoned up within my head by then was severing all communication and ties with him at some point. I was resigned to let him rot in the dingy, smelly prison he believes is a good life. The only question was: when?

"You might be right," I admitted.

"I know I am."

Something happened, however, not long after this conversation. A change in me occurred. Intrusions into my sleep and while eating out with friends and family were the norm by now, and I expected Jesperson's influence to infiltrate my social life. I guess, in employing a serial killer and interviewing him for as many years as I had about his crimes, one has signed up for an invasion of his emotional and personal space. But as he got to know more about my life by the few things I'd let slip and admitted, or perhaps what others were sending him upon request, he used this to further deepen our relationship.

"Let's talk about your sister-in-law's murder," he said next time we spoke. He'd mentioned this from time to time and I'd let it pass. But he was adamant. "I can help you. I can give you some answers. I know from our last conversation that this is an uncomfortable subject for you, but I want you to know I will help in whatever way I can."

"What are you talking about? You know *nothing* about her or what happened. I've explained how I feel talking to you about this."

"Right, but all those cases we talked about on *Dark Minds,* I knew nothing about those, either, until you sent me research and filled me in. Let's treat her case as one more *Dark Minds* episode. Send me what you have and let's see where it takes us."

It was a subject I did not want to discuss, with him or anybody. I'd been slammed by certain family members after the first season of *Dark Minds* aired (which Jesperson was not involved with—we used a serial killer codenamed "13," a guy John Kelly had groomed as a killer consultant), after I spoke my opinions and shared certain facts about Diane's life. Her and my brother's children wanted my head after the episode premiered. There were things I shared on "The Woodsmen" episode during season one that the kids were not prepared to hear. They had been so young when everything happened. They were unclear about certain facts. I should have discussed what I was going to say with them before I aired it on national television. That was my mistake. I owned it.

In defense of what had been edited into that episode, however, when you're out on the road for months filming such a personal series as *Dark Minds* had been, living it around the clock, you get caught up in your own pathos. The episode weighed on me because it had hit so close to home, in more ways than just logistics (Worcester, Massachusetts, is about forty-five minutes from my office). After sitting with the family—two sisters and mother—of a victim, interviewing them for the episode, sharing in their heartbreak, taking in all of their pain, crying with them, trading personal anecdotes, the crew and I went out and shot some scenes of me sitting on a bench in the woods talking through my brother and Diane and what happened. Without realizing how much honesty poured out of me (we shot about an hour's worth of material), in the throes of nostalgic emotion, I said some things I shouldn't have.

Now I had the Devil whispering in my ear, wanting to step inside that world and help untangle it. He, nor anyone else, knew I'd been digging into the case myself for years. I'd spoken to a cop in Hartford I knew. "Let it go," he told me after I asked how the investigation into Diane's murder was coming along. I was even told back in the day that I couldn't go into the prison and run my alcohol/drug abuse meeting because Diane's killer was thought to be one of the inmates attending. So I quit going up to the prison altogether. These types of family tragedies, especially those that involve the murder of a loved one, become messy, sensitive, and difficult to come to terms with for immediate family. I understood that directly as a writer dealing with victims' families every day. As you immerse yourself in the heartbreak, the pain, the darkness, you need to sometimes trick yourself into believing it happened to someone else.

I'd go to morning Mass, sit, pray, and think about Diane, the tumultuous history I'd had with her and my brother at the end, how much they meant to me, their kids, what had transpired among all of us, but could never find solace or answers, spiritual or otherwise. Every time I went back, I'd end up at the same place: All of us wanted Diane out of our lives for good and, suddenly, unexpectedly, shockingly, one day she was gone. Like my old neighborhood, it was an emotional powder keg. Revisiting it would no doubt blow things up for me. So as I dug into Diane's murder over the years and didn't get very far, I pushed it all into a corner, placed a sheet over it.

Now here I was one afternoon, talking to Jesperson, him pressing me to explain what had happened.

So I told him.

26

THE TERROR OF DAMNATION

"He will never have true friends who is afraid of
making enemies."
—William Hazlitt

JULIE WINNINGHAM EXPLAINED TO JESPERSON THAT IF SHE WOUND UP behind bars, it was up to him to come up with bail money. The least he could do. As they discussed this while driving away from Julie's mother's house, Jesperson looked Julie in the eye and said, "I have an idea how to keep you from going to jail." They were traveling east on Highway 14, just outside Portland, not far from where it had all begun five years before with Taunja Bennett.

"I need you to keep me from jail," Julie reiterated. "You will have to bail me out."

As he drove, Jesperson's thoughts wandered into an unforgiving litany: *Bail money! She expects me to bail her out. They all want something from me.*

"The only way I knew how to keep Julie from jail was to kill her," he told me, smiling, as if his plan was clever and humorous.

"You always promised to keep me out of jail," Julie pleaded. "You need to follow through with that." As she spoke, Jesperson drove, picturing himself taking Julie by the neck, staring into her eyes and watching her die, telling himself she was nothing more than a "leech" and "money pit." In searching for the right reason, Happy Face had found a purpose and motive to take another life.

"I used my hands to strangle her," he explained, before uttering that common phrase, "and put her out of her misery—or *my* misery, I guess is the way I looked at it."

On my computer screen, inside the confines of my office, this crazy son of a bitch described killing Julie Winningham as if it were another day in the life of an over-the-road long-haul trucker. Here he was, twenty years later, laughing about it.

After deciding he'd had enough of Julie, Jesperson pulled over. He could not recall exactly where. He grabbed her in a fit of rage, took her into the back of his sleeper cab (just as he'd pictured moments before), and, without uttering a word, placed his hands around her neck and squeezed. She fought back. Her arms flailed. Her legs thrashed. Mucus came out of her nose and mouth as she gasped for air. A small woman of five feet four inches, 120 pounds, Julie Winningham was no match for an experienced serial killer. It took five minutes. Jesperson said he never broke a sweat, adding, "She would not have to worry about court any longer."

SOME MEMORIES ARE SEARED into my brain with eidetic clarity. When I go to that place, I see those recollections completely and entirely. I hear those involved speaking. Perhaps it is the way I recall the incident, or how it really happened, but the memory is unchanging and unblemished. It feels genuine.

By the spring of 1994, my first wife and I took Mark and Diane to family court and won custody of their kids. They were in no condition to raise children. The tipping point was when I found my six-year-old nephew playing on the side of a busy road near their apartment at midnight. He wore only underpants and a T-shirt. He was alone. My brother and Diane, along with several transients who were forever coming and going and sleeping at their apartment, were upstairs, passed out. Empty bottles and cans, dirty laundry, dishes piled all over, and drug paraphernalia filled their living space. The smell of stale crack cocaine, booze, and cigarette butts was absorbed into the curtains and linens. No one in the apartment had any idea my nephew had wandered off.

Scheduled visitations, at our discretion, were set up after we were awarded custody. If we believed Mark or Diane were under the influence, we had the right to deny a visit. So many times they'd take the kids on Friday and not bring them back per the state's order on Sunday night. We'd have to call child services and the police, or I would go out and track them down myself, engage in a confrontation, and haul the kids back to my home. By now, they'd been kicked out of that apartment and were living in motels and moving around a lot, deeply ensconced in their addictions. We thought the kids being taken away would have been a bottom, but it became, instead, a glass ceiling. We argued with Diane every time my wife and I ran into her. Diane was vulgar. She could be nasty and hurtful. I know at this time she hated us.

One Friday, they showed up and my brother was drunk. Diane had driven and seemed, for the most part, somewhat with it. My niece, Meranda, was in the backseat.

"You're not taking the kids. Come back when you're *both* sober." Diane stood at my front door. She was not allowed on the property. Just ringing the bell was a violation of our agreement with the court.

"You need to leave, Diane."

I cannot tell you exactly what she said in response because the memory becomes blurry here. I'm sure her rage included a multitude of the usual obscenities and threats: *I can easily have you killed. . . . You're going to pay for this. . . . Your brother knows people who can have your legs broken.*

Diane was upset because we wouldn't allow her into the house to see the kids. After a time, she calmed down. I then escorted her to the end of the driveway, where her car was parked, and my brother, now awake, stared at me, shaking his head. "You're an asshole, you know that," Mark said.

"Just leave, man. Come on. Show up sober. That's *all* you have to do."

As we approached the end of the driveway, Diane looked inside my recycling bin sitting on the lawn. Stopping, lifting her eyes away from the bin, she stared at me without saying anything at first. Then: "Take a look at yourself! You're not so fucking different than me and Mark," she said, kicking the bin as she got into the car.

"Just leave," I said. "Get out of here."

I watched them drive away. Walking back to the house, passing the bin, I stopped and stared at the contents: *Bitch doesn't know anything about me.*

Yet, here's the thing about Diane: she *did* know.

It's easy to deny your own problems or even consider they exist when you focus on someone else's. Inside my recycling bin were several empty twelve-pack Bud Light cartons, wine, and vodka bottles. What Diane articulated in a moment of clarity and observation while standing at the end of my driveway was that I'd taken them to court, won custody of their children, but all I'd done was remove the children from one dysfunctional home and place them into another. Diane could be perceptive at times; she understood life; she knew what suffering and growing up struggling was. She comprehended the idea that your adult self is a product of your familial DNA—this was what she'd tried to say.

I was not anywhere near the bottom of the hellhole Mark and Diane had been swallowed up into, but I was on my way. Who was I to judge her, when my life was on a course of destruction? I was on a path accelerated by the stress of now, at twenty-seven, raising four boys, with a wife I took for granted and treated as though she would always be there, did not matter to me, and would never leave?

I never wanted to be estranged, dislike, or fight with Diane, and certainly deny her and my brother visitations with their children. I loved her—and always viewed Diane as (or maybe hoped her to be) a big sister to confide in. As a teenager, when Mark and Diane had a somewhat normal life and nice apartment, their daughter, Meranda, just five years old, my oldest nephew, Mark, just starting to walk, I babysat. They'd buy me a six-pack. Sitting on their couch, I'd drink my Pabst, smoke cigarettes, and watch Cinemax (when it actually had value for a boy of sixteen). I was the youngest of four boys, but my oldest brother and his wife treated me like an adult, leaving me in charge of their family. I felt honored and grown-up.

I'm not sure where the scales tipped for them and social use turned into addiction, but that was the way it turned out. Just two years and change from the day Diane and Mark drove away from me as I stood on Susan Road and watched them leave without their kids, Mark and I would be face-to-face in my kitchen, Diane dead, the task in front of me left to explain to him what had happened to the woman he loved all his life.

27

GHOST STORIES

"The tragedy in a man's life is what dies inside of him
while he lives."
—Albert Schweitzer

*L*ES JESPERSON TOOK A DRIVE ONE DAY FROM HIS HOME IN WASH-
ington to the OSP in Salem. A visit with his son was in order. As
Happy Face later described him, Les was forever looking for ways
to strike it rich. Land. An invention. Machining business. The pro-
prietor of a trailer park. One of the first businesses Les operated
was a rental service: he bought a bunch of bicycles and leased them
to servicemen on an army base near his Chilliwack home. Whatever way he could facilitate finding the end of the rainbow, Les
was willing to begin the journey.

"A book," Les said after the two of them settled in for a prison
visit.

"Book?" Happy Face asked, confused.

"Yeah, the father of a serial killer writes a book about his son."

Jesperson liked the idea. Jeffrey Dahmer's father had published a book the previous year. What was good for Dahmer was
good for Happy Face.

Jesperson wrote eighty pages of material for his father and sent
it off.

They spoke on the phone a few days after the package arrived.

"What do you think?"

"You're blaming me for everything," Les stated. He was livid.

"No, I'm not. You asked for my perspective and I am giving it to you."

But if what Jesperson sent to his dad included a whiff of what he shared with me (the manifesto), Les was spot-on: Les was the source of planting the demon seed in the Jesperson family.

"He didn't like the way things turned out, and he wanted to whitewash the Jesperson effect," Happy Face told me.

"I can clearly see, in all you've written to me," I countered, "that Les plays a large role in your anger. Whether it's how you perceived it then, see it now, or how it was, your father was right. You blame him for *everything*."

"Dad was so afraid that he would come off as a monster and that he created me," Jesperson explained, speaking of their book (which was never completed or published). "There was a lot of me that *wasn't* created by him . . . but he always told me to be hard on people because people will run over you. My father had this idea to *use* a person. That was his nature. A friend to him was someone who had something he could use that he wanted. That's the way he saw life. Dad saw people as assets. A friend to him is someone that has something to offer. Dad is a taker. And hates all who take from us."

One story that Jesperson shared, hoping to place some of the responsibility for who he turned out to be on his father, occurred around a campfire "back in the early 1960s." The Jespersons would sit around an outdoor fire and talk. "We told ghost stories," Jesperson said.

One by one, they'd share. On this night, when it came time for Les, he nestled up close to the fire, rubbed his hands together over the flame, and asked everyone to pay close attention. What he was about to say, he preferred calling a "premonition story."

As Les got going, he explained how he was out driving along a dark country road one early morning as the sun was coming up.

"He got a bad feeling and needed to stop on the side of the road," Jesperson said.

So Les parked his vehicle, got out, and took a walk around.

As he approached the back bumper, an RCMP cruiser pulled up.

Why are you stopped here, sir? the RCMP supposedly asked.

I have this premonition that something bad happened here, Les said. *Just cannot get it out of my head.*

The cop seemed mystified. *Just about twelve hours ago, a man was stopped on this very spot, changing a flat tire in the dark, when a vehicle came by and struck and killed him.*

No kidding.

Yes! So I suggest you get back into your vehicle and get going now.

Aspiring one day to be mayor, at this time Les was a prominent member of the city council. It was one more reason, Jesperson said, to be protective of the family name and reputation.

Les concluded his campfire tale there, leaving it as the story of a man with a sharp sense of perception. The kids were thrilled. Dad had special powers.

As the years passed, the story nagged at Happy Face. Les had told it several times, changing certain, however minor, details. Happy would look at the old man and think: *Why would you change that?* Such subtle facts. Over a period of time, Happy wondered if there was any truth to his father's story. The tale had to be based on a real event, or was it a story Les had heard?

One night, they sat, together, in back of their Durr Road home at High Valley Ranch near Yakima/Ellensburg, Washington, again around a campfire. Les was rip-roaring drunk.

"Why is it you only had *one* premonition and no more since then?" the son asked the father. "There *has* to be something you're not saying."

According to Jesperson, his father "began to tremble" and his teeth "chattered."

"What he was about to tell me," Jesperson recalled, "no one else had ever heard."

"What is it?" the son asked the father.

Les explained how "he had been drinking that night before and drove around a corner, his eyes only seeing a flash of something standing up in front of him, before he felt and heard a loud thud."

So Les stopped the vehicle. He got out to see what he'd hit. He looked in all directions, making sure no one was around.

Just as he did that, however, "he turned to see a car coming and took off."

Les pulled over several miles ahead, drove into the brush, and slept off his bender.

"Wait a minute," I said as Jesperson related the story. "Are you telling me that your father hit—"

"Let me finish!"

When Les woke, he examined the bumper and then drove back to where he'd heard the thud and saw the flash. He hoped it had been a deer or another type of animal.

As he returned to the scene, it was in that moment the RCMP came upon Les and explained that on the same spot the previous night someone had hit a person and taken off.

"My father had killed a man and confessed it to me," Jesperson claimed. "In the morning, I tried to bring it up again, to get more facts. All he said was 'Keith, you need to forget what I talked about last night. I shouldn't have said it. It was a mistake.' So it was his word against mine. Whenever we sat around and told ghost stories after that, Les never said a word."

I NEEDED TO TAKE a trip to Washington and sit down with Les. Get his version of the life his son had scripted. The conversation would answer a growing list of questions. What would Les say about Keith all these years later?

"Go ahead," Jesperson told me. "I'd be interested in hearing his response."

By now, Les had stopped communicating with his son. He'd send a short note, or his second wife would write to say Les was not up to talking about the past or visiting anymore. He was too old, sick, tired. A man in his eighties, he didn't want to deal with it. In 2012, Les wrote one of his final letters to his son, opening the missive with how "hard" it was for him to "start" writing be-cause "feelings run so deep." He mentioned how he chose to remember his son: A picture hanging over his bed, for which every time he looked at, Les explained, "My head says, 'Why Keith, why?'" The one comforting feeling Les could die with, he added, was that "your mother did not know about you before her passing."

Jesperson gave me his father's address and phone number.

"I'll make plans right away," I promised.

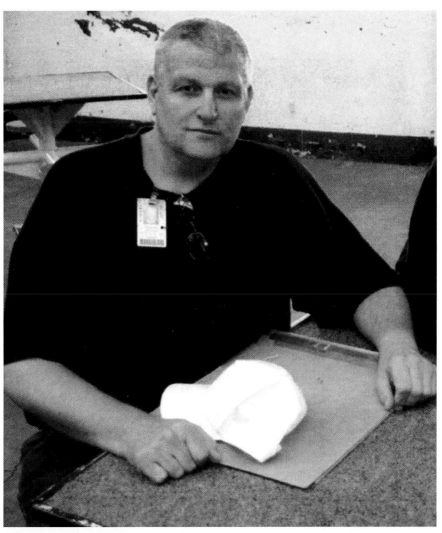

Keith Jesperson (left) in his teens and (above) in 2016. Also called the Happy Face Killer, he became an anonymous, secret source, known to viewers only as Raven, on my Investigation Discovery series *Dark Minds*.

From 2011 to 2016, I maintained an unexpected friendship with this convicted serial killer that tested my limits. The relationship included countless emails, letters, Skypes, and prison visits.

Behind the scenes of *Dark Minds*: Interviewing a source for the Long Island Serial Killer episode. *(Photo Courtesy of Peter Heap)*

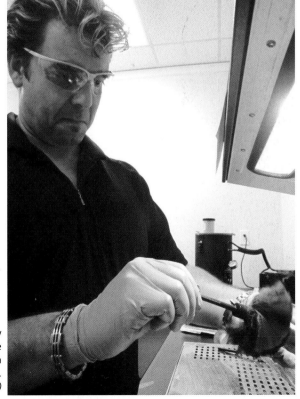

Filming a TV reality show sometimes required me to learn hands-on crime-solving techniques. *(Photo Courtesy of Peter Heap)*

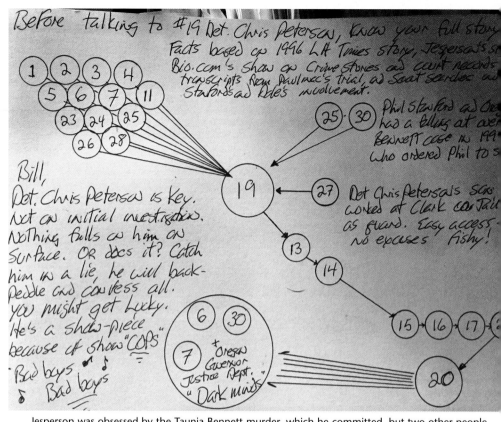

Before talking to #19 Det. Chris Peterson, know your full story. Facts based on 1996 LA Times story, Jesperson's story, Bio.com's show on Crime Stories and court records, transcripts from Pauline's trial, and Court records and Stanfords and Kyle's involvement.

1 2 3 4
5 6 7 11
23 24 25
26 28

25 30 Phil Stanford and Oregon had a falling at over Bennett case in 199_ who ordered Phil to s_

19

27 Det Chris Peterson's son worked at Clark county Jail as guard. Easy access no excuses. Fishy!

Bill,
Det. Chris Peterson is key. Not on initial investigation. Nothing falls on him on surface. OR does it? Catch him in a lie, he will back-pedddle and confess all. You might get lucky. He's a show-piece because of show "COPS" ♪♫ "Bad boys ♪ ♫ Bad boys"

13
14

6 30
7 + Oregon Governor Justice Dept. "Dark minds"

15 16 17
20

Jesperson was obsessed by the Taunja Bennett murder, which he committed, but two other people were convicted of the crime. He sent me copious letters, drawings, and narratives that depicted, in his view, how investigators botched the case.

Jesperson created colored-pencil and charcoal drawings showing where he dumped Taunja Bennett's personal belongings — information only her killer would know.

Here is my oldest brother, Mark, in 1968, holding me up on his shoulders, while our brothers Thomas (left) and Frank (right) ham it up for the photo.

The four Phelps boys in 1969 standing near our home on Hollister Drive in East Hartford, Connecticut (From left to right, Mark, Frank, Thomas, and me)

On my sixth birthday,
I lived my dream of being a cowboy.

I was seventeen in 1983—yes, that's a mullet!
—and my brother Mark was twenty-eight
when I realized that something wasn't
quite right with him.

My brother Thomas (in back of me, eating)
and I are the closest in age. We would later
share responsibilities for caring for my
brother Mark's children when he and
his wife could not.

I want to remember Mark as he was in 1962,
when he was six: innocent, happy, safe,
and sheltered from life's demons.

Before drug addiction took control
of his life, Mark was a wonderful,
doting father and loving family member.

Mark made a handsome usher
during my first wedding in 1987.

Little Meranda at 3½ months old.

Mark met his wife Diane Ferris when she was thirteen. Here is Diane at seventeen holding her three-and-a-half-month-old daughter, Meranda.

Before addiction took over, Diane was a loving and proud mother.

Diane with her family.
From left to right:
Mark, Jr., Diane, Tyler, and Mark.

This is the last photo taken of Diane, two months pregnant at the time, twelve weeks before she was murdered.

UNSOLVED HOMICIDE

Diana Ferris
34 Year Old Female

On April 11, 1996, Diana Ferris was found strangled to death in her Garden Street apartment in Hartford.

If You Have Any Info
Regarding This Case
Call Connecticut Cold Case
1-866-623-8058

Diane Ferris was murdered on April 11, 1996. She became the Ten of Hearts in Connecticut's second edition deck of the Cold Case Playing Cards.
(Photo Courtesy of State of Connecticut)

Although Mark was terribly troubled by his wife's murder and suffered from bipolar disorder, he smiled for this photo.

Not long after this photo was taken, my brother, Mark Anthony Phelps, Sr., died from liver failure at age 47.

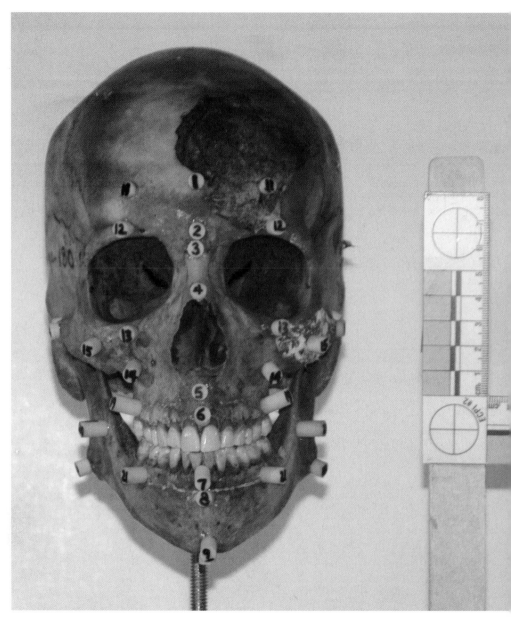

Jane Doe (Florida) was one of Jesperson's victims. He discussed her with me at length.
I worked with law enforcement to re-investigate and try to identify her. This photo shows Jane's actual skull.
(Photo Courtesy of the Palm Beach County Sheriff's Office)

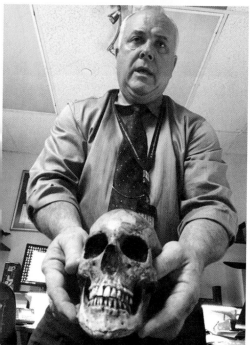

Ken Robinson (left) has become one of my best friends, a mentor, and an important part of my investigative reporting team.

Palm Beach County Sheriff's Office Forensic Imaging Specialist Paul Moody holds an exact scaled resin replica of Jane Doe's skull, which he later gave me.

Florida Department of Law Enforcement Special Agent Dennis Haley was instrumental in seeking to identify Jesperson's Jane Doe (Florida) victim.

This is the first drawing Jesperson created of Jane Doe (Florida), which he sent to me.

White woman with Blonde hair

Kur Jespor
Florida case
? 1994 ?

After I convinced him he wouldn't face the death penalty for helping Florida law enforcement identify Jane Doe, Jesperson sent this drawing with greater detail.

Jesperson rendered this pencil/charcoal drawing for PBSO Forensic Imaging Specialist Paul Moody. *(Photo Courtesy of the Palm Beach County Sheriff's Office)*

This computerized identikit rendering of Jane Doe (Florida), composed by Forensic Imaging Specialist Paul Moody with help from serial killer Keith Jesperson, is the most accurate depiction to date of Jane Doe, a five foot, four inch, 110-pound, 20-something, blond, blue-eyed female going by the name Suzette, Suzanne, Sue, Sue-Ellen, or Susan. The sash and bracelet in this photo are Jane's actual belongings.
(Photo Courtesy of the Palm Beach County Sheriff's Office)

If you have any information about Jane Doe—think you know who she is or recognize her jewelry—please contact Special Agent Dennis Haley, Pensacola Regional Operations Center, 1301 North Palafox St., Pensacola, Florida 32501; phone: 850-595-2149; dennishaley@fdle.state.fl.us

No matter where I was, Keith "Raven" Jesperson called me incessantly on my cell phone. While I was shooting the Israel Keyes episode of *Dark Minds* in Alaska, Jesperson claimed he had a "major breakthrough." *(Photo Courtesy of Peter Heap)*

28

TEN OF HEARTS

"The meaning of life is that it stops."
—Franz Kafka

MARK WALKED INTO THE HOUSE. I STOOD IN THE KITCHEN, NOT far from where the side door opened (we never used the front door). He had groceries in both hands, cigarette hanging from his lips. It was April 12, 1996, two years after Diane and I had the recycling bin conversation at the end of my driveway. Mark and I had been living together in this empty house in Vernon, Connecticut, on Susan Road, which the bank was going to take any day. I was glad to walk away, honestly. So much misery had occurred within these walls. My wife had been gone about a year by then. I was devastated, depressed, sober, not eating much, about 150 pounds. It was time to move on, to accept my life had changed and that my wife was gone and never coming back, and start over.

"What happened to her?" Mark asked, staring at me, dropping both bags of groceries.

How the hell did he know? I had not said a word.

While he was out, I'd sat and questioned where he'd gone the night before. The guy never went out. His methadone maintenance program wouldn't allow it. But the previous night—near the same time we believed that Diane had been murdered—Mark left the house. I'd convinced myself he'd played a role in her death. Yet, by the time he walked through the door, looking into his eyes and feeling the pain surround him like a force field, I knew my brother wasn't a killer. Those thoughts were nothing more than the soul's rapid reaction to tragedy, when every deleterious scenario possible takes over your senses, as if you have no control over your own thoughts. It's like hearing a bump in the middle of the night. During the day, you wouldn't think twice about it, but in the darkened silence of early morning, a branch squeaking up against a windowpane becomes a home invader sneaking in to commit deplorable acts of violence against your family.

I wouldn't find out until many years later why Mark seemed to know before I opened my mouth. He'd taken a phone call from Diane two days before she was murdered. She said something about needing five hundred dollars before the weekend—or else. Going out that night before, Mark had been working on getting her the money.

"She's dead, Mark, I'm sorry," I explained, landing the blow as soft as I could, adding how our other brother Tommy had called. "Strangled. That's about all we know."

My brother's body language personified his addictions. At times, Mark moved around as though he'd been paralyzed and was learning how to walk again. His gait reminded me of Ozzy on *The Osbournes:* stiff legs, like Pinocchio, except where they bent at the joints, a perpetual look of him falling over. He'd nod, in and out of it, like opiate addicts do, with the lethargy and consistency of a narcoleptic. I'd find him passed out all over the house: sitting on the toilet, at the kitchen table, outside on the deck, on the stairs going down into his section of the house, leaning against the handrail. I'd once pulled into the driveway to find him standing with his house key in the lock, his forehead leaning against the windowpane, a steam of nostril exhaust fogging up the glass in rhythm with his labored breathing, the screen door butted up against his back.

In those days before she was murdered, Diane was a woman all of us had wished would disappear. Now she *was* gone. Now her death was beginning to settle on my brother. Now Mark was broken.

After sitting, smoking several cigarettes, Mark tried to stand. I can still see his face, his body rubbery, melting as if all his bones had been removed. He and Diane had been estranged for close to five months on that night I told him, but he still loved her. He'd been living with me while Diane stayed in Hartford, inside the apartment of a "friend." Yet, he was still seeing and sleeping with her. I'd asked him about this many times: "Why not just let her go, man. You two together, you self-destruct. The worst possible person for you to be around is Diane, and her, you."

"I know," he said. "But I can't abandon her. She needs me—especially right now. I love her. I could not live without Diane in my life."

My brother was one of those kids who hit home runs in Little League, and every other kid wanted to be on his team, though he gave up on sports. He quit school and yet excelled later in accounting college, able to work numbers like a savant. But he gave up on that, too, and appropriated his genius math skills to thinking he could somehow beat the horse and dog track. He was one of those dads his kids loved. He was kind, a heart as soft as a poem. His smile made everything all right. He bought his children toys, took them on vacations, made them dinners, taught them how to swim. But he gave up on that also. When the booze and drugs took over, Mark checked out of life. He became unavailable to everyone. He never wanted help. He never wanted to stop. He never wanted for his life to turn out the way it did.

Although he and Diane could scream at each other and rattle windowpanes, Mark was quiet, even when he got high or drunk. Diane, alternatively, was obstreperous. Her voice raised an octave when she got splashed. When she smoked crack, paranoia set in. She'd draw the shades, stand in the corner, freaking out, thinking there were bugs crawling in her hair. At times, she'd be belligerent, vicious, and nasty, but she could also show tremendous love and affection in ways that any mother, wife, and sister-in-law might. She had a deep connection, as did Mark, with their youngest child, Tyler.

"It's funny because, as kids, they made each of us feel as if we were their favorite, as if we were special," Meranda recalled. "That was one of their greatest gifts as parents."

The first published report of Diane's murder painted a gruesome picture. It claimed she was found "strangled" to death inside a Garden Street apartment in Hartford's north end "after neighbors and family members had not seen her for days." In one version, she had been lying on a bed, a pillowcase over her head, a telephone cord wrapped around her neck, bruises on one leg.

I'd heard several varieties of this as time passed. One was that she'd been found wearing only panties. The other was that she was murdered inside the bathtub (no water).

What cannot be disputed is the fact that she was five months pregnant and she'd been in that apartment, dead, for several days before anyone had found her. The fetus, news reports claimed, was stillborn. Blood was never taken from the baby to find out who had fathered the child.

Diane called her oldest, Meranda, in the weeks before she was murdered: "I'm not sure if it's Mark's or [the other guy's]," she said of the baby. "We'll see when the baby is born."

"She really felt that it was Mark's baby," Meranda said.

In this same *Hartford Courant* article about her murder, for the first time it was reported publicly that "police believe she was at the scene of" Thomas Myers's 1993 Dutch Point housing project murder. By then, three years after his death, Diane had stiff-armed cops enough to where they had let her be. The Myers murder went cold, unsolved.

In the early 2000s, the Connecticut Division of Criminal Justice, working with the Connecticut Department of Correction and law enforcement agencies across the state, created a cold case deck of playing cards "highlighting fifty-two unsolved homicides, missing persons, and unidentified remains cases" statewide. Each of the fifty-two cards in the deck represented one case, featured details about the crime, a photo of the victim, and a phone number to call with any anonymous tips or important information. In subsequent years, other decks (editions) were printed. The state distributes the cards, mainly, to prisoners in Connecticut state prisons. It is an unconventional method of generating tips and initiating conversation among inmates about unsolved cases. Thus far, I've been told, eight murders have been resolved because of information from the cards. In a second-edition playing-card deck, Diane is featured as the ten of hearts.[5]

[5]You can see Diane's card and each cold case deck here: http://www.ct.gov/doc/lib/doc/images/coldcasecards2.jPG. If you have any information about any of these cases, please come forward.

29

SMOKED

"What strange creatures brothers are!"
—Jane Austen

*T*HE HAPPY FACE KILLER WAS SEVEN WHEN HIS FATHER OPENED THE door to his room one afternoon in 1962 and ordered him downstairs, pronto.

Little Keith sat as his dad thought for a minute. Then Les came out with it: "Have you been taking my cigarettes?"

"No."

"Don't you lie to me, boy."

Keith broke down.

Les took a cigarette out of the pack, lit it, and handed it to his son. "Inhale that like a *real* man. Come on, I want to see you smoke one."

Keith thought: *The belt or cigarette?*

As the child puffed, Les demanded he inhale and stop faking it. Take a big drag, suck that smoke into both lungs, and then "hold it."

"Before long, I was puking my guts out," Jesperson recalled. "But it did not stop me from wanting to smoke. I still stole cigarettes from Dad's stash."

By the early 1970s, the Jesperson household was used to hearing Les hack and cough for most of the day, as if something had gone down the wrong pipe. During one coughing fit, Les was rushed to the ER because he couldn't stop. He was diagnosed with pneumonia. Smoking was killing him, his doctors told him. That night, Les coughed so violently he broke three ribs, one of which punctured a lung.

"When his doctors went in to save his life, they found he had lung cancer," Jesperson explained. "They fixed him and he was told to stop smoking or he'd die." Les quit and, after a brief battle, was free of cancer. "And my cigarettes disappeared. So I stopped mostly because it was killing my dad."

In 2012, Les ended a brief letter to his boy explaining he was "on oxygen 24/7," a "50-foot hose" attached to the tank "long enough to reach the bed and toilet." Les was in bad shape. Life had caught up to him.

Jesperson told me the cancer story to put his dad into context. Years after he'd quit smoking, Les would sit around, bragging to anyone listening, that he "stopped smoking because he wanted to be a good dad and be around for [his kids]—lead by example."

"I would tell him much later that he stopped smoking because he stared death in the face, quit or die."

According to Happy Face, the story demonstrated the deceptive nature his father had instilled in him. He took note: learning that one could twist and shape a life to fit an agenda.

This conversation got me thinking. I was interested in what scared Jesperson. What was it that a seasoned serial killer, doing life behind bars, feared most? Death by disease? The electric chair? Being shanked by some young punk looking to make a name for himself in the prison yard by taking out the resident serial?

Jesperson's answer surprised me. "Being caught," he said. "Being found out. That was my biggest fear. Once I realized people would know who I *truly* was, it terrified me. Everything was fine and dandy until everyone *knew* I was a killer."

He enjoyed harboring the secret; walking around, stopping at the table of four cops as they ate lunch, asking for directions; holding the door for an attractive female; pumping diesel fuel into his rig, smiling, waving at fellow truckers. All while knowing the corpse of a woman he'd just strangled to death was lying inside his rig. He got a rush. He felt omnipotent. It gave him a sense of superiority and power: being smarter and having more confidence than anyone else. It was all a component of the drug keeping the psychopath high.

This led to taking greater risks. Like, for example, when he was at home in Portland, Jesperson jogged regularly at a nearby park. One day, while running down a popular trail, a woman passed, jogging in the opposite direction. Happy Face stopped, turned around, ran back, and caught up. They jogged, side by side, for a short distance before she looked him in the eye and said, "Not interested."

Before turning and taking off in the direction he'd been going, Jesperson told her she was "beautiful." In response, he claimed, "she blushed and smiled."

Looking back over his shoulder as he ran away, he caught her doing the same. "She is watching *me*."

As she ran out of sight, he looked at his watch, noting the time.

The next day, he jogged the same route, same time, hoping to run into the woman again. As they passed each other, he waved.

She smiled.

He did it again the following day.

Then, per his carefully designed plan, he didn't go back for a week.

Next time he jogged, he saw the woman. She smiled, waved. He responded with the same gesture. Over the next four weeks, he saw her every third day. By then, she felt comfortable and knew him by sight. He was grooming her. "Building a rapport." Charming her defenses. Allowing her to feel safe within his presence. He'd murdered several women just like her by then. In fact, it was during this period when he'd initiated a cat-and-mouse bait with law enforcement by leaving a note on a restroom wall after Laverne Pavlinac and John Sosnovske were convicted: JAN 21 . . . KILLED TAUNJA BENNETT IN PORTLAND – TOO [SIC] PEOPLE GOT THE BLAME SO I CAN KILL AGAIN – CUT BUTTON OFF JEANS PROOF.

One afternoon, as Jesperson jogged down a narrow part of the trail, he came upon the woman. She was standing, "blocking my path."

He knew he had her complete trust.

"Name?" she said, smiling.

"Keith."

"We should have coffee."

"I'd like that."

As they sat and talked inside a nearby coffee shop, Jesperson picked up on what he later referred to as a "sexual hint to the meeting." She was "flirting." As they chitchatted, he couldn't stop thinking: *I could take you home right now and kill you. You have no idea who you are sitting with.* This gave him a thrill, sure, but also a profound sense of being in total control of this woman without her knowing (a major element of his preferred fantasy). Being a serial killer in this moment energized him.

After coffee, they jogged together a few additional times. They'd sit on a park bench afterward, sweaty and out of breath, talking.

"I'm married," she confessed. "I have children. My husband doesn't work out."

Jesperson smiled.

"I made her feel safe," he recalled, laughing at the thought. "She was easy prey."

He needed to act on the situation or take himself out of it. Because in the weeks that followed, he fantasized about one day waiting for her to run down a secluded section of the trail as he stealthily waited in the brush. As she ran by, he saw himself grab her with the intention of raping and killing her in the woods. It was the moment when she realized she'd been duped, tricked by a predator, that he sought most. Seeing her face—her eyes, especially—change as she understood she'd allowed a monster into her life would have been a bigger high than killing her, he claimed.

"But that wasn't me," he said, after I asked why he never acted. "Too many things can go wrong in that scenario."

As he thought about it later, he said, "Here I was, a serial murderer of women, *protecting* a woman."

In the office of the trucking company he worked for, there was a woman Jesperson walked to her car every evening when he was in town. This was after one of his bodies had been discovered and it had been reported in the news that a potential serial killer was on the loose in the Pacific Northwest.

"I protected her from the serial killer in the news . . . me!"

Jesperson had a way of desensitizing himself to certain behaviors he understood to be ruthless, demeaning, and resentful. He thought it nothing, for example, to set up a scenario in the house when he was married to Rose—during that period when she'd allegedly refused to have sex—where she would walk in on him while he masturbated to photographs of other women, including her friends.

"It's no wonder why I don't miss her," he said.

As a youngster, Jesperson once received a telescope for Christmas. He used it to peep on the female neighbors. One particular house had the perfect view for him to watch as a woman undressed every night. He'd ogle her as she took off her clothes, convincing himself she knew he was watching.

But after a short while, he said, "It was just old news. The telescope was put away. Later on, I kept a pair of binoculars in my truck to be able to observe the goings-on in various areas I parked at. My life was full of spare time just to *watch* people."

Specifically, he enjoyed studying women who weren't "aware they were being watched." (This was from a man who told me several times he never stalked anyone.)

As the middle of March (1995) dawned, Jesperson felt as though his immediate family, children, ex-wife, and society in general were pointing a finger in his face, backing him into a corner. He anticipated the moment when they realized he was a serial killer. Thinking about that, he couldn't face the rejection, ridicule, and public scorn about to fall on him. This was what kept him up at night. The only way out, he reconciled, was suicide.

"If that comment is the truth, take me back there then," I told him, unconvinced. "When you were caught, or, rather, when you gave yourself up, why was it Brad—the one brother you were more at odds with throughout your childhood—you decided to write a letter to and admit what you'd done?"

"Brothers," he said, taking a deep breath. "Siblings. What an interesting topic."

WE DID NOT GROW up religious. Being born into an Irish-Italian family, growing up in East Hartford, Connecticut, I was expected to attend catechism, follow through with First Communion and Confirmation. Yet, I have little memory of attending Mass on Sundays as a family. In grammar school, after class, we walked from McCartin School on Handel Road to Blessed Sacrament Church on Millbrook, where I studied the sacraments and, when the sisters weren't looking, carved my initials, same as my catechetical classmates, into the wooden pews. Unlike most Catholic youths, however, I severed my involvement with the Church *before* I was confirmed (when I realized drinking beer from a keg in the woods did far more for my soul than Jesus could). It wasn't until my midthirties that I was able to sort everything out and understand the grace within the Catholic Church did not have to be muddled by those larger, divisive social issues driving scores of cradle Catholics away. It was the church's archaic roots in Judaism and its dedication to custom—love that incense—I felt most at home with. Sure, I was repulsed by the disregard for human life that any pedophile priest displayed, but I was able to set aside those feelings for the sake of my faith—for which, not long after my conversations with Jesperson began, took a serious hit as questions began to surface.

Going to Mass was a Band-Aid holding me together. I leaned on it when I felt the need to bring some light into the darkness, and my dialogue with Jesperson had manifested into physical ailments. Confession, simple meditation and prayer, fasting (we have such an obsession with food in this country, the burn of hunger once in a while, for me, keeps it real), Penance (because, of course, I hate myself), Holy Days of Obligation, and the sheer silence, relaxation, and peaceful solemnity I experienced while sitting before, during, and after Mass, became a balm, keeping my anxiety levels, diverticulitis episodes, and panic attacks to a minimum.

As Jesperson and I discussed his demons, feeling I was getting closer to my Jane Doe goals, my semidaily Mass routine, which I'd been accustomed to for years before I met him, seemed to work in tandem with something else. In order to help me quit smoking in 2007, my doctor put me on .5 mils of Lexapro, an antidepressant. "It'll keep you calm and help to alleviate the stress of breaking the habit." And it did the job: I quit and never picked up a cigarette again. Yet, after the whirlwind my health got swept up into not long after *Dark Minds* started shooting in 2010, after prescribing yet another round of antibiotics for an "episode," my doctor wondered if upping the dosage to .10 mils a day might help me achieve stability. "But I don't want to take your edge or intensity away," he warned. "I want you to stay who you are."

The .10 mils seemed to be the magic number. Along with Mass, prayer, and a renewed dedication to lifting weights, the balance I sought arrived in small chunks. I also accepted that along the path of a journey, such as the one I'd embarked upon, especially when seeking specific answers, you have to prepare yourself for the reality that they might not be there in the end. No matter how hard it is we want to make sense of what happens in life, the violence and evil perpetrated by one human being against another, sometimes you have to be content that moving forward is the only response, and the answers lie in the fact that you were willing to take the journey to begin with and, in the end, saw it through.

Still, as I continued believing that I was halfway to heaven, making it all somehow work, it soon became apparent I was, in fact, only a few steps from hell.

30

NOSTALGIA AS CAMOUFLAGE

"Remembrance of things past is not necessarily the
remembrance of things as they were."
—Marcel Proust

MY BROTHER CRUMBLED AFTER DIANE'S MURDER. HER FUNERAL
was one of the more somber moments of my life. It was pouring
rain. Buckets. A hard, slanted rain that makes a lot of noise.
Everything drenched. It was gloomy and overcast, like Seattle.
Crawling all over the funeral home and later, at the cemetery,
were plainclothes cops. Looking for what, I do not know. Not
once was Mark questioned or asked to produce an alibi, as far as I
was told. His and Diane's daughter, Meranda, was a month shy of
her seventeenth birthday. At thirteen, Meranda had walked out of
her parents' lives, fed up with babysitting them, and went to live
with an aunt.

The two boys, my nephews Mark and Tyler, seemed resolute;
being so young (Mark Jr., thirteen, and Tyler, eight), they responded to what happened by putting up an emotional barrier.
My brother Tommy, whom the boys were living with at the time of
Diane's murder, called them down from their room. My mother
and stepfather had come over to break the news.

"Your mother has been in an accident," my stepfather told
them, leaning on the old cliché we gravitate to in times of distress
because we are so scared to face death in any form.

"Can we visit her?" Mark Jr. asked.

"I'm sorry, we can't—she's gone. She died."

"Can I go play now?" Tyler asked.

At the funeral home, before heading to the cemetery, Meranda read a eulogy she'd prepared. Afterward, she stood at peace behind the lectern while a song she and Diane used to sing to each other played: Whitney Houston's "I Will Always Love You."

"My mom always sends me signs that she's near," Meranda said later. "That same song played in the dressing room as I tried on my wedding dress."

Most everyone sat motionless and stunned, many crying. I thought: *Here is a young girl, headstrong and unwavering, much like her mother, honoring the woman who'd given birth to her at nearly the same age* she *was now eulogizing her.*

There is so much of Diane in Meranda. Not only do they look alike, but they share the same hard-nosed will and temperamental drive, only Meranda harnessed hers into a path of devout Christianity, teaching, marriage, and motherhood to three children. On that day, as she read her eulogy and stood strong in front of everyone, Whitney belting out that familiar, sad song, I could feel the final arc of that "vicious cycle" we all hear about, one of which Meranda had been locked in, dissolve. Meranda was a survivor. Some bumps and bruises along the way, but she would come through this.

As we headed to Silver Lane Cemetery in East Hartford, less than a mile down the road from a restaurant/bar, The Family Affair, that my parents once owned, and the cape-style home Diane grew up in with a brother, Terry, and sister, Kelly, the rain came down sideways, in piercing strands. As I look back now, it feels as though I'd stepped into a scene from *The Killing.* Dark. Damp. Cold. Raw. Everyone suspiciously gazing at each other: *What the hell happened?* I see the memory in slow motion.

My brother wore sunglasses, an empty shell of a man. He had to be held up by a friend on each arm, as if his body had given up. I'd been mourning a marriage of seven years, on top of all else that had happened. I was sober a year by then, so I had a different outlook on life. But losing my oldest brother because he was no longer emotionally available, and now this, a murder in the family, most everyone thunderstruck and crushed, no answers in sight, felt final, the pain so crippling my legs heavy as stone. This was not an end to a chapter, but the closing of a book.

Still, as I stood there afterward, thinking about our lives, an intense feeling of closure came up. This could be a new beginning. In the months and years ahead, our family could step back, mourn in whatever way he or she chose, and hit restart.

Hope. I was beginning to see it had always been available.

I HAD NO IDEA how sick my brother would become. The hep C was only part of it. Diane's death was the true disease he battled. It was as though he'd shut off a fan after her murder by not taking care of himself, its blade, although still spinning, turning slower each day. In due time, we all knew without saying, the blade would stop. And as I walked away from the cemetery that day, I could see in Mark's eyes that he didn't care any longer when that day came. Perhaps the sooner, the better.

I decided to take a ride by my childhood home on Hollister Drive, not far away from the cemetery. When you haven't seen the house where you grew up for a long time, your initial reaction is one of shock. Everything seemed so much bigger as a child: the house itself, the street, the yard, the distance between your home and your best friend's. Parked out front, staring, I wondered how four of us boys (ranging in ages from one to eleven) and my parents ever managed to fit into such a small space. But that was the rub where nostalgia and reality met: in memory it was all perfect; in person it was as though someone else had lived it.

The house where Mark, our brothers Tommy and Frank, and I grew up in East Hartford was one of hundreds of cookie-cutter, Pratt & Whitney "dorms," I'll call them, built on slabs of concrete in the 1940s and 1950s to house a growing number of immigrant workers flocking to the Hartford region to work on the war effort.

That wistful desire, the inner yearning to step back into those childhood moments when life, in retrospect, seemed "so much simpler," as they say, tugged at me. Just over my shoulder, twenty-three years before, I had sat atop a pony on my sixth birthday, decked out in full cowboy regalia, my ten-gallon hat and holstered cap gun, pretending to be James West from my favorite childhood TV series, *The Wild Wild West.*

I could still see the bookshelf on the first floor inside the old house with several random volumes of *The Encyclopedia Britannica—DEM* to *EDW* and *GIC* to *HAR—*my mom purchased from an endcap display at Andy's Supermarket, a pink carbon copy receipt on the table she placed next to the invoice for the white aluminum siding and Kirby vacuum she bought from men who came to the door while my dad was at work.

Dad is a Korean War vet. He climbed his way up from inside a Hartford steel company warehouse to drive a truck and then took an office job, where he sat, hunched over his desk inside a cubicle, for close to forty years. Mom worked retail, Topps and Two Guys, stayed home with us kids, and then went to work, oddly and embarrassingly, for a paving company, tarring driveways, working with a guy who picked her up while Dad was at work.

Just the look and feel of the old neighborhood, staring at all the houses of old friends, where passing notes with that first crush made you feel devious and lustful for the first time, where we played football and wrestled in the circle, was enough to bring me to tears, which I understood for maybe the first time were shed on this day for Mark and Diane (I couldn't cry in front of everyone else because I was supposed to hate her). The neighborhood back in the day seemed so big, so community-oriented and segregated by ethnicity. Grandma Castellassi, from my mom's side, lived a mile away, in the Italian section; "Kitty" Grandma Phelps, from dad's side, had a house just around the corner, next to the Irish. Blessed Sacrament Church was a five-minute walk; McCartin School, where I walked to and from every morning and afternoon with my *Six Million Dollar Man* metal lunch box with the stumpy matching thermos, was three blocks away. In my mind I went back to those days at McCartin putting on actual plays, celebrating those precious holidays we were allowed to call Thanksgiving, Halloween, and Christmas; where we had Field Day outside on the last day of school (and not every damn kid won a ribbon).

Our neighbors were like family. We played kick-the-can and terrorized Mr. Softie. Fastened playing cards by clothespins to the spokes of our bicycles. Hung around the grassy circle in front of my house. Made fun of the old lady drunk who never showed her face or cut her lawn or ponied up five bucks for us to shovel her driveway. Ran from the "project" kids when they hopped the fence and came looking for fresh ass to beat. The road where my brother Tommy—begging our parents for a minibike one summer—crashed the thing into the neighbor's fence upon first ride. I can still hear the loose chain on the thing rattling, the engine puffing *putt-putt-putt-putt*, and feel the spongy grip of the throttle, the smell of gasoline fluttering out of the exhaust.

I was obsessed with Bruce Lee (that iconic velvet *Enter the Dragon* poster hung over my headboard) and *jai alai* (I badgered Dad until he bought me a *cesta*). Our "special," once-in-a-while dinner was cube steak, surely *not* organic or grass-fed, but a piece of meat tough as rubber bands and no doubt loaded with antibiotics and other chemicals—and we fucking *loved* it. I remember *Jeopardy, Adam-12,* Walter Cronkite and the Daily Number every night at 7:30 P.M. Tang, Kool-Aid and Sea Monkeys.

Some things never leave you.

I MET A WOMAN five months after Diane's funeral. We were married on New Year's Eve, twelve weeks later. Moving in with her, I gifted Mark the apartment I'd moved into after coming home from an AA meeting one night to find a yellow summons to vacate the Susan Road premises wedged in the front door.

Mark shifted his focus in the months that followed. He didn't much want to talk about what happened, at least not with me. He drank beer and maintained his opiate addiction, yet I will say this: He made a staunch effort to pull back and be the father he could manage to be. His kids grew. They lived with our brothers, but Mark spent more time with them every year. They got to know one another again. They did things together. They didn't focus on the past, but they somehow managed to stay in the present. It was as though a barrier had been torn down between them. Strangely, in Diane's passing, they started to be a family again.

Amends. Forgiveness. Isn't that the only way to move forward?

We all knew the hepatitis was worsening. Mark settled into a new apartment in Rockville (a small urban section of Vernon) after being tossed from the one I'd gifted him. He was closer to his kids. He lived courtesy of state and city welfare. He took so many pills I couldn't keep track of which were keeping him alive and which were killing him.

I'd stop by and say hello. My first book had come out.

"I'm proud of you," he said one day. "You published a book."

I walked away that day wiping my eyes on my sleeve.

"Why don't you go see him more often?" my wife asked from time to time, my mother and brothers echoing. I knew everyone in my family—including my niece and nephews—wondered why I'd distanced myself. Part of it was keeping my sobriety in check. But there was also a voice inside me insisting that I not be a party to watching my brother, the oldest, fade into dust. I couldn't stand to see him bloated and sickly, his eyes sunken into his skull or bulged like a bullfrog, his teeth falling out and rotting. It was selfish, maybe. But I couldn't be around someone I loved who was dying. I didn't want to remember him this way.

Mark had turned thirty-nine a few weeks before Diane's death. As he hit his forties, the hep C attacked his body like an out-of-control brushfire. I'd look at him as we sat and talked and would think: *He won't see fifty.* He looked like an old man. Frail. Wrinkled. Hunched over. His stomach so big on some days, he couldn't move, literally. As I think back now, I can see his fingernails, abnormally long and white, the tips grungy, like a mechanic, a blue hospital pajama top he wore all the time. The way he'd lean to his left side and force a smile. I'd leave his apartment with a dreaded sense of isolation—that same feeling you get when summoned in the middle of the night and, driving alone in the quiet darkness, you feel like you're the only person left in the world.

31

OH, BROTHER . . .

"It's a fool that looks for logic in the chambers of the
human heart."
—Joel Coen

*D*URING THE PERIOD WHEN HE KILLED EIGHT WOMEN, KEITH JESPER-
son trusted no one. He'd murdered Julie Winningham on March
10, 1995, in Washington State. By March 13, Jesperson was in
Utah. By the fourteenth, eating NoDoz like Mentos, he'd managed to cross into Pennsylvania, where he dropped a haul and
watched as forklifts loaded yards of stainless steel for delivery to
Deming, New Mexico. Leaving Pennsylvania, with a new form of
paranoia settling on him, Jesperson said, "I expected to meet up
with cops everywhere I went."

In Julie Winningham's case, it was simple, common laziness
(complacency or absolute hubris) that got the best of him. He'd
tossed her body about fifteen feet off the side of the freeway, over
a guardrail, on the opposite side of the Columbia River Gorge, directly across the river from where he'd put Taunja Bennett. He'd
planned to drag her down the embankment and hide her later
on that night, but he never got around to it. A passerby ran across
Winningham's body the following day, March 11. From there, it
took cops fewer than twenty-four hours to identify her and find
out she'd been traveling with a man her friends named, describing Jesperson as "creepy," and that Julie had been telling every-

one he was her "fiancé." Law enforcement then descended upon Jesperson's employer.

Going over this turning point in Jesperson's life—as cops moved in and he sensed an end nearing—became frustrating, sending me in different directions. This man has lied so much, to so many people over twenty years, it's hard to decipher which tales regarding the end of his murder spree are accurate, simply because of the intensity those fabrications took on as law enforcement circled around him.

"The lies, man," I said. "Why so many?"

"I began lying the moment I started talking to cops and did not stop for many, many years. Crossing that line of lying to police was like crossing that line to kill Bennett. The more I lied to them, the easier it was to lie to everyone."

For the serial killer, once the jig is up, he settles in and initiates a game plan. Jesperson made an important point when he told me: "As a serial murderer, I can tell stories and it is up to investigators to prove what is true or not. If it turns out to be a lie, no one can be mad because I am a *known* liar. If it turns out to be true, I'm credible." He found this exhilarating. It gave him a sense of power and control, even after he was finished killing.

On March 17, Jesperson called his daughter to wish her happy birthday. They cried, he remembered, because calling home was emotional and difficult.

My bet is, he was upset over the fact that he was about to go to jail and everything he had done would be exposed.

After calling his daughter, feeling "a weight," Jesperson stopped in Texarkana, an Arkansas-Texas border town, while on his way to Deming to dump that load of Pennsylvania mining steel. From Texarkana, he drove into Dallas, then headed west on the 40, crossing the state line into New Mexico, near Amarillo.

Entering New Mexico, he stopped at the port of entry. After reading through his paperwork, the man behind the counter asked, "What is your full name?"

Jesperson looked around, expecting the troops to swarm in.

"That's not something they *ever* ask."

But no cops, so he drove into Deming.

On March 19, Happy Face dropped his load of steel and called dispatch to find out about another. They told him to call back later that day.

Highly unusual.

Jesperson phoned: "We'll have something for you in the next day or two," dispatch said. He held the phone away from his ear and stared. "Last thing they want is for a truck to sit around. They were putting me off all day. Now I knew for *sure* they were working with law enforcement."

Leaving the facility, as he drove into town, two cruisers pulled up alongside, slowed down, took a good look at him, and sped off.

It's over.

Hanging around Deming for a few days at a local truck stop, by March 22, Jesperson still hadn't received orders from dispatch. He sensed they were trying to figure out with cops where to send him next so he could be arrested without incident.

Over the past twenty-four hours, he'd noticed a black-and-red Ford Bronco tailing him, sitting where he parked or up ahead in traffic, always within sight.

Before leaving the Deming truck stop, he decided to wash his rig.

"Closed," the man said. "Might reopen later."

Those rig-washing stations never shut down.

"They were afraid I'd wash evidence off the truck."

Finally, dispatch gave him an address and told him to drive into Las Cruces, New Mexico.

As he pulled up to a closed gate in Las Cruces, the Bronco parked next to him. A man got out and told Jesperson the business was closed. He needed to pull around to the other gate, in back.

Jesperson went along with the charade. He parked the rig near a shed. The man beckoned Happy Face down from his cab: "Follow me."

As they walked around the corner, two more men stepped out from the shadows. Both had weapons pointed at Jesperson's head.

They patted him down.

At the local sheriff's office, one of the detectives explained: "We're investigating the death of your fiancée, Julie Winningham. We're from Clark County, Washington. I'm Detective Rick Buckner."

Jesperson withstood five hours of interrogation, both detectives telling him they knew he'd murdered his girlfriend. They took hair and blood samples and fingerprinted him. But they could not charge Happy Face and released him.

"I don't think Buckner had anything on him then," Thomas Phelan said. "I know Buckner." He was a cop who could get murderers to crack. "He didn't have enough then to pop Keith. It wasn't a question of letting him go."

Over the next two days, Jesperson was followed wherever he went. Then Buckner cornered Jesperson one afternoon, stuck an arrest warrant affidavit in his face, telling him: "I just filed that." As soon as the judge signed off, Buckner made clear, Jesperson was going to jail.

Detective Buckner and his partner walked back to their vehicle and took off.

"I had a day, two, maybe three, tops, before they took me in," Jesperson recalled. "I had to do what I'd planned all that week— take my life. The kills weren't doing it. Suicide was the only answer."

ACTIVE ADDICTION IS A painful, costly (to family and friends), deceitful, prolonged suicide. I'd made the decision to end my alcohol dependence on April 1, 1994—and never looked back. Getting sober once was Everest; there was no way I could summit twice.

"The key to sobriety is that you never have to do it a second time. Just don't pick up that first drink again," a friend had told me early on.

I live by that one piece of advice.

One of the regrets I live with is never knowing the source of my brother's pain: Why did he drink and drug? What was he medicating all those years? What trauma had he stuffed? Our grandfather on my dad's side gave us the alcoholic gene, but my dad never touched a drop. Was Mark, like the rest of us, simply wired to be an addict? Once he got a whiff, *boom,* off and running he went. I knew, somewhat, why Diane had chosen drugs and alcohol. I'd heard stories about her childhood, many of which were later verified by family. But Mark? I never understood. He was, at a young age, involved on a low level in a chapter of organized crime in Hartford run by the late Louis Failla. Mark was never a "made" guy, but he came close. Was what he'd done in that respect the source of his pain? Had he committed sins he couldn't reconcile? Things he couldn't escape no matter how much poison he injected and ingested?

When my brother started using hard-core drugs, it was as though he stepped on a land mine. After Diane died, I think he gave in to the idea that, as each day passed, an uncontrollable weakness forced him to lift his foot, however little at a time, knowing the explosion that would someday follow.

What struck me during those years after Diane was murdered was the way I changed. But that's how life goes, right? You think you've got it figured out, but then faced with a tragedy, your response is not what you thought it would have been. Within the dynamic of brotherhood, there is a lumpy emotional landscape connecting siblings, one that you have to manage walking through by yourself, at your own pace. The way I viewed my childhood might not be the same way in which my brother viewed his, or even mine. In this sense, you believe you know your sibling because you share his DNA, grew up in the same house. When, point in fact, you really don't.

As the hep C ate away at Mark from the inside out, I sensed a clarity emerge from him. I'd ask how it was going. "Fine," he'd say. "Why don't you come to the casino with us?" He sounded different, almost at peace. Mark lived on disability after being diagnosed with bipolar disorder. Being a bookie once, having never held down a full-time job for more than a few weeks, Mark loved Foxwoods, playing poker and roulette, betting on sports. My brothers, Meranda, his two sons, my mother, and my stepfather were forever taking him gambling, shopping, out to eat, to end-less doctors' appointments, helping him run errands. Mark was one of those guys who sued everyone. He spent a lot of time doing research for those lawsuits. Tagging along on any of these trips wasn't something I was interested in. As I said, I couldn't stand to see my brother melt. I had also started a second chapter: raising a daughter. Watching my blood germinate into life at home and fizzle out elsewhere was not something I could face.

IN SEPTEMBER 2000, THE *Hartford Courant* published an article, CAN POLICE CONNECT THE CASES?—"City Investigators Looking for Links in 11 Unsolved Killings." It detailed the murders of eleven "prostitutes and drug addicts" over a six-year period, all of whom were found in a two- to three-mile radius, the bull's-eye being Asy-lum Hill. Among those counted as a potential serial killer's "third" victim was Diane. Three years after her murder, in 1999, not far from where she had been killed, on the same street, twenty-eight-year-old LaDawn Roberts was found beaten to death and left on the rear porch of an apartment building. Roberts was five months pregnant.

"Can you imagine?" Mark said. "That headline pisses me off."

"I was irritated," Meranda recalled. "Like many reporters, they don't really care about what or who they are writing about. They are just going for the salacious headline."

All of the victims' photos (including Diane's) were published on the front page of the newspaper, with a detailed map showing where they'd been found. It was as if the newspaper linked the eleven murders by proximity and victimology. Investigators were skeptical: some of the murders were definitely connected, while others did not share the same signature. There was even a male among the eleven. Me, I looked at it and thought the story made for a great headline, but that was all. Murders that happened in the same specific area of a city, with similar circumstances, no known suspect, sounded neatly packaged for the nightly news, but where was the evidence linking a serial killer? Perhaps it was all just coincidence, despite Jesperson's harebrained theory there are no coincidences in murder.

That one part of the article upset my brother and his kids: Diane being labeled a prostitute and drug addict. It was unfair to label any of them in this way. All victims of murder are human beings, somebody's children; friends and family love them, despite how their lives turned out. No young girl, having tea in plastic cups and playing with her Barbie, dreams of becoming a drug-addicted street hooker. Your life should not be distilled into a noun. Moreover, from a law enforcement perspective, labels smother and tunnel an investigation at its fundamental core.

Still, we considered that her case was moving. It had been four years since Diane's murder and nobody in the family had heard anything. We felt for the first time Diane had not been singled out; her murder had been part of a spree of murders, spanning years, and her case, with the others, might one day be solved because of that alone.

Apparently the *Courant* received the memo from victims' family members, including ours. Five days after that article published, the newspaper printed a "correction" within the body of a second article: THE SLAYING OF 5 HARTFORD WOMEN, ONE WITH A DIFFERENCE— "The Link: Violent Death." The retraction corrected that four of the women had "never [been] convicted of prostitution or drug offenses," and "Diana Ferris was never convicted of prostitution," adding, "If it turns out there is a serial killer preying on women involved with the illegal sex or drug trade—something police appear far from concluding—Hartford would join the ranks of many communities with such a problem."

The killing of addicts and streetwalkers hit off-the-chart levels in America during the 1980s and 1990s. Serial killers have told me that preying on those types of victims lessen their chances tenfold of being caught, not to mention how easy it is for a predator to wave a fifty-dollar bill in front of a dope addict or sex worker and get him or her into his comfort zone.

Jesperson had killed several "prostitutes." I asked him why he chose sex workers.

"Because nobody gives a shit. They're not missed. Cops don't care. They say they're investigating your sister-in-law's murder, but a rich white girl goes missing and they pull out all stops. It's all over the news. Not so with drug addicts and street whores."

"My sister-in-law was *not* a street whore."

"You get what I am saying."

I call it the "Natalee Holloway Effect." Some blond, blue-eyed college girl goes missing and television networks park their trucks in front of the family McMansion. But a dozen prostitutes found murdered all over a city, beaten, raped, strangled, mutilated, and we don't see anything about it until a transient is on trial—a judicial process of which, in turn, becomes all about him.

"The point I am making is: who you kill matters," Jesperson added. "We pay attention to the victims we choose."

Overnight, whoever was murdering Hartford area women and one male was given a catchy Hollywood nickname: "The Asylum Hill Killer." From that day forward, it became apparent to us that Diane was likely one of his victims. We couldn't overlook all of the links, however circumstantial. The *Courant* had made it an easy concept to grasp.

In September 2001, thirty-eight-year-old Matthew Steven Johnson, a man described as a cocaine-addicted "homeless drifter with an IQ of 69," was arrested and connected to three of the eleven cases, with good reason to believe he'd committed that murder on Garden Street, LaDawn Roberts. His DNA had been part of the sex offender's database registry. The Asylum Hill Killer had left semen—from masturbating on each of them—and blood at each scene. An identical twin, Johnson was a troubled youth who grew up in the Asylum Hill section of Hartford and spent a majority of his life in group homes. He'd done serious time at Long Lane School, a juvenile detention center in Middletown, Connecticut. Long Lane, where Diane had herself spent time, had one of those legendary reputations among us kids. There was not a parent in my neighborhood that had not threatened: "You better stop or you'll end up in Long Lane."

Johnson had a vast criminal history: from assault to theft to vandalism. His most recent obsession, however, was attacking women. A massive and obese black man, Johnson was identified and arrested after abducting a woman from a Hartford street, dragging her into a bush, and holding her hostage for two hours, while repeatedly and violently raping and beating her.

It was said Johnson rode a bicycle to and from each murder and rape, was good for at least three, yet had likely done many of the others, including Diane.

"Not sure," Mark told me when I asked him about Johnson. Then a week later, changing his mind: "Glad they got that piece of shit. I got people in prison. He'll pay for what he did to Diane."

At first, police could not say definitively yes or no whether Johnson was connected to Diane's murder, giving us the proverbial line—"We're waiting on DNA"—so many families hear when a loved one has been murdered and a suspect emerges.[6]

In February 2004, Johnson was convicted of those three murders, all of which were thought to be "similar deaths," based on DNA results and medical examiners' reports. Johnson was sentenced to life for killing two women, Aida Quinones and Rosali Jimenez, both aged thirty-three, and thirty-seven-year-old Alesia Ford. All were killed by blunt-force trauma to the neck, their faces beaten into an unrecognizable bloody pulp, their skulls crushed.

I'd been considering writing a book about another Hartford-area serial killer, Berlin native Edwin "Ned" Snelgrove. While looking into the Snelgrove case, I met many of the same cops working the Johnson investigation. Sitting inside the office of one, talking about Snelgrove, when we finished, I made a passing comment: "Johnson's good for my sister-in-law, don't you think?"

The investigator sat, glaring at me. I felt he was weighing how much to share. He was still working the Johnson investigation, which made him an expert on Diane's case.

---

[6]As of this writing, we're still waiting. I e-mailed a good friend in the state's attorney's office in 2016. I asked for an update. It's been twenty years now since Diane was murdered. Insultingly, in an e-mail, he replied, "They are looking at the case and going through everything. That's the best I can tell you."

"No," he said.

"No? Come on. It's all there."

"Turn around. Take a look at that picture on my wall behind the door."

The photo had been blown up, poster-sized, if memory serves me, and tucked behind the door because of its graphic nature. To see it, you had to know it was there.

Walking over, taking a close look, I wondered what the hell he was talking about.

"That's one of Johnson's victims," he said, standing in back of me, arms folded.

And I knew, as I stood there taking in this brutal crime scene photograph, displaying that distinctive signature—the victim's grotesquely beaten face and his DNA—he had left at every one of his scenes, that Matthew Steven Johnson had not murdered Diane.

32

RISKY UNCERTAINTY

"The incidence of suicide in rampage murderers (34.7%)
is much higher than in serial killers (4.4%). . . . [Fifty-two
percent] of the suicides in the serial killers occurred
after arrest."
—David Lester, Ph.D., The Richard Stockton College of New Jersey

*H*E PARKED AT THE FOOT OF AN ARIZONA MOUNTAIN RANGE JUST over the New Mexican border outside Road Forks, likely somewhere near the Dos Cabezas Peaks off the I-10, though he could not recall exactly where. He sat in his truck and stared at the snowcapped points. It was time to put an end to the madness: swallow a bag of over-the-counter sleeping pills and drift off into eternal sleep. Jesperson couldn't stop himself. Having committed eight murders over the span of five years, each one easier and more violent than the last, he no longer had the control he did when he met that jogger along the trail.

"There was once, when I was on the East Coast, I felt I could easily kill as many as eighty before anyone caught on," he told me, explaining further how being a cross-country trucker afforded him the opportunity to pick up a woman in, say, Ohio, drive her to North Carolina, kill her there, and dump her body in Georgia. Without any DNA, there would be no connection back to him or her anywhere.

A number associated with Jesperson's body count has been as

high as 166. And Jesperson once told a cellmate (snitch) he killed twenty-two.

"I named dates and places, filled in the time line . . . pulling it all from a hat."

In making bold admissions, Jesperson knew it would send scores of detectives from all over to interview him in prison. He relished the attention. It kept him busy while behind bars. He'd be written about in newspapers and magazines and books; he'd be talked about on television. A celebrity.

Manson. Bundy. Gacy.

Jesperson.

"They lie, too," he said, referring to law enforcement. "I killed one hundred sixty-six in thirteen years, seven in Nevada, I told them. There is a story called 'a tale of two tails.'" (It's actually an academic article from a March 1990 issue of the *Journal of Risk and Uncertainty*.) "I sent it to [someone] in 1996 and he shared it with the Green River Task Force. I got letters from [the Task Force] begging me to confess to being the Green River Killer. I was messing with them all."

Jesperson said much of what he told ABC's *20/20*, during its 2010 "exclusive" interview with him from inside the prison (the last time cameras were allowed into OSP to interview Jesperson), "was all bullshit lies," adding how "documentation" and "just a little bit of research" would have proven most of what he said on ABC to have been fabricated. "But when a killer speaks, everyone accepts what he says and takes him for his word. *Nobody* checks it out."

BEFORE HEADING INTO THAT mountain range to end his life, Jesperson parked at a nearby truck stop. He took out a piece of paper and wrote a letter to his brother Brad. He'd tried to kill himself two separate times since Buckner shoved that affidavit in his face, but only had gotten ill from taking all the pills at once. After writing and mailing the letter to Brad, however, he was determined to succeed. Dated March 24, 1995, the short missive began with Jesperson—in his humdrum narcissistic vitriol—saying how his "luck" had "run out."

> *I will never be able to enjoy life on the outside again. I got into a bad situation and got caught up with emotion. I killed a woman in my truck during an argument. With all the evidence against me, it looks like I truly am a black sheep. The court will appoint me a lawyer and there will be a trial. I am sure they will kill me for this. I am sorry that I turned out this way. I have been a killer for 5 years. And have killed 8 people. Assaulted more. I guess I haven't learned anything.*

"Tell me about this letter?" I asked.

"You see, right there, in the letter, I say eight. Remember, I believed I was going to be dead not long after writing it, so why not, at this time, take credit for ten, fifteen, twenty? It's because I only killed eight. But later, even though this letter was published, they still wanted to put one hundred sixty-six and twenty-two or whatever number they came up with on me."

> *Dad always worried about me. Because of what I had gone through in the divorce and finances, etc. . . . As I saw it I was hoping they would catch me. I took 48 sleeping pills last night and I woke up well-rested. . . . Keith.*

Jesperson intended it to be a suicide note to his family, he told me. He needed them to hear the "truth" from him, not what would come out in the media.

My interest was in the addressee. Why Brad? They had been in conflict, very competitive as kids. As much as Jesperson maintained that his greatest fear was to disappoint the Jesperson clan and his kids, why reach out to Brad?

"Brad was an accountant," Jesperson said. "He took care of our finances. He would have known how to get hold of everyone in the family for me. I still had a connection with Brad. Bruce, I mean, you know, he was an *asshole*. Even though Brad and I were always at odds with each other, there was always some kind of connection."

After mailing the letter, sitting in his truck with a fresh bag of pills, Happy Face got out and started what he believed to be a final ascent up "Suicide Mountain."

"I was looking up and I saw snow. I thought, 'Go hiking, take the pills, it was going to get cold, and I was just going to fall asleep and die. Let nature take its course.'"

He failed to go through with it, however. Jesperson could not end his life with over-the-counter medications because he was too big. Every time he tried, it made him sick to his stomach, nothing more. So, after the mountain air "cleared" his mind and he watched a man on a horse tend to his cattle, Happy Face decided to "act like a man for a change" and turn himself in.

This was the coward's way of explaining he didn't have the nerve to complete the task. Anyone bent on killing himself, especially a guy who had murdered eight human beings, can find a way to get the job done. In addition, Jesperson was no doubt thinking about the fame in becoming a notorious serial killer was about to bring him. He was a big fan of *True Detective* magazine. He knew what type of celebrity certain killers had attained by becoming what the public perceived as the ultimate evil. He'd even written to *True Detective* and by then had read about himself (as Happy Face) in magazines and newspapers.

Forty-eight hours after Detective Buckner had shoved that affidavit into his face, the over-the-road trucker stopped at a rest stop and called Buckner. One report had it as a voice mail Jesperson left, while Jesperson insisted he spoke directly to the detective: "Hi, Rick. This is Keith. I'd like to talk to you. I'll be in Phoenix tomorrow morning. You were right. I've been fighting with myself for the last two days. Tried to kill myself a couple of times and it hasn't worked. Not enough pills in this damn country. I'll talk to you in the morning. I want to turn myself in."

The next day, Buckner asked where he was, then demanded details.

Jesperson explained he was in Cochise County, Arizona, before saying he'd taped Julie Winningham's "mouth shut and strangled her to death as [I] raped her in [my] truck cab." Afterward, he drove down Highway 14 and, just outside Camas, dumped her body.

There was enough "nonpublic" information in the admission to prove Jesperson was Julie's killer.

"But wait," I asked him, "why would you say you raped Julie? Wasn't she your girlfriend?"

"I made it up. I gave Buckner a story he wanted to hear."

Happy Face, the celebrity serial killer, was born.

"Why did you turn yourself in?" This was important. Serial killers do not turn themselves in; Jesperson is an anomaly in that respect. His case remains unique in that he actually played the Hollywood card: *Here I am, come and get me. I did it.*

"I don't *know* why. I was up there walking through [the mountains] and my rationale wasn't altogether right, and I thought, 'Why kill myself when I can let the system kill me?' I thought that turning myself in, I was just going to get the death penalty and that was going to be that. I thought the system worked quickly."

"Why not continue to kill?"

"I didn't *want* to be a killer. I thought about it all the time: I. Did. Not. Want. To. Kill. Anymore. I was fighting this. I didn't want to be a killer. I just wanted to be Keith, the nice guy."

"Why did you end up killing Julie?" I reckoned it wasn't to keep her from court. That answer was classic Jesperson, the smart-ass quote machine.

"It . . . it just got to that point where I wanted to . . ." Then he stopped. "She was a user. I wanted to rid the world of a user. I knew the moment she got into the truck with me, there was a plan. Something in her head. She was always looking out for Julie."

He went on, blaming Julie Winningham, knowing how I felt about this. Yet it was, perhaps, the first time I understood he was speaking of his actual thought process. It was how Jesperson saw the world: Bad people needed to disappear (or pay, or own up to their mistakes) before they hurt anyone else. He had designated himself the gatekeeper, the hand of God, making sure whatever punishment came to pass.

"It was, like, in 1995, when I picked Julie up again. She got into the truck and I was just, like, waiting for a drumroll. I was, like, why is she so in love with me again? And it came down to, she had two DUIs and she needed somebody to bail her out. I just felt that . . . well, I'd get rid of her. I just felt I needed to destroy all that was left of her." He then explained, without realizing, the predominant trigger regulating his thirst for blood: "This is the punch line. After we went out . . . everything was going to be hunky-dory now and it was all good that she was a changed woman. And later that night, as we sat in the truck stop, she said, 'We got to get married.' I'm like, '*Excuse* me?'" He laughed. "It was one of those, you know, deal breakers."

He'd brought it up, so I asked about the death penalty. He'd given me the impression that when he first turned himself in, he'd welcome the needle. He was arrested later that day (after calling Buckner) and subsequently admitted to eight murders, pleading those cases out over many years. Attorney Thomas Phelan worked diligently and successfully to make certain the death penalty was off the table for Jesperson. From there, he became comfortable in OSP as System Identification Number 11620304—and even more comfortable as Happy Face.

"They think it's a deterrent to give the death penalty, when, in fact, it's actually a welcome sight because death row is protective custody all the way." He spoke of automatic appeals, millions of dollars of "taxpayer money spent on trials and appellate lawyers and courts—all for *nothing*. I *saved* the taxpayers money by pleading my cases. I could've dragged each [case] out."

He'd done us all a favor, in other words.

Settling into prison was easier for Jesperson than he expected. The letters he and his cellies receive from women all over the world kept him occupied. Jesperson has shared many of them with me. Pen pals from Australia, Germany, England, Italy, and other countries—women writing to men either doing life or condemned to die.

"Basically, I am a trophy. That's how they see serial killers in prison—trophies. We're like the trophy husband. We're always where we're supposed to be. They have control over us. I really don't like those types of women. I had one come in here to visit me and she wanted me to be on *Jerry Springer.* She made it out where she was the dominating woman and I was just the bitch." He terminated the visit and told her to never contact him again. "They use us to catapult their careers. There is a girl in Texas who writes me and she is actually infatuated with Jeffrey Dahmer, even though he is dead. Even on the recording of her phone, she says she is 'Mrs. Dahmer.'"

I asked if his pen pals were the type of women he would have killed.

"I figured you'd ask that question. I'm not sure. But it could very well be."

His state of mind was important. It's quite a cliché to say that the serial killer has no conscience. Yet, what does this actually mean in terms of how Keith Jesperson viewed the world?

"We have one when it pertains to *us,*" Jesperson concluded. "To *our* needs. To what *we* value in *our* lives. Our victims are collateral damage in dealing with our own personal demons in the baggage that we carry."

WHEN YOU ARE IN their presence, serial killers project a nervous, calculating, saturating energy, draining your vitality. They understand that the public, mostly, fears them in some way. They tend to have a look of guarded satisfaction; they recognize society views them as a scourge, but they are able to play off it, instead of allowing it to affect them negatively.

Jesperson agreed he was hated. He knew that the majority saw him as a vile, inhumane creature. Yet, he was okay with that and, in many ways, embraced it, feeding into the public perception of him.

After years of talking, I noticed there was a visceral, childlike intensity about Happy Face. This constant and aggressive inner dialogue running on a loop inside his head, which I could, at times, almost hear. He was motivated to figure me and the public out.

Where was I coming from? What was my hidden agenda? What had people said about him? What did people think of him?

"You're my last hope, Phelps," he said many times.

One has to keep in mind that in befriending a serial killer, you are entering into a pact with the Devil, allowing him a portal into your life and soul. I never once discounted or underestimated this fact, however much I probably convinced myself it wasn't real. And as Jesperson tried, to no avail, to help me understand the mind-set of the man who had murdered my sister-in-law, which I felt by this time I understood already, I stepped up my presence at Mass (even with my faith slipping), took to fasting more often, read and meditated more. I dreaded that if I did not have an antidote to evil, it would take control of my life. Even though I now understood that the imperturbable calm I chased, so contrary to all of my anxiety, didn't exist for me.

33

WHEN GRACE ABANDONS

"No one ever told me that grief felt so like fear."
—C.S. Lewis

Mark LIKED TO CATCH THE BUS FROM A STOP OUTSIDE HIS APART-ment in Rockville, across the street from a Dunkin' Donuts, Dollar Store, and CVS. One day in early March 2004, my brother stood at what he perceived was that bus stop.

On this day, however, Mark waited, unknowingly, about twenty yards away from the designated stop. The bus driver came to a complete halt near him, puffed the air door open, and shouted, "This isn't the bus stop!" Then closed the door. Took off.

My brother must have tripped—or perhaps he jumped in front of the thing, possibly it was nothing more than an accident, or the bus driver didn't see him—and somehow got tangled up with the bus, which flung him against the curb, dragging Mark for a short distance.

The accident tore a grotesque gouge down to the bone in Mark's arm. He had black eyes. Scrapes and scratches. Cuts and bruises. He left the scene in an ambulance, bloodied and beaten up, and was admitted to Rockville General Hospital.

By now, the hep C had developed into a disease, consuming his liver like salt on ice. Falling within one-fourth of all hep C patients who experience symptoms, Mark, also being one of the percent-age points between 5 and 20 who suffer from an actual infection, wound up with advanced cirrhosis, no doubt expedited by the amount of alcohol and drugs he consumed before and after his diagnosis.

With a simple blood test, doctors gauge liver disease status by the percentage the liver functions at any given time. The liver is a miraculous organ, the only one in the human body that can regenerate itself under proper, otherwise healthy conditions. Whereas all other organs scar when damage occurs, the liver replaces any damage with functioning cells. But once liver disease of any kind sets in, that same liver, I recall Mark's doctor once explaining, becomes like a crumb cake, disintegrating a little bit each day.

Mark was admitted to the hospital after the bus incident, sewed and bandaged up, and released. A few weeks later, my brother Tommy called. Mark was back in the hospital. His liver function was low, under 20 percent, maybe less. After a few days in Rockville General Hospital, Mark's liver function slipped once again and he was moved to hospice.

The cirrhosis swelled my brother's face and puffed his cheeks, tightened his skin like a latex glove stretched over a melon. Mark always had these deep, distinctive lines in his face; pockmarks, too, old acne scars. Those were gone now, as he became gaunt as an anorexic, frail as a ninety-year-old man. His stomach had always been bloated—another symptom of the liver not functioning as it should—but now it was so big it looked deformed, his waistline skin taut and stretched, seemingly ready to tear. A terrible situation to witness.

It was spring, the start of a new season. Flowers and fresh air. Blue skies. Birds. The smell of life. But we knew it was over for my forty-seven-year-old big brother. His time was up.

My mother, God bless her (who I deeply love), was there every day, along with my stepfather, himself suffering from prostate cancer. Mom had taken over as legal conservator to Mark's affairs. She made the decisions. He was her baby. Seeing her during this time, I felt as though she'd been down in a foxhole all our lives with Mark, afraid to stick her head out anymore in fear of being struck by whatever stray tragedy that might whiz by next. I recall her not wanting the doctors to allow Mark to have morphine. "He's done drugs his whole life." He'd stopped using heroin many years before this. He was far from sober, but did the best he could. I thought: *Man, now is the time when the guy actually* needs *the drug that had put him here, and she doesn't want him to have it? Insane. Completely insane.*

Then Mom called one day and said, "For now, when you see him, don't talk about him dying." She explained that she didn't want Mark to know how close he was to death.

"I think he realizes."

Actually, I went to see him one night not long after. He said, "I'm hoping to go home," he told me. "I'm on the list for a liver. Who knows?" He spoke almost in a whisper, his voice phlegmy and cracking, tired.

Chicago Bear Hall of Fame running back Walter Payton had died of liver disease in 1999. I thought if a Hall of Famer couldn't get a liver, my brother wasn't.

At home that night, I made the decision to tell him myself. I would want to know. I was certain there were things he needed to tell his kids before he died. He deserved the opportunity to make that decision. He also needed to see a priest, in case he wanted to confess his sins (which he ultimately did).

He was leaned over to one side in his bed when I arrived, a blanket covering him, shivering. "I'm so cold," he said. "So cold." His eyes were opened halfway. His bottom lip drooped, his mouth unable to close. He stared out the window. Meranda was there. She was *always* there. She had become so close to her dad at the end; it was inspiring to witness the love between them. The two boys, now grown and on their own, spent as much time as they could visiting their dad. They seemed so content, the four of them together. I could feel the forgiveness. It was real, and it energized that room.

"I won't be leaving here," Mark told me next time we were able to talk alone. By now, cousins and uncles and aunts and Mark's friends were visiting—coming to say good-bye, I knew. His best friend, Gary Saccocia, was there, too.

"I'm so sorry, Mark," I said. It was obvious he had been reevaluating his life and thinking about what he'd do differently, had he been given the chance. I could see in his eyes how sorry he was for everything. "You know, what you need to do is forget about the past. I know it's on your mind." He'd told me he wished like hell he could fix the mistakes he'd made. "Forget about all that. You're sorry for it—I know that, your kids know that. Focus on right now. Today. You're a good person. You always have been. I love you."

I called my sons and told them to go see their uncle.

Immediately.

"Take [our daughter] and go visit him now," I told my wife when I got home that night.

TALKING TO JESPERSON BECAME a necessary inconvenience, a chore. He was sucking the life out of me. After that last conversation about his conscience, I went to Mass. As I sat, staring at the life-sized crucifix in back of the altar, a sudden feeling struck me. My stomach turned with an acidic sourness of panic—a feeling similar to when you sense bad news coming, maybe a message about someone you love leaving. A terrible feeling of dread. A colossal regret. All at once. I'd experienced this before, but nowhere near as profound. As my heart raced, I felt an adrenaline rush, a panic attack coming on.

None of this is real, I thought. Jesus and God are two more gods throughout history. It was all a story, passed down, written for those gullible enough to buy into it. When it's over, that's it—over. Rotting flesh and earthworms, as Jesperson had said. There was no eternal reward. No pearly gates and soft clouds and family members and happy people wearing robes, smiling and hugging everyone. It was all a damn dream sold by old men with white hair. We were pathetic fools for believing such bombast.

I must have turned pale, because I felt sick to my stomach. I questioned my faith once a day. However, as I continued to accept Jesperson's calls and became immersed in his life, those moments of question lasted longer, came on more often, and felt more intense.

Such momentary lapses (or, rather, spasms of disbelief) were generally followed by an immediate thrust of conviction, as was the case on this day, subtle as it turned out to be. I never had blind faith, like many I know. Yet, I was always able to talk myself away from the ledge—where at the bottom of that cliff I knew the late Christopher Hitchens' spirit, Richard Dawkins, and scores of atheists I'd met working in television were waiting to catch my fall from grace.

Whether it was my need for a bit of light to illuminate so much darkness around me, or just my sheer will, I continued going to Mass, kept praying (though the prayers felt empty, as if I was talking to myself), and searching, forcing myself to believe, same as we sometimes force ourselves to love.

"Can you imagine not questioning any of it?" a priest said to me in the confessional after one of my more traumatic religious hiccups. "You've been given a gift. Anyone who doesn't question his faith is a liar. That moment you come out of the disbelief will be filled with joy."

I understood, but did not believe him.

If there was no such thing as religious redemption, no Jesus, no God, no Great Unknown, what was left? It meant I was alone. That was where the panic existed for me: in being alone. What I wanted was to believe, unhindered, uninterrupted, like a child. But that gift of faith, given to me in childhood, was slithering away. As it did, I asked myself: Was Jesperson's evil edge cutting into me? Because if I *truly* believed in redemption, salvation, divinity, and everything discussed at that altar and in the Bible, including the core teaching that no soul is unreachable, why was it that I'd never gotten on my knees inside that church and prayed for Jesperson's soul?

Slowly, over the next few months, I noticed my psychosomatic pain disappear as each spiritual crisis arose and seemingly resolved itself. Much of it was the result of dealing with a madman, being sucked into his world, and trying to unpack his self-reliant, parasitic, skewed philosophies of life and murder. Perhaps there *was* no answer? Maybe I was searching for reconciliation within my life that did not exist?

I'd been thinking about making plans to visit Les. I needed to do that. I wanted his input and opinions of his son. I'd put it off long enough. My plan was to visit the old man, get a few comments from him to round out Jesperson's parental smackdown, and then focus on what I could do to make use out of all the time I'd invested in interviewing Happy Face—my main objective being, of course, to convince Jesperson to help identify a Jane Doe in Florida and sort out a mess of a situation he claimed existed in California surrounding one of his kills, a victim named Cynthia Lynn Rose.

My belief was that he had to know who his Florida Jane Doe was, where she lived. I pondered whether he could have hidden her identification cards or purse, same as Bennett. Was it possible that a serial killer could murder a woman and not know any identifying markers about her?

I decided to go behind Jesperson's back and make contact with the detectives investigating the Florida case. I knew one detective had reached out to Jesperson the year before I started communicating with him for *Dark Minds*. But Jesperson had ignored the cop's pleas. Hell, Jesperson had sent me the original copy of every letter Florida law enforcement had sent him. I wanted to see if maybe I could help in some way. Being as close to Jesperson as I had become, having spent years building his trust, perhaps I could get him to open up and divulge secrets about the case. Act as a liaison between Jesperson and Florida law enforcement.

"Convincing him to help us would be huge," forensic imaging specialist (FIS) Paul Moody, of the Palm Beach County Sheriff's Office (PBSO), told me during one of our first conversations.

"We're hoping he can draw a picture of what she looked like." Moody explained that Jesperson thought they might be tricking him. That once he helped identify Jane Doe, they were coming after him with the death penalty.

"Let me see what I can do," I told Moody.

34

YOU CAN SEE WITH THOSE EYES

"Everyone is a moon, and has a dark side which he
never shows to anybody."
—Mark Twain

WATCHING MY BROTHER DIE WAS EXCRUCIATING. THOSE FEW DAYS
when we knew death was in the room, pacing, waiting for the
right moment, it was as though we existed underwater, forever
trying to sluggishly wade our way through each twenty-four hours,
screaming, not being able to hear one another. You thought
about *nothing* else. Your life was on hold. You sat and stared at the
television, didn't see a thing or hear a word. You ate and didn't
taste the food. You slept with your eyes and ears halfway open.

When Meranda realized Mark's time had come, she phoned a
priest and asked him to pay a visit. That same night, when Meranda
went up to see her dad, the priest was on his way out. "He doesn't
have long," he said. "I'm so sorry."

Mark suffered during his final days. He held tough, but the
pain burned and pounded every cell of his body. His kids were
there, loving him, talking to him, reassuring my oldest brother
that they knew he'd done the best he could. I recall him saying,
over and over, how "cold" he was inside his skin. He could never
get warm enough. Meranda sat and held his hand for hours, listening to him breathe. No words needed to be spoken. He had
one friend, a woman, who slept by his side at night, held his hand
during the day.

One evening, as the end drew near, Mark whispered to me: "My entire body throbs. The pain is unbearable. I am so, so cold." That last time I saw him, his legs flailed under the sheets as if some unknown entity controlled them with strings. He thrashed. Mumbled. Skinny as an AIDS patient, his entire body was as yellow as morning piss.

Mark needed that morphine.

As I looked back, the black-and-white photo we existed in when Mark and Diane ripped terror throughout our family had come into full color. I saw it there inside my brother's room during his final hours. The love between my brother and his kids. You could feel it suspended in that stuffy, sterile air. They had all forgiven him—and meant it.

After saying good-bye to the priest, Meranda sat and held her father's hand. Mark Jr. and Tyler, along with Meranda's husband, Mike, stood bedside.

"We're all here," Meranda told him. "You can go now and be with Diana."

On March 24, 2004, I was in the middle of teaching an adult education creative writing/publishing course at Rockville High School. When my phone rang as I was lecturing, I knew he was gone. It was my brother Tommy calling, once again delivering the bad news, a guy who'd somehow been designated all our lives as the Phelps bullhorn of tragedy.

I said hello and Tommy, a six-one, two-hundred-pound, hard-bodied, third-degree–black-belt tough guy, cried, saying nothing more.

When I arrived at the hospital, Mark looked serene, at total rest.

Finally.

It had been the morphine. They'd given it to him and he lasted not long after because the drug slowed his heart rate and body function down, made him comfortable, and allowed him to die at peace.

I understood in that moment why Mom had held off the morphine: She knew not giving it to him, he'd be around longer. Life would never be the same for her, I realized while standing, staring at my dead brother. Her firstborn, the child she favored over all of us, and had taken care of most of his life, was gone. It was the opposite of natural order—he had gone before her. Mark's death, not to mention burying him on her birthday and the death of her husband a few years later, would break my mother into thousands of tiny pieces.

I cannot hear George Harrison's "My Sweet Lord" without thinking of Mark. Not sure if it was his favorite song, or it was on the radio once when he played the role of big brother, holding me up on his shoulders, carrying me around our yard in East Hartford, protecting me from falling. The person I need to remember.

One of the strangest things about my oldest brother being dead today is that I am now older than he was when he died. I never considered this. He was always the eldest, the big brother, the unspoken guardian. Regardless how his life turned out, Mark Anthony Phelps Sr. was our brother; he was a father and a son. Throughout the course of the thirty-seven years of my life leading up to Mark's passing, I'd never seen our father cry. Not one tear. Yet, while we sat, as families do, in the front row, inside the same funeral home where we'd said good-bye to Diane eight years earlier, I looked on as my dad, his shoulders bouncing up and down, cried. It was as though he'd held back the tears all his life, each one reserved for this day he undoubtedly knew—as far back as Mark's teenage years—he'd bear witness to.

PART THREE

FAITH

35

A NEW PURPOSE

"You cannot be a man of faith unless you know how
to doubt. . . . Faith is . . . a decision, a judgment that is
fully and deliberately taken in the light of a truth that
cannot be proven. . . ."
—Thomas Merton, *New Seeds of Contemplation*

*O*SCAR PATTERSON (PSEUDONYM) STOOD AND STARED AT THE BLOWN
radiator in his truck. He'd been waiting for a serviceman to come
out and have a look since about two o'clock, on the morning of
September 4, 1992. Now somewhere near 9:00 A.M., Oscar wondered when in the hell the guy was going to show up.

On Highway 99, in Livingston, California, the Blueberry Hill
Café was a popular stopover for truckers looking for a bite to eat,
fuel, some road porn, a shower, paid female company, and maybe
even what they needed most: rest. The joint had changed over
the years. In the 1990s, the front of the café faced Highway 99.
Well-known by truckers, the Blueberry functioned more along
the lines of your traditional truck stop with access directly off the
highway. It had a large, unpaved, powdered-dirt parking area in
back. The southbound side of Highway 99 ran out front of the
main entrance; the northbound side just beyond that; there was a
dirt connector in between the north and south lanes, allowing
traffic on either side to pull in. The Blueberry was a bona fide
greasy spoon, with hookers roaming the lot and amphetamine

dealers waiting in cars, looking to unload Black Beauties, Tick-Tock, Redneck Cocaine and, of course, heroin for the working girls.

As Oscar waited, he grew bored. He was parked one hundred *feet* south of the restaurant building. About 150 *yards* from there was a field with a few stray walnut trees and what looked to be an abandoned house some distance away from one of the trees. Near the nine o'clock hour, his repairman nowhere in sight, Oscar walked out into the field to find a tree he could sit under. It wasn't hot yet, but the sun was out and that scorching California dry heat was coming.

After walking through the dirt parking lot and into the field, happening upon a walnut tree, its limbs draped down like spider legs, several nearly touching the ground, Oscar saw something. Positioned in an area near the trunk of the tree, in a section with no hanging limbs or other debris, Oscar adjusted his eyes and was shocked to be staring at a dead woman. She lay faceup, her head leaning to her left. From a distance, because of the hanging limbs and foliage, "[she would have been] difficult to see unless you were very close," a report of the crime scene said. Standing next to Oscar's truck, or in the Blueberry parking lot, there was no chance of seeing her.

She'd been dead for some time. Her corpse was bloated and bugs had gotten to her, with "a high concentration of maggots on the head and facial area." This initial report claimed a "large amount of blood in the head . . . and in the victim's vaginal area." Her dark brown skirt was "rolled up above her waist." She had foxtails—common meadow grass, small, brushlike, pointy spikes, found all over this particular region of the west—stuck to her clothes and hair. She wore socks, but no shoes. There were no footprints, other than Oscar's, anywhere. That vacant house stood about forty yards east of her body, where "a sandal, a pair of men's underwear, a lunch box, assorted business letters and a Sty-rofoam coffee cup" would be uncovered, ultimately written off by investigators as "nothing . . . related to the body."

Without giving any indication as to how it was known, the report said that "the victim sustained her injuries and died at another location," but "was then left . . . where she was found."

She was initially described as a "Hispanic female adult" between twenty and thirty. She wore a red pullover short-sleeved top, red panties, white, woolen, ankle-high socks. Her shoes were not at the scene (nor would they be recovered). She had one tattoo: a "bird flying into the sun" (on her lower-left abdomen). She wore a wristwatch on her left arm, along with a wedding band. Two gold chains hung around her neck, an earring in her right ear. There was an empty Budweiser can on the ground, close to her head. Eight inches south of her body was a "piece of cloth material."

Upon removing her from the scene, investigators found no blood underneath her head or vaginal area, leading them to believe that what, at first, seemed to be bloodied areas (face and vagina) was decomposition fluids leaking from those areas, both locations on the ground slithering with maggots.

It didn't take long to identify thirty-two-year-old Cynthia Lynn (Rose) Wilcox (her married name). She was actually a "white" female (not Hispanic), five-two, about one hundred pounds (though an accompanying photograph of her in the report claimed she was 120 pounds), brown hair, hazel eyes. Cynthia had a distinctive mole on the right side of her cheek. Investigators learned the last time anyone had seen her alive was August 27, 1992. Cynthia's husband had reported her missing. He told police his "wife was a prostitute and she was supposed to meet with an old friend named 'Charlie' at the Highway 99 rest stop in Turlock to 'turn a trick.'"

With no clear indication of how she died, investigators sent Cynthia's body off to the Delta Pathology Associates Medical Group in Stockton for complete toxicology analysis and autopsy. If she had been murdered, a manner of death many investigators believed to be a strong possibility, an autopsy would, by showing cause, give them good reason to begin searching for a suspect.

* * *

BEYOND KEITH JESPERSON'S WORK on *Dark Minds*—the insight into
the mind of the serial killer he shared—beyond all the stress,
physical, spiritual, mental, and medical complications I battled,
beyond anything we discussed between 2011 and 2014, the next
two years of our "friendship" would prove to be the most important
I'd spend interviewing him—work that began with, of course, yet
another telephone call.

"I'm ready to talk about some things I've kept from you," Jesperson said. It was early May 2015. He sounded out of breath and
frenzied, unable to get the words out fast enough.

"Is that right?"

"Yeah. I mean, I haven't told you *everything,* obviously."

I'd never gotten around to interviewing Les. One thing led to
another, writing books and filming several television shows got in
the way. I put it off. Then a report crossed the wire one morning:
Les had died.

"Listen, Phelps," Jesperson added, "Dad's dead now. I'm ready."

"Explain what you mean."

"With Dad gone, I can clear up a few things."

Les had served in the Canadian Merchant Navy. He wasn't a
large man like his son, but Keith and Les looked a lot alike. Les
had said publicly and in print he did not understand why his son
blamed him for the way he turned out and denied any of the
abuse Happy Face accused him of. He was well appreciated by his
surviving family and eulogized as if he was a simple outdoorsman,
a man who loved nothing more than riding his four-wheeler on
the property he owned, running businesses, and being a loving
father and grandfather to seventeen grandchildren and thirteen
great-grandchildren—someone who adored life and contributed
to his community, many of his later years living in the shadow of
having a serial killer for a son.

My focus was not—nor had it ever been—on Les and how
many stories Jesperson could spin in order to trash the old man,

but rather on something Jesperson had said a few times throughout the years in passing. Now, as he brought up the topic again, it seemed urgent. I'd paid little attention to the comment until 2015. To me, it fell into that scatological category of the serial killer jabbering about another law enforcement mess-up. Still, as I sensed a natural end to our friendship approaching, it was the first of several salient comments Jesperson made that reinvigorated me: "Number three, Cynthia Lynn Rose [Wilcox][7]—I did not kill her."

"What?"

"Cynthia Rose. I've been trying to tell people for years. I had no part in her death."

Cynthia Lynn (Rose) Wilcox lived in Modesto, California. The Blueberry Hill Café was six miles south of Turlock, where she had last been seen. Jesperson had told investigators (and me) he picked up a victim in Turlock at the Highway 99 rest area, killed her, and dumped her body in back of the Blueberry Hill Café. All of the available information since that admission would lead anyone reviewing the case, along with what Jesperson had said, in addition to the accessible facts, to believe that he had, in fact, murdered Cynthia Wilcox.

"I picked a woman up in Turlock at a rest area, strangled her right away, but it wasn't Cynthia," Jesperson explained. He described his Turlock victim as petite, blond, in her twenties. In a common Jesperson restatement pertaining to his victims, he said she was "in need of a shower and a comb." One more way to debase them, I guess.

[7] I should note that no one ever knew Cynthia Lynn Rose, the victim Jesperson has always been connected to, by her married name, Cynthia Wilcox. Her name, as connected to Jesperson in print, online and in other public places, has always been Cynthia Rose or Cynthia Lynn Rose. Thus, she will be known as Cynthia Lynn (Rose) Wilcox, Cynthia Wilcox, or, more simply, Wilcox, throughout the remainder of the book. But Cynthia Lynn Rose and Cynthia Wilcox are the same person.

In studying her autopsy report, which I obtained in 2016 but did not tell Jesperson right away, Cynthia Lynn (Rose) Wilcox was 120 pounds. She had Peter Pan–styled brown hair. She might not have been on any shortlist for a hygiene award, but she kept herself clean. These two women (Cynthia Lynn (Rose) Wilcox and Jesperson's Turlock victim), at least by outward appearances, shared polarizing contrasts. I would come to find out, those minor discrepancies were just the beginning.

Jesperson has always been attached to her murder, admitting to it in 1995, after he started talking to investigators about cases they'd been trying to close for years. He was never charged with Wilcox's murder, but she is on the books as one of his eight victims.

"How can you be so sure?" I asked. For years, I'd worked under the assumption that he'd killed Cynthia Wilcox and anything he said to the contrary was the psychopath, pathological liar inside of him flexing his muscle, trying to send me down a rabbit hole.

"Because, in 2009, while answering a separate case in Riverside County, I saw a photo of [Cynthia] a detective had out in front of me. I saw her face. I did not kill her. Her murderer is still out there. Somebody else did it. They mixed her up with my victim. But I didn't know this until I saw her photo for the first time in 2009."

Through several channels, it took me nearly five years, but I'd managed to get hold of Cynthia Wilcox's photo and, on top of her autopsy, the entire case report. Getting these documents was a pivotal part of proving or disproving what Jesperson had maintained. I didn't tell him I had the photo or reports. I needed to question him with the knowledge I now had access to.

An even bigger find, however, maybe the most significant from our five years, was getting my hands on something Jesperson never thought I'd be able to locate: his logbooks. He'd kind of rubbed it in my face many times, knowing the logs were a part of his case history only lawyers and law enforcement had access to.

With all of this new information, I could compare it to what he'd told me over the years in his letters and phone calls and see where we stood.

"So, then, the woman you killed, the victim they think *is* Cynthia, where is she?" I asked. He'd never denied killing a woman from Turlock.

"She should still be where I put her." In a rut in the Blueberry Hill Café parking lot, twenty-five feet south, 150 feet west of the building's back corner, he explained. "Just on the edge of a grassy section of land that dropped off into a ravine." It was an area trucks used as a turnaround to park or head back out on the road.

I knew from the reports, Cynthia Wilcox had been found 150 *yards* (three times the distance) south of the building, in a field, underneath a walnut tree. According to the reports, during his first interview about his Turlock/Blueberry Hill victim, Jesperson said that "he placed the victim's body on the ground . . . facedown amongst some tumbleweeds near the tree . . . stood on the back of the victim's head to make sure she was dead . . . and may have kicked some dirt on the victim." The reporting detective had questions, indicating how "Jesperson's statements were completely inconsistent with the facts of the case."

The tree was on the edge of the parking lot, Jesperson told me. Nowhere near where he positioned his victim facedown in the dirt. Jesperson drew police a map showing where the café was located, the parking lot, and where he put his victim.

"Again inconsistent with the facts of the case," the detective concluded.

Jesperson pushed me to go out there and dig. He was desperate for me to find his Turlock victim. Was he setting me up? I considered. In bed one sleepless night, my anxiety projected a situation on the ceiling: Me in Livingston with a shovel, standing behind the Blueberry Hill Café, cameras over my shoulder, digging and digging, not finding anything. This would be my Al Capone/Geraldo Rivera empty-vault moment. I'd be ridiculed and laughed at by trolls and true-crime aficionados.

"Come on, dude, you expect me to believe this bullshit?" I said. Whenever he'd bring it up, the same thoughts plagued me: *A serial killer saying he didn't kill one of his victims*—que sera, sera. *He wants more publicity.*

"I have no reason to lie to you about this," he insisted.

I thought about his answer. He's not saying he didn't kill the woman; he's saying the woman he killed was not the same victim he's accused of killing. Maybe he was confused?

"Why now?" I asked. "Just because your dad is dead?"

Jesperson wanted this resolved, he explained, all these years later, for the purpose of transparency: "Growing up, kids would say, 'Keith did this . . . Keith did that.' Then my father . . . I was blamed for things I never did. I took it. I was even punished for what I *didn't* do. And that kind of ran into this part of my life after I gave myself up. All of a sudden, they're coming to me saying I did this and that. And I'm saying no, I didn't. I had a Florida cop come visit me once. He asked me to admit to a body he found in Florida so he could close the case. He came over three thousand miles to ask me to lie. He said I would be more famous if I admitted it. That's ridiculous."

I understood his argument. His obsession with "righting these wrongs" stemmed from being blamed throughout his youth and into early adulthood for things he didn't do. Psychologically speaking, it made sense. It was how he was raised. His brothers were given cars and boats by Dad; Keith had to earn money and buy his own. He was viewed as an outcast, not a true family member. When there was a problem, "Keith was always to blame," he claimed.

Whether blaming his family was irrelevant or they saw it a different way, it was Jesperson's truth. It shaped who he became. Thus, it didn't matter to me why he needed to do this, or if his retrospective view of childhood was accurate. If I could prove a missing person was actually one of his victims, and the woman everyone thought he'd killed wasn't, it was worth listening to whatever twisted logic he spewed. Bottom line: was the Happy Face Killer telling me the body of a woman he'd murdered was still where he dumped her and Cynthia Wilcox's killer—if, in fact, she had been murdered—had not answered for that crime?

36

TRUE BLUE

"We are all in the same boat, in a stormy sea, and we owe
each other a terrible loyalty."
—G.K. Chesterton

WHENEVER *DARK MINDS* AIRED, I RECEIVED SCORES OF FACEBOOK
and Twitter messages, voice- and e-mail from fans, armchair and
Web sleuths, viewers interested in pursuing careers as investigative
journalists and in law enforcement, along with people who wanted
nothing more than to poke fun at aspects of the show (along with
my hair, clothes, how I pronounced certain words, and just about
everything in between). There were trolls, tipsters, and knuckle-
heads, some of whom threatened me. But also caring people
looking to vent their opinions and frustrations, not to mention
many well-balanced, inspiring individuals looking to help make
the world a better place by reporting a neighbor, friend, family
member, or spouse as a potential serial killer.

During the winter of 2014, one such message came from Ken
Robinson, a retired twenty-plus-year New York Police Department
(NYPD) detective, first grade. At one time, Ken, a hulking man of
six-three, 275 pounds, blue eyes and short-cropped, brown cop hair,
had worked security for Lenny Kravitz, Sheryl Crow, Stevie Nicks,
and a host of other celebrities. Ken is one of those "just-in-case"
guys anyone in my business loves to have backing him up. Once,
Ken was the face of the NYPD, his picture plastered on the sides
of buses and across billboards, his gentle personality, insightful

spirit, and traditional "New Yawk" accent heard on radio and television ads, encouraging those searching for a career in the nation's most recognized police force to sign up.

In that first, brief e-mail, Ken offered to help. The idleness of
forced retirement had gotten to him. He was still young, just
under fifty. He'd hurt his hand, arm, back, and suffered severely
from post-9/11 breathing issues. But his mind had not stopped
working; he was interested in sharing and offering his expertise
and experience as a mentor, which can be a blessing or a curse for
a guy in my position, depending on who the individual making
the offer is.

Over the course of that winter and spring, Ken and I talked many
times, and communicated almost daily by e-mail. Even though *Dark
Minds* was over, I brought Ken in on several cases from the series I
felt his vast knowledge and contacts could help. Ken developed
new threads and came up with new theories. He was a godsend.

As we chatted, I recognized his integrity and loyalty. For one, I'd
checked Ken out with a source close to the department. Within
twelve hours, the report back was flawless: "Ken is a top-notch cop.
You won't find a better person or investigator anywhere."

A partnership was born.

I'd kept the secret of Raven's identity from many in my inner
circle. My road crew knew. Execs at Investigation Discovery and
my production company knew. A few immediate family members
knew. But that was it. After several months, I let Ken in on everything I'd been working on regarding Jesperson—and that one
gesture, by itself, built a level of trust between us that has only
grown.

After I got hold of the logbooks and some of Jesperson's ATM
transactions and the other reports, I sent copies to Ken and asked
him to dig in, find me a missing person from that Blueberry Hill
Café/Turlock area that could fit Jesperson's description of his
supposed Turlock victim and match any logistics we could prove
with the documents and logs. I then asked him to put together a
lineup—with Cynthia Wilcox's picture—so I could present it to
Jesperson when I next went out to visit him. If Jesperson identi-

fied her in the lineup, we'd know he'd killed her. He was confused. I've always worked under the assumption that, though it
had been twenty-plus years, a serial killer of Jesperson's caliber
would have a hard time forgetting the face of a victim if he saw
her again.

"One more thing," I told Ken. "Jane Doe, in Florida. I need
your help there? I've involved the Palm Beach County Sheriff's
Office behind Jesperson's back. Can you talk cop-to-cop with
those guys and get us a starting point? Introduce yourself. Let's
try to do everything we can to force Jesperson's hand on that
case. He knows something about Florida he's not saying."

Ken thought about it.

"Does Jesperson know I'm working with you?"

"No. He knows nothing about you."

"Good, because I have a plan for Florida."

Sometime later, we were back discussing Cynthia Wilcox. By now,
Ken had a chance to go through the documents. I'd also expressed
some excitement to Ken that I was leaning toward believing Jesperson. The autopsy report, after all, claimed Cynthia Wilcox died of
an opiate/heroin overdose. She had *not* been murdered.

"This is the first of several inconsistencies I'd found between
Jesperson's Turlock victim and Cynthia's death," I told Ken.

"Well, I must admit that I was leaning toward being with you as
I read through everything . . . but not anymore," Ken said. "Jesperson killed Cynthia Wilcox. I'm sure of it. Give me some time
to explain."

For almost five years, I was certain Jesperson was playing me
where this case was concerned. When those reports came in—especially the autopsy and Cynthia Wilcox's photo—I grew more
certain every time I opened the case that Jesperson was telling the
truth. Now my right-hand man, whom I trusted more than anyone, said I was wrong.

JESPERSON "ASSUMED" FOR SIXTEEN years—1993 until 2009—that the
woman he killed at a Turlock, California, rest stop and dumped in
Livingston, in back of the Blueberry Hill Café, was Cynthia Wilcox,

a woman he knew by her maiden name, Cynthia Rose. Throughout that entire period, he never questioned it. When Merced, Colusa, Riverside, and Multnomah County (Oregon) investigators presented him with the case after he gave his Turlock/Blueberry Hill account, at face value it all fit.

"I had *no* reason not to think I killed her," he said. "Until I saw a photograph in 2009." It was a photo, according to him, that changed everything.

In 1995, after turning himself in, investigators in the jurisdictions where he'd claimed bodies came to interview him about each case. Jesperson gave details about the eight he'd murdered: how, where he met each woman and dumped each body, sharing specifics only the killer could know. During the course of those admissions, he mentioned the woman from a Turlock southbound rest area he'd met and murdered and dumped in back of the Blueberry Hill Café. She was petite, he told investigators. He called her "the blond hooker." Her hair was short, just above the shoulders. He claimed she did not have any identification on her (Cynthia Wilcox had left her purse inside the car her husband had dropped her at the Turlock rest area). He said she wore a red sweater, blue jeans, and tennis sneakers.

Cynthia Lynn (Rose) Wilcox had dark hair ("seven inches in length," according to the coroner's measurements). On the night she went missing, she was wearing a brown skirt, "slip-on, flat, black shoes, with a small bow on the toe and very low heels," and a jean jacket.

Jesperson never mentioned any of this during his Turlock admission.

Fast-forward to when he saw that crime scene photo in 2009 that he was told was Cynthia Lynn Rose, shown to him by investigators—and he knew he hadn't killed her.

My goal was to disprove Jesperson's claim. One fact kept reemerging, however, as I went about this confusing, gargantuan task. I've learned in five years of dealing with Jesperson that there can be no mistaking a victim he put his hands on. Also, I would come to find out in 2016 that Jesperson had left a second signature never pub-

licly reported: many of his victims were found with a zip tie or ligature (rope, tape) fastened around their necks. When asked why
he did this, Jesperson told investigators, "So I could mark them as
mine."

In his first interview (1996) regarding Turlock/Blueberry Hill,
Jesperson said he arrived at the Turlock "southbound rest area"
at 4:00 A.M. "Jesperson told us he was 'contacted' by a 'gal' who
asked him if he wanted company. . . . He parked his truck . . . the
woman got into his truck and got into his sleeper," the MCSO reported. "Jesperson said a 'scuffle' ended with [him] strangling
the woman." He panicked because he heard voices and two more
ladies "peering in" his cab. His victim had been dead by then for
"possibly twenty seconds." Spooked by the two girls, he took off,
merged onto Highway 99, and stopped at the next off-ramp to
"make sure the victim was dead." The entire scenario took about
thirty minutes.

I asked him what "contacted" meant. The reports clearly indicate Cynthia Wilcox used a CB radio to set up a lot of her dates.
Was this how Jesperson met his victim that night?

"No. I *never* used the CB for that. She jumped up on my running boards. That's how we met."

Leaving the off-ramp, his Turlock victim dead inside the
sleeper cab, Jesperson came upon a familiar place: the Blueberry
Hill Café. *It's late,* he thought. *No one is up. Perfect spot to get rid of her.*

He parked in back of the restaurant, with the front end of his
truck about fifteen feet away from the back of the building. He
got out to see if anyone was around and to search for the best
place to dump her. As he walked, he realized that near the back
of the lot, along the edge of grass (the borderline of that field), a
tree in the field just beyond that, there was a rut where trucks
pulled into the lot and made a turn to face the exit, so they
wouldn't have to back up and turn their trucks around when they
decided to leave. He told investigators it was "eight inches of powdered dirt."

"Jesperson described he placed the victim's body in the tumbleweeds near a tree in the parking lot . . . facedown into the dust and

stood on the victim's head 'to make damn sure' she was dead," investigators reported. He denied having sexual intercourse with her before or after she was dead.

Pressed further for details about the actual murder, Jesperson explained to investigators how he "either strangled [her] with his hands or 'my normal way,' pushing my fist down into [her] throat." He claimed not to have beaten her, but after he stopped at the off-ramp on the way to the Blueberry, unsure if she was still alive, he "held his hands on her [throat] for a good five minutes . . . to make sure she was dead." All of this was consistent with the versions he had given me over the years of discussing the case.

Wilcox's autopsy reported remarkable inconsistencies with the narrative Jesperson gave to police and me. Additionally, in a report I was able to obtain about Julie Winningham's murder, as told by Jesperson after he was arrested and charged, "The victim [Winningham] was duct-taped around the face and mouth and was beaten about her torso." Here we have, nevertheless, another signature of Jesperson's: binding and taping up his victims, beating them about their bodies and face. He told me, "I duct-taped my Turlock victim's hands and then tore that tape off, thinking I was going to leave fingerprints behind."

The autopsy mentioned nothing about Cynthia Wilcox's wrists having ever been bound.

"Yes, I have to admit to you that I did do this to all of them," he told me in 2015, after denying binding any of his victims all the years we talked. "I lied to you."

Between 1992, when Wilcox was found, and 1995 (when Happy Face, still out killing, started communicating with newspapers and police via letters, detailing several of his crimes), her case was ruled an overdose and closed. Her autopsy report, furthermore, proves she had more than toxic amounts of opiates, methadone, and benzodiazepines ("benzos" on the street, tranquilizers) in her system. Toxic levels of morphine/heroin come in at .10 to 1.0; Cynthia's morphine blood level was .27.

"There is a dense infestation of maggots, particularly about the head and neck," reported the autopsy. Her brain had been eaten by "three generations" of maggots. Fly ova was present. All of which—in addition to evidence backing up a report of her last being seen during the early morning hours of August 27, 1992— gave investigators a time frame for when Cynthia Wilcox died: one week before she was found, putting her death on or around August 27 (the same day Jesperson was in Turlock). Confusing matters ever more, Cynthia Wilcox was last seen by her husband, who had searched for his wife all that night and into the next morning, after dropping her off, at the *same* Turlock southbound rest area (where Jesperson met his victim) at 1:30 A.M., just hours before Jesperson arrived.

Jesperson logged himself being at the Blueberry Hill Café on August 1, 1992, almost a full month before she went missing. Fuel and ATM receipts, however, along with additional entries in his log, place him driving through Turlock on August 27. He knew this area well and traveled through it routinely during that entire year.

"There is no obvious trauma to the nose, lips, or neck, although decomposition and maggot infestation could obscure *minor* (emphasis mine) bruises or abrasions," claimed Wilcox's autopsy report. She had no rib fractures (Wilcox weighed one hundred pounds at autopsy [twenty pounds of water weight evaporated from decomposition]; Jesperson 275). All of her jewelry was accounted for: two gold necklaces, earring, watch, and wedding ring. She was menstruating at the time of her death and the coroner found a tampon with "pink bloodstaining" inside her vagina. There was "no external or internal evidence of vaginal trauma." She did have a few soft bruises on her right shin and thigh, but "no other" blunt-force injuries. No trauma to her head, chest, or abdomen. What's more, and perhaps most important to me, after her neck was "removed as a block," the coroner found "no soft tissue hemorrhages. Serial sectioning of the paraspinous musculature [that area of muscle around the neck we use to turn and hold up our head] was also negative for hemorrhage." Significantly, there was "no trauma to the carotid sheaths [that area to the left of your throat] . . . the cartilages and"—the most important factor leading me to believe there is no way she could have been strangled by Jesperson—"hyoid bone are intact. . . ."

Jesperson could not strangle a woman by placing his massive hands around her neck (twice, with one of those for "a good five minutes") and not bruise or crack her hyoid bone, on top of leaving no other signs of trauma to any of her neck muscles. Impossible for a man of his size and strength, especially taking into account he was in the beginning stages of his murder spree and not yet an experienced killer.

According to her autopsy, Wilcox had not been strangled. Shot. Stabbed. Drowned. Raped. Assaulted. Or murdered by any means.

It had taken me four-plus years, but I was confident Jesperson was being straight with me; he'd had nothing to do with the death of the woman he had always known as Cynthia Lynn Rose (her maiden and online name), but whose full name when she died was Cynthia Lynn Wilcox. If proven, this was beyond momentous. Not only did it mean a serial killer had not murdered a victim he'd been accountable for (he'd said he'd killed a blond prostitute and had always believed that Cynthia Lynn [Rose] Wilcox was that person); but the woman Jesperson *had* murdered could (and should) still be buried in back of the Blueberry Hill Café.

As I was about to celebrate the find, my voice of reason, Ken Robinson, called. He'd found more, he said. Going through interviews with former Jesperson coworkers and Jesperson's bank and ATM records, Ken could not wrap his mind around the fact that Jesperson, near the *exact* time Cynthia Wilcox went missing, in the *exact* Turlock location, passed through within hours of the same time and had *not* killed her. What were the chances a serial killer was at the *same* rest area where a woman went missing, that *same* woman was later found dead (where the serial killer had said he'd left her), and he was *not* responsible? Ken could not overlook these facts.

"Well—" I started to say.

"Zero chance, Phelps," Ken interrupted.

"But . . ."

"No, listen. I have much more. You say Cynthia Wilcox wasn't murdered—that the autopsy says she overdosed, but I am having issues with that, too."

Ken had found an aerial photo from the 1960s of the Blueberry Hill Café. He sent it to me. He asked me to send the photo to Jesperson so he could show us where he'd dumped his Turlock victim. This was important. If he drew an *X* on the same spot (which we were certain of) where Wilcox had been found, regardless of the maps Jesperson drew for me and investigators, it would indicate that Jesperson had killed her.

I got it back from Jesperson weeks later. He was angry I'd sent him a photo from the 1960s. The entire setup was different from the 1992 café. Still, he sketched in where he might have dumped his victim. Looking at it, I shook my head.

Shit.

37

BABY DOLL

"Your every new journey is your new window opening to
new ideas."
—Mehmet Murat ildan

*I*N MY VIEW, UNIMPEACHABLE EVIDENCE PROVING HAPPY FACE DID NOT
murder Cynthia Lynn Wilcox can be found in the autopsy report.
I don't like to argue with science. After receiving that document,
there was no question in my mind Wilcox had died of an overdose.

Jesperson told me he kept at least three logbooks (I only saw
one). From a stop in Oregon on August 1, 1992, Jesperson traveled
to San Jose (stopping at the Blueberry Hill Café along the way),
San Francisco, Stockdale, Phoenix, back up to Yoncalla, Oregon
(August 22), Portland, Wallula (Washington), and then down to
Fresno (on August 27) via Highway 99. The trip to Fresno became
the link that kept me up at night wondering if what I believed and
what science seemed to prove was wrong. I kept going back to the
obvious: a serial killer admitting to a murder, admitting to dumping her body at a location where law enforcement uncovered a
body, and that same serial killer admitting he was in the exact location where the victim went missing—all on the same day, within
hours. It seemed ridiculous not to make the connection.

Complicating matters even further, I asked a retired ME, a
woman I've known for years, to take a look at the autopsy report.

I gave her no other details other than asking, "How did this woman die?"

"It appears to be a mixed drug toxicity case, but the condition of the clothing is suspicious. . . . In opiate overdoses, respiratory depression and cessation is the mechanism of death, which manifests as pulmonary edema (which she has)."

Because of the autopsy results, the MCSO labeled Wilcox's death—from 1992 until 1995, when Jesperson started talking—a drug overdose and publicly stated as much. The Associated Press reported Cynthia Wilcox's death in the same manner. The police report detailing the intense investigation into her death seized on the notion of a trucker from Livingston named Charlie, a regular Cynthia Wilcox customer, who might have killed her, but he was ruled out after the autopsy proved otherwise and his alibi checked out. Even her husband was looked at as a potential suspect, but then also was ruled out. The husband claimed it was August 27, about 1:30 A.M., when he'd dropped his wife off at the southbound Turlock rest stop. He watched her exit the vehicle and walk near a "light blue van," which he considered "suspicious." It was the last time he saw his wife.

Cynthia Wilcox and her husband had been camping at Oakdale Lake, in Eugene, California, about forty miles east, an hour outside Livingston, for three weeks leading up to that early August morning. They'd lived in Modesto with someone she called "Grandpa." Since June 3, 1992, every day up to her death, her husband drove her to Modesto, where, between 6:30 and 8:00 A.M., a clinic provided her with a daily dose of methadone. She'd never missed a day. Her husband believed she was off heroin; but after she went missing and he questioned friends, they told him she was "back on . . . and getting loaded." She'd failed three drug screens given by the clinic: June 3, July 4, and August 6.

On August 26, she phoned Charlie. The first call she made was at 6:00 P.M. from a pay phone near the Oakdale Lake campground restrooms. Charlie wasn't home. She left a message: "I want you to meet me at the rest area."

Charlie knew that meant Turlock. Charlie, who drove a white

cab-over truck, had been meeting her for years at the same Turlock rest stop. She sought Charlie out on this night because she needed money to give to her husband, who was involved in a green card immigration issue. She knew Charlie to be good for "thirty to forty dollars" whenever they met. All they ever did "was talk," the report claimed.

She and her husband went back to the campsite, ate, and slept. They awoke near 11:00 P.M. on the twenty-sixth and drove into Turlock. At 1:00/1:15 A.M. on the twenty-seventh, according to the husband, they parked at the AM/PM on Taylor Road in town, where she called Charlie a second time. Taylor Road ran underneath Highway 99, not far from the rest stop.

Charlie didn't answer.

"Charlie, this is Baby Doll. I'm at the rest area on the southbound side," Charlie's answering machine recorded. "Baby Doll" was Cynthia Wilcox's CB handle many of the truckers passing through the region knew her by.

"No," Jesperson told me. "I have never heard that name. Nor would I ever communicate over my CB with one of the girls who worked the radio."

Baby Doll and her husband arrived at the Turlock southbound-side rest stop moments later. After parking, she turned to her husband: "I'll be back in fifteen to twenty minutes."

It was near 1:30 A.M. She was expected back by two o'clock, at the latest.

She got out. Her husband leaned back, tipped his cap down over his eyes, and fell asleep.

He woke up at 2:30 A.M. She had not returned. So he walked around the lot to see if he could find her. He searched for hours. He ran into a friend of his wife's, another "working girl," who said, "No, I have not seen her."

As he stood near his vehicle, he thought he heard "someone calling his name from a distance." This made him think his wife had walked across the interstate and was trying to get his attention from the northbound-side rest area.

He looked across the freeway and didn't see much. So he drove from the southbound to the northbound side. By 6:30 A.M., he still had no idea where his wife had gone off to or whom she was with. He then drove to the methadone clinic in Modesto to see if Cynthia had shown up for her daily dose. After speaking with several people in line, however, he was at a great loss, because no one claimed to have seen her.

JESPERSON WAS IN BIGGS Junction, Oregon, on August 26; he drove "all night" to Fresno, into early the next morning, August 27, purchasing fuel in the amount of $180.05 at the Grantland Exxon in Fresno, hustling on a tight schedule to deliver meat. He made it to the southbound-side (Highway 99) Turlock rest stop at 4:00 A.M., a few hours after Cynthia reportedly went missing.

The time line rules him out of being involved in Cynthia Wilcox's disappearance—that is, if it's accurate. Even more compelling evidence against Happy Face's involvement is that detectives proved Cynthia Wilcox was still alive later that day, past 8:00 A.M., because the methadone clinic claimed she came for her methadone maintenance after the prescribed time frame (6:30 to 8:00 A.M.), and arrived alone to take the dose. Even more convincing, she was heard throughout the night and into the morning of August 27 on the CB by several other girls: "This is Baby Doll. . . ."

Still, to be certain I wasn't missing anything, I asked Jesperson for a detailed account of killing his Turlock victim, who, by his account, should still be buried behind the Blueberry Hill Café, a woman whose identity is a mystery. I also wanted to see how consistent he was with his previous statements to law enforcement (which he did not know I had).

"I pulled into the Turlock rest area going southbound on Highway 99 at about three thirty in the morning," he began (not having seen any of the reports or been able to review his interviews). He couldn't recall the exact date, but he agreed the log should be accurate. "If it says I passed through the area on the twenty-seventh, then I did."

Just after stopping his truck near the car park section of the rest stop, nowhere near a truck slot, his Turlock victim "stepped up on" the running boards of his truck and asked if he wanted company. He told her no. "Get away. I'm tired. Move on."

This wouldn't match Cynthia Wilcox's husband's account of his wife going there to meet someone she knew as Charlie. If Charlie, who went by the last name Brown, was a CB handle, maybe Jesperson had one that the girls knew him by.

"What name did you use with the girls?"

"I never gave them a name. Keith, if they needed to know."

"You didn't have a nickname?"

"I had a CB handle."

"What was it?"

"Kingpin."

Not even close.

With a steely affect I'd seldom heard, Jesperson's account of the murder became one of the more chilling he'd ever shared. After telling the Turlock prostitute to beat it, she stepped off the running board and left. (This differs a bit from his original account to law enforcement, where he talked about negotiating a price for sex after they made contact, before she started to argue with him.)

Twenty minutes later, she returned.

He was now parked and asleep.

So she opened the door, climbed into the cab, and startled him awake.

"I had basically told her I didn't want company and she wanted company, anyway," he explained to me, "so she got into the truck and I strangled her and put her out of her misery. I took her down to the Blueberry Hill Café, where I left her body in the back parking lot. And that's about it . . . it wasn't no big thing. I had just taken care of this. It was done. I put her facedown in the dirt. Kicked the back of her head and put tumbleweeds over the top of her and drove off. I assumed they would have found her, but they didn't, and that's where we stand right now." It was an account that mostly matched what he had said all those years before when interviewed by law enforcement.

Cynthia Wilcox had a fractured jaw the coroner believed occurred postmortem. Was it from that kick he said he gave his victim? But she was found faceup underneath a walnut tree, her
head leaning to her left, 150 yards from the parking lot. Jesperson
claimed to have dumped his victim in the opposite direction, in the
parking lot itself, covering her with powdered dirt and tumbleweeds.

"And you think she is still there?" I asked him.

"Well, I think she would be still there. The powdered dirt was
about six inches deep. If someone drove over the top of her, she
could be like a foot down in the ground." Tossing her out of his
truck and into that soft dirt was "like throwing a watch" onto
meadow grass and looking on as it "disappears—I mean, it had the
same results."

This area he described was a well-trafficked section of the lot
that trucks drove over all the time. That was part of the reason
why he chose it. It was nowhere near that walnut tree, which from
this location would have been about three hundred feet to the
southeast, in a grassy meadow.

Our conversation took place over a Video Visit. I looked at
him. I shook my head in disgust at his predictable, egotistical
smugness while describing how he had killed and dumped the
Turlock victim. Talking about murder to him was so common, so
casual. I never got used to this.

Because the Blueberry Hill Café was a popular trucking area,
he dumped her in a rut trucks drove in, hoping that "all her body
juices and blood" would dissolve, thus allowing her to "dissipate
and petrify." His hope was that trucks drove over her body, forcing it deeper into the powdered dirt. It had been a week before
Cynthia Wilcox was found. One would have to believe a truck
would have driven over the victim if she had been dumped where
he claimed he placed the Turlock prostitute.

There was zero indication in her autopsy report that Wilcox
had been run over by a truck. She was found in an area far from
where trucks would have driven.

Jesperson's account, which never changed, was in total contrast to how and where she had been found.

"Why her?" I asked, referring to the Turlock kill.

"Because she was there. She was the one that got onto *my* truck. When I pulled into the parking lot, she was the first one to jump up on the side of my truck."

"You never set up a date with your Turlock victim?"

"No! Would I set up a date and then kill the girl? That's ridiculous. It'd be a sure way of getting caught."

While he was in the process of strangling his Turlock victim, "two more [women] jumped up on the side of the truck and tried to get in." This spooked Happy Face, so he drove off, which became the only reason he wound up at the Blueberry Hill Café.

Several of her regular girlfriends said they never saw Baby Doll that night at the Turlock rest stop. If either of these two women knew Jesperson's Turlock victim and she was Cynthia Wilcox, why wouldn't they claim to have seen her get into Jesperson's truck?

Still, I had many questions, not to mention Ken Robinson sitting on my shoulder, wagging a finger.

"All right, explain the confusion," I said.

Jesperson shuffled a bit in his seat, displaying body language that told me he was excited and, for him, setting the record straight was important. He said, "Well, they told me initially it was Cindy [Wilcox]. When detectives came and saw me in 1996, they told me they were working the Cynthia [Wilcox] case and I *assumed* that *that* was the case we were talking about—the one I left in Livingston. I had no knowledge that it wasn't the real case. Only in 2009, when I was going down to Riverside County, did they show me the victim's picture, and when they asked me who that was, I said, 'I don't know who that is.' They said it was Cynthia [Wilcox]. I said, 'Well, that may be [Cynthia], but it's not mine. I didn't do her. Mine is still there.' I then heard a detective [say], 'It doesn't sound like we're talking about the same case.' And I heard another detective say, 'Oh, well, just shut [that] for now. We'll deal with this later.'"

Later never came for investigators because they knew he was not involved. That's why he did not recognize the photo of Cynthia Lynn (Rose) Wilcox. Still, her case—even though her married name of Wilcox had been dropped from any reporting of it—has stuck to Jesperson all these years.

In November 2015, as I amped up pressure, Jesperson asked again if I was going out to the Blueberry Hill Café with a shovel.

"Well, not exactly," I said. "Not for nothing, but that area where you claim you put her is now a paved parking lot."

Sometime later, I received a letter. Jesperson spoke of a great need to ask me a "serious question," apparently ignoring what I'd said about the paved parking lot and not going there. "Let's say you discover the victim is still there, buried in the back of the lot. . . . You open ground and see she is still there. What will you do? Document the find with photographs and cover her back up until your book is ready to go? Or will you document it with photos and call in the sheriffs to document them uncovering her and hopefully identifying her? She would be there since August 1992—what is another few months?"

This comment further helped me understand how different his thinking is from the average human being's. The indication that he'd consider the possibility existed for me to hold on to the location of a murder victim (if I dug her up) to use as a publicity stunt for a book proved how far beneath any moral ground he slithered.

Further along, after encouraging me to hold on to the info if I located her, his paranoia let loose. He talked about how Merced County might have "buried" their reports and how I would need witnesses, if I went out there, to "verify the find." As he continued, it became obvious what this was about: spitting in the face of law enforcement again. We were back at Taunja Bennett.

One of his goals was to get "police to quit sitting on the Cynthia [Wilcox] case and run the DNA to find her real killer and quit blaming [me] for it." He indicated how "stupid" the police would look if his Turlock victim turned up buried in back of the old Blueberry Hill Café. Why? Because "[they] offered a life sentence for a murder that never happened—and to fulfill the deal they have filled the [toe] tag with Cynthia [Wilcox]."

He wasn't exactly wrong. But not right, either. There were no cops on record claiming Jesperson had murdered Cynthia Wilcox. Nor was he ever charged with killing her.

Sometime later: "Call me crazy, Phelps. Paranoid again. But what if Merced [County] police went to the Blueberry Hill Café and found my victim and disposed of it, just to be able to point at me for the [Wilcox] case? But destroyed the report in favor of pointing at me for the [Wilcox] case?"

That was ridiculous. Here was the serial killer hating on cops again, now trying to put me in the middle. He still had no idea I had all the reports he was referring to.

"I'll look into all that," I told him.

Ken Robison had a plan and contacted me about it. When I got him that photo of Cynthia Wilcox he'd asked for, he put together a lineup of missing California girls from the time frame of Cynthia's case so I could deliver it to Jesperson in person, ask him if he could point out his Turlock victim, and then gauge his reaction. The photo of Cynthia Wilcox—which Jesperson didn't know we had—was number 1 on that list.

38

CASE CLOSED

"We trouble our life by thoughts about death, and our
death by thoughts about life."
—Michel de Montaigne

*T*HE SCENARIO I KEPT RETURNING TO WHILE SPENDING MONTHS
going through all of the available information pertaining to Cynthia Lynn (Rose) Wilcox's death and Jesperson's Turlock victim—including all he'd written and said to me over the years—became that in Turlock, Livingston, and along that Highway 99 corridor in Merced County during the 1990s, confined to truck and rest stop zones, there was a bustling criminal culture ebbing and flowing on a regular basis. Drug dealing, prostitution, assault, rape, murder, and other crimes were common fare. So when we look at the (Rose) Wilcox/Turlock cases (if they are separate) and consider how improbable a coincidence it could be that a serial killer crossed paths with the victim of an overdose, but murdered another woman, dumping her in the same general location the overdose victim was later found, we need to bring into the argument that this section of California was a busy and felonious world of criminals and violent crime. Thus, I believe the odds for such a coincidence taking place—when Jesperson himself is the one who told me many times, "There are no coincidences in murder"—become impossible to ignore.

As additional evidence of the crime culture existing in that area at the time, the police reports claim Cynthia Wilcox had been choked once to the point "where she almost passed out" by drug dealers to whom she owed money. She'd been threatened. Beaten. Many of the working girls whom police spoke to in the days after her body was found did not seem all that surprised a working girl within this crowd of prostitutes, drug dealers, and truckers had gone missing and wound up dead. They also weren't shocked the dead girl turned out to be Wilcox, who many described as working in a high-risk atmosphere. Wilcox had reportedly stolen nine hundred dollars from a trucker. In addition, an anonymous witness explained to police a "Mexican truck driver in a white cattle truck" had been giving her trouble for months. He'd been seen at local rest stops on several occasions, grabbing her by the arm, pulling her along, slapping her around. She'd owed him money for drugs. Another witness claimed the Mexican truck driver took Wilcox out to breakfast early that morning (August 27), fed her, and then killed her. It would not have been all that difficult to gift her a few bags of tainted dope and let her kill herself. A kitchen worker at the Blueberry Hill Café told police he saw a white cattle truck (Jesperson's rig was blue) parked where her body was later found, around the date her body would have been dumped. There was a tablecloth located at the Oakdale Lake campsite where she was staying with her husband. One interview claimed the tablecloth had blood on it and reeked of a terrible "death" stench. Both Cynthia Wilcox and Jesperson's Turlock victim wore red tops—consistent with what some later called the "red top girls" of Highway 99, a group of prostitutes, all of whom wore red tops to indicate who they were to truckers.

Had Cynthia Wilcox, who was said to have taken her methadone dose late in the day, August 27, fired up a few bags, OD'd in someone's truck, and that person dumped her at the Blueberry Hill Café? To make her death look suspicious, hoping to perhaps cause confusion for police, maybe the person who'd dumped her rolled up her skirt? Furthermore, why hadn't Jesperson ever been charged with her murder? Thomas Phelan had cut deals and done a good job of getting the death penalty off the table in exchange for information, but still, California never pursued Jesperson in Cynthia Lynn (Rose) Wilcox's case. The last line of the forty-nine-page report concluded that "Jesperson marked the area where he placed [his Turlock] victim's body, again inconsistent with the facts of the case. . . . This is the end of the report." The case was closed; the report "approved" on December 1, 1996.

WHEN JESPERSON CAME FORWARD and said he'd killed a woman in Turlock and dumped her in back of the Blueberry Hill Café, it's easy to see how investigators from several agencies looked to pin Cynthia Wilcox's death on him. Once you see the light on the other side, it's not hard to convince yourself the tunnel in front of you can get you there.

Ken Robinson had even gone down this same road when he first looked at the case for me, calling and saying, "While the autopsy shows no evidence of homicide, it really doesn't need to, if we have the killer saying he killed her and she is dead."

The problem with that statement is its close-minded vision and the fact that we now had a killer saying he *hadn't* killed this particular victim. Further complicating the Wilcox/Turlock cases was that another victim from California, a Jane Doe whom Jesperson called "Claudia," a woman he admitted killing and dumping ten miles north of Blythe (five hundred miles south of Livingston), was found on August 30, 1992. A third body was then found ten months later, on June 3, 1993, by a trucker, according to the Associated Press, about "twenty-four miles southwest of Livingston" (still Merced County). She was said to be in her thirties. In one of his Happy Face letters to the press, Jesperson talked about meeting this woman at a truck stop in Corning. His logbook shows he was in Corning on May 31, 1993, backing up what he said. She was hungry and needed a ride (typical Jesperson victim, but quite atypical of Cynthia Wilcox's MO). He called her "attractive," save for her unkempt hair, adding, "She needed to run a comb through it." Jesperson said he killed her in Williams, an hour south of Corning, at a rest stop; yet he never logged the location. After logging

Corning, his log shows he drove north, not south, up through Ashland, Oregon (June 1), Vancouver and Yakima, Washington (June 2).

In those two cases, there was never any question: Jesperson admitted killing both women and gave investigators unequivocal proof that he'd committed both crimes.

My conclusion is that Jesperson is likely telling the truth with regard to Cynthia Wilcox/Turlock, which is to say, then, that his Turlock victim, if anything is left of her, should still be buried in Livingston, California, where the old Blueberry Hill Café stood in 1992.

39

QUESTION

"Truth never damages a cause that is just."
—Mahatma Gandhi

I FLEW TO PORTLAND/SALEM AND SAT WITH JESPERSON ON MARCH 29, 2016. We talked for three hours inside the OSP visiting room. It was one of the more emotional visits/conversations I'd ever had with him. He was a different man from when I'd last seen him in person, in 2012. Yes, he looked older and walked slower. His hair was a bit grayer. He wasn't wearing his trademark glasses. He seemed softer, mellower, his anxiety in check. We talked through the Blueberry Hill case. He drew maps on scraps of paper and explained how he'd picked up the Turlock hooker and dumped her in back of the Blueberry. I'd heard all this before.

"I obtained all the reports," I interrupted as he talked.

He put the short golfer's pencil down, sat back, his jaw on his chest. Stared at me.

"Merced County reports?"

"Yes. I've been using them to question you about everything."

"Blows my paranoid theory of the cops covering it all up," he said.

"Sure does. And there's more—Cynthia Wilcox's autopsy report proves she died of an overdose. There's no indication she was murdered. None."

He looked relieved. It was as though he'd wrestled with himself since 2009: *Maybe I did kill Cynthia?* He did not gloat. I thought he would. He said he felt vindicated. "I don't like being blamed for things I didn't do. Les did it to me all my life."

I had not mentioned the photo of Cynthia Wilcox. I had the lineup I'd smuggled into the prison in my back pocket: six photos of six different women. Number 1: Cynthia Lynn (Rose) Wilcox. Number 4: a woman, Lori Thiel, Ken Robinson had found. Ken and I believed Lori was a good candidate for the Jane Doe whom Jesperson referred to as Claudia. The composite drawing of Claudia is an identical match to Lori's photo. Even the circumstances surrounding Lori's disappearance, and where she'd supposedly run off to, fit.

He looked at the lineup as I gauged his reaction; it was the main reason I'd flown three thousand miles. A visceral response can indicate truth: the body and mind reacting on their own after seeing a woman he'd killed. It was something he would not be able to contain.

He glanced at each image, passing over Cynthia's photo without a dash of hesitation. He shook his head back and forth.

"Nothing?" I asked.

After a second scan, he stopped at Number 4, Lori Thiel. "She looks like Claudia." He stared at her face.

"I thought you'd say that." I then explained that I'd just spoken to the detective investigating Lori's disappearance. He said the DNA match to Claudia did not check out, adding how he had a solid suspect for Lori's disappearance.

"The DNA *doesn't* match?" Jesperson asked, puzzled.

"Nope. It's been checked. So have dental, I've been told. Listen, forget that. No one else in the lineup seems familiar to you?"

He looked down again. Studied each face a second time. "None of them, besides number four, looks even vaguely familiar."

I took a moment to focus on his face. Then: "Number one, what do you see there—anything?"

He was at a loss. "Just a woman. Have no idea who she is."

"That's . . . Cynthia Lynn Rose . . . Wilcox, man. Her married name is Wilcox."

He looked down quickly. His face never changed. "Never seen

her before. That's not even the woman I saw in the 2009 photo they showed me when they told me I was looking at the Cynthia Lynn Rose crime scene."

I was more than convinced. I called Ken later that day. He was far from sold. He'd put together a list of "similarities" and "inconsistencies" regarding Turlock and Cynthia Wilcox and e-mailed it to me before my trip.

"You read that report I sent you?" Ken asked.

"I did."

"Let's discuss it. Look, your scenario is certainly possible, and could even be likely," Ken said.

"It's not *my* scenario, Ken. I'm just going by what the reports indicate."

"After reading the final summation by the detective from the Jesperson interview," Ken explained, "that first one they did with him, it leads me to believe it's *not* his body. But it really doesn't tell us what all of the inconsistencies are that lead them to draw this conclusion, and they don't look into a lot of it."

"I think what they saw was enough, Ken. They interviewed scores of people. Cynthia's husband. Those girls. The methadone clinic people."

"Okay, here's why he didn't kill her. The autopsy report *not* showing strangulation. Cynthia had toxic levels of drugs in her system. Police saying Jesperson's case does *not* match Cynthia's death. Police say the location of Jesperson's victim does *not* match Cynthia's location. And he said the picture he was shown of Cynthia did *not* match his victim."

There was a lot more, Ken added, but for the sake of our conversation, he kept it brief, sticking to major points.

I asked: "How do you explain the timing of the methadone? She got her methadone *after* the eight A.M. window closed. Jesperson, we know from the logs and fuel receipts, was well on his way by then, dropping that meat delivery and out of the state."

"I don't buy this," Ken said of the methadone report. "I don't feel she showed up for the methadone later—I don't think she *ever* showed up."

The report was not as detailed in this regard as we would have liked; yet, that being said, the director of the Stanislaus County Heroin Treatment Center, where Wilcox received her daily methadone, claimed she "received her daily dose on [August 27, 1992] and did not return after that date." The problem they had was that no one wrote down the time. Moreover, the initial entry for that date showed she "missed" her 6:30 to 8:00 A.M. dose, but then the entry was crossed out, indicating she'd been given the dose after hours.

"I look at that," I told Ken, "as a simple, undeniable fact. They said she was there on August twenty-seven, *after* eight A.M. They have no reason or motive to fudge that."

We moved on. I asked Ken for his reasons backing up that Jesperson killed Wilcox. What was he basing his opinion on?

"Cynthia went missing the same time of night, on the same day Jesperson was in the area, probably within a two-hour window. He was not only just in the area, but he admits to stopping in the Turlock rest stop. He was in the *same* rest stop on the *same* night a girl was reported missing from this rest stop. After stopping at the Turlock rest stop, he killed a woman who got into his truck and then dumped her behind the Blueberry Hill Café. Cynthia was found *behind* the Blueberry, next to a shack by a tree. He has said he stepped on the head or throat of the victim *after* she was dead. Cynthia's jaw was fractured after death. Jesperson described his Turlock victim as a petite, white, maybe one hundred pounds, red top, with short hair above her shoulders, and a prostitute. Cynthia was a petite female, white (despite the picture we have), one hundred pounds, red top, with short hair above her shoulders—and a prostitute! The hair colors described don't match, I know. Neither do the blue jeans/skirt. I realize Cynthia may have looked Hispanic. Still, no other bodies were found behind the Blueberry Hill Café, *despite* Jesperson dumping a victim there, and *despite* a police search in this same area for evidence. Just Cynthia Wilcox."

To me, undeniable evidence that Keith Jesperson *did not* kill Cynthia Lynn (Rose) Wilcox can be found in the autopsy report—because she overdosed. What's more, she showed up for her methadone maintenance long after Happy Face was out of the area. Anything beyond those two facts, in my opinion, is speculation.

BACK A FEW DAYS after visiting Jesperson, I made a call I'd not felt the need to make in at least twenty years. A constant knot, my stomach muscles were perpetually clenched, tightened, and stressed. I called my doctor and he told me to up my Lexapro intake by .5 mils. I didn't. I also recognized (and felt guilty) that over the course of the past few months my Mass routine had fallen off. When I did go, I sat and stared at the stained-glass windows, statues, Stations of the Cross along the sidewalls, and took in nothing presented at the altar. My faith was nearly gone. I felt like a shell, a body walking through the motions of life, no soul. My anxiety was back at full throttle. I was torn, broken. I cried when no one was around for no particular reason I could discern. I'd never felt so profoundly different, so sad, so lost. I was desperate to find out why.

40

AS MUCH AS I EVER COULD

"Although an act of help done timely might be small in
nature, it is truly larger than the world itself."
—Thiruvalluvar

A GOAL OF MINE WAS TO CONVINCE JESPERSON TO DO EVERYTHING
in his power to help identify his Florida Jane Doe. This kept me
going. I believed he knew more than he'd shared all these years.
So behind Jesperson's back, I'd initiated a dialogue with PBSO
FIS Paul Moody, while explaining to Jesperson I didn't have much
time presently to devote to his cases and agenda. Without promis-
ing anything, Moody said Jesperson would "not likely" be prosecuted under the death penalty if he helped identify Jane. The
Florida Department of Law Enforcement (FDLE), lead agency in
the case, was not looking to reopen the investigation; they, like
me, wanted to bring Jane home to her family, giving a name and
place of final rest to a box of bones and a skull sitting on a shelf
inside a brick building in Okaloosa County. All this time, Jane
had been floating in the universe, a nameless murder victim, her
legacy and memory a twenty-year phantom. It was time for her to
be at peace.

"They are not interested in prosecuting you," I told Jesperson
one afternoon.

"That's all bullshit. No. Not helping."

Back in 2012, Jesperson wrote to Thomas Phelan, explaining

that he'd received a letter from the FDLE indicating they wanted his help identifying Jane Doe (Florida). Jesperson told Phelan his "instinct" was to ignore the request. No matter what they promised, Florida could haul him back into court and charge him with the death penalty, especially if Jane's family pushed the case after she was identified.

In his first letter to Jesperson, dated June 22, 2012, Special Agent (SA) Dennis Haley, of the FDLE, asked about Jane, basing his questions on an interview Jesperson had given on February 17, 1996, to SA Glen Barberree, then FDLE lead detective in Jane's case. In that letter, Haley said, "Florida has declined to seek any prosecution against you because you are already doing multiple life sentences." From there, the SA outlined what the FDLE "knew" about the case.

Phelan advised Jesperson to consider how the prosecutor in the case was not offering "immunity" for his help; thus, with no statute of limitations on murder, trusting the State of Florida in this regard would be foolish—and perhaps deadly. Phelan warned that investigators were "motivated by a 'do-gooder' attitude." Or maybe they *were* looking to prosecute. He encouraged Jesperson to "simply not respond to [Haley's] letter."

Far too egocentric, forever needing the last word on anything, Jesperson, of course, couldn't help himself. He wrote back to Haley, before forwarding both letters (Haley and Phelan's) to me, which I received in July (2012), along with one of Jesperson's classic soliloquies regarding his feelings about it all. In his diatribe to me, Jesperson's suspicion ran amuck: "Why now?" he asked, before blaming his daughter, Melissa, for "disturbing the waters," forcing cops to "look back at me" and all the old cases, by writing a book about her life with a serial killer dad. He mentioned being "in the news" more these days than after his arrest.

"Be honest, had she [Melissa] not gotten me into the news, you would have never written?" he asked.

"Wrong," I told him. John Kelly, my *Dark Minds* colleague, knew Jesperson could not refuse getting involved with the series and suggested I write to him on that basis alone.

"Let's say they locate her family, then what?" he said. "Florida changes its mind and prosecutes me."

"They say they won't."

"Lies. Of course, they will, Phelps. I'm a killer. I have no rights. Little bit of pressure from some victim's family and I'm looking at the chair."

He went through SA Haley's letter, line by line, picking out where he believed Haley had baited him by sending misinformation. Jesperson saw through each blatant, orchestrated error Haley had purposely made.

"That first letter was designed to get Jesperson talking," SA Dennis Haley told me, laughing. "And it worked."

In his return letter to Haley, Jesperson pointed out the errors. He'd not decided to help, but he was open to discussing it. This is typical serial killer behavior: *I am smarter than the police.*

After that initial correspondence between Haley and Jesperson, using his familiar flippant, patronizing tone, Jesperson sent me another letter: "What Dennis Haley doesn't know is, Mr. Phelps is doing a book and he [Haley] just became a topic to cover in it. Your book will show the truth." He assumed that if he helped Florida and kept me in the loop, Florida couldn't turn around and burn him because I would be monitoring the situation. I became Jesperson's insurance policy.

After that, he ripped Haley, calling him a liar. He presumed Haley would "take the stand, on principle," if Jane's case ever went to trial, and would perjure himself if need be: "Any lie is okay to get to the truth of the case."

I saw my opening: Act as though I was on Jesperson's side. He trusted me. Play the middleman. His "yes" man. Tell him what he wanted to hear so we could move forward with identifying Jane Doe. If I needed to lie, well, the guy was a serial killer. He deserved nothing less.

41

THE GIRL WITH THE FAMILIAR LAST NAME

"'Great idea,' I said. 'Call the police. Call the fucking
police.'"
—Ava Gardner, *Ava: My Story*

SA DENNIS HALEY IS AN OLD-SCHOOL COP. A HARDENED FLORIDA
transplant from Illinois, who unintentionally projects himself to
be a bit backcountry, but once you get to know Haley, you realize
a superior intelligence and boundless charm lurks underneath
that Southern veneer. Haley sports a familiar Florida red face,
white goatee, mustache. His laugh is deep, phlegmy, unique. He
speaks from a place of experience when discussing murderers
and serial killers and has tangled with the worst of them. He's per-
sonable and real. Meeting SA Haley for the first time, I knew that
if there was a cop in Florida who could identify Jesperson's Jane
Doe, he was that person.

During the fall of 2014 and into early 2015, I made Jane a priority. Since 2012, Happy Face and the FDLE wrote back and
forth, while I watched over the situation as a third party. I knew
from my own investigative experience, this was a case that, with a
few breaks, could be resolved. I also felt my contribution to it
would increase the chances of there being a resolution. First
thing I did was go through all of the paperwork involved, including hundreds of pages of letters Jesperson had written to me
about the case over the years (to see how consistent he'd been),
and all of the letters Haley, FIS Paul Moody, and Jesperson had

exchanged since. Between 2012 and 2014, Jesperson played hard-to-get with Florida. He'd claim he wanted to help, but didn't do much to back up his word. My thought was Jesperson had been holding on to information. Afraid of facing the death penalty, he knew identifying markers about Jane he hadn't shared. Conversely, if this was true, why hadn't he, like many serials in this same position, used that carrot to deal the death penalty off the table?

"Do you *know* who she is?" I asked, looking for a starting point. "No bullshit here. I need to know."

"No."

"Come on. You have a history of hiding licenses and rifling through your victims' luggage and personal belongings. Who is she, man? Let's do this. Be a 'good guy' here. If for no one else, do it for me."

"I have no idea. All I know is what I've been saying: Suzette, Suzanne, Susan, maybe Sue-Ellen. We met in Tampa. She was coming from Miami, heading to Lake Tahoe. She pissed me off. I strangled the bitch."[8]

I got my hands on the original reports, including an interview FDLE SA Glen Barberree conducted with Jesperson in 1996. I again resisted telling Jesperson. Instead, I questioned him about Jane with the knowledge the FDLE had uncovered, along with Jesperson's version of events all those years ago.

What he'd told me—in letters, Video Visit chats, and calls—did not differ all that much from what he'd said throughout the years, nor what he'd told the FDLE in 1996.

"They gave me their word about the death penalty," I told him. "They will not prosecute."

I was pushing the bar on this; I never got that promise. With his help, finding Jane's family was a possibility; without it, not a chance.

---

[8]There has been some confusion about where Jane Doe was heading; Jesperson also said it could have been Reno. He used both during various interviews over the years. With me, recently, he's certain it was Lake Tahoe. According to SA Haley, "I believe it is going to be Reno. That was in his first statements and in his first letters. It later became Lake Tahoe and in the one letter he wrote as the Happy Face Killer, he said, 'Reno.'"

Jesperson had become a decent artist in prison. Could he draw a portrait from memory of Jane? If so, FIS Paul Moody could take that drawing and, armed with the reports, autopsy, and Jane's actual skull, construct a computerized rendering of Jane similar to the clay busts used in forensic-art identification. Moody could then send Jesperson the computer composite images and, gauging his reaction, tweak the image to Jesperson's specs until an accurate composite of Jane emerged, one that the man who had killed her agreed with.

"How can you be so sure?" Jesperson asked, adding that he'd been unable to get any Florida cop to write to him on official law enforcement agency stationery telling him they weren't interested in seeking the death penalty or further prosecution.

It was policy, I told him. Cops don't write to convicts using department letterhead. Haley had explained this to Jesperson in a letter.

"You're serving all those life sentences," I said. "It won't matter. They just want to find her family and bring her home."

"I want to help."

"Then do it."

"I trust you, Phelps."

"What about Phelan?" I asked.

"[Screw] him. He does *not* tell me what to do—he *never* did. I make up my *own* mind."

Phelan wasn't even his official lawyer any longer.

"You're doing a good thing here. You always talk about people not understanding you. The general public looking at you and judging you as some sort of monster—only a killer. This can begin to change that perspective. You follow me?"

He didn't sound convinced. "I guess" was all Jesperson said in response.

PERSPECTIVE IS EVERYTHING WHEN trying to analyze a serial killer: his motivations, what drove him to it, carried him through the kill, how he turned into a killer, and the way in which he views life in general. That said, we have to keep in mind that serial killers are manipulative, glib, charismatic, and superficial, entirely devoid of remorse or empathy. When they lie, those untruths feel real to them and, subsequently, to us. We're easily fooled, because serials are experts at playing psychological mind games.

To our advantage, however, difficult, abstract concepts that non-psychopaths can manage their way around quite easily are where psychopaths become confused and get tripped up by.

"Do you argue with the idea that you were a professional killer?" I asked Jesperson one afternoon, trying to mine deeper into who he is. I was looking for him to think differently, to begin to consider empathy—even if he didn't *feel* it—or, at least, view himself under a different light.

"I would. I *knew* what I was doing. I wasn't bashful about what I did. No one really knew what I was doing because I was good at it."

When we got onto the subject of God—good versus evil—Jesperson would often wax philosophical in some of his letters and on the telephone. Not that anyone would agree with his sometimes bizarre cultural and spiritual viewpoints or ideas, or even make sense out of them. However, as part of my research, I wanted to understand where he stood on the larger questions of spirituality and faith, especially as my own faith was sinking. I'd read in some of his old letters to the media and other writings long before we met that he was a God-fearing man. I wanted to know where his faith stood these days. We've all heard the stories of Bible-thumping prisoners finding the light and falling into Jesus' waiting arms. I wondered where Jesperson was in this regard.

"Not really [a believer]," he responded. "I've read the Bible. I think the Bible is a book orchestrated for the fact of giving [people] hope there's something beyond death. I think the book was written by people who were persecuted and they decided to write something so they could be forgiven along the way, when the only one who could forgive them would be God. [The Bible] is kind of an okey-dokey type story. You commit a crime and the only one that is going to forgive you is the guy that's going to allow you into heaven? No, I don't really think there's a God."

The Devil is hard to kill and certainly would never give God any credit, I thought. Even though my faith had taken a tremendous blow by this point, I was still firm on the conviction that there was something beyond death, and I had not totally abandoned the Church or God. To think that this—our lives—is the end, I will always believe, is an egotistical, narcissistic stance—that we have evolved into the superior beings of the universe is beyond the megalomania Jesus has often been accused of by the atheistic community. Still, my faith was dissolving in a pool of indifference; I had entirely stopped going to Mass. I wasn't on one side or the other, but in limbo, not thinking about God or sins or eternal damnation.

"So what about evil?" I asked. If there was no God, "how do you explain evil in this world? Not necessarily an evil doer, like Satan, but an evil *presence*—like *you,* for example?"

He paused. "I . . . I don't believe there's an actual Satan. I believe there's people out there who just have an 'evil' heart and will go out of their way to be evil to people, just because they can."

"And do you believe that you were one of those people?"

No hesitation whatsoever: "I believe that I was a *very* nice guy most of the time, and one that didn't care about people part of the time. I could be evil if I wanted to."

I asked him about ghosts. He'd once told me he saw himself as a ghost—an invisible figure roaming through the world, able to pluck any woman out of society he wanted and end her life. I understood the metaphor, but I wanted clarification.

"Yes, I *was* a ghost. Nobody knew who I was. I was somebody who was there and gone. Nobody had an idea what I was—if I even existed in the first place. Most of the time, ghosts . . . that's what they are—a figment of our imaginations. And, of course, if evil happens, somebody *must* be responsible, so why not blame the ghost?"

Jesperson had pulled aside a friend one day in 1994 and told him, "I'm a serial killer. I have killed women. No one can stop me."

The friend laughed it off.

"See, right there, I was invisible to him as this person, this killer."

We'd routinely discuss the serial killer's opinion of law enforcement. Hollywood projects part of this serial killer–cop relationship as a cat-and-mouse chase. Fiction and film play this up for dramatic purposes, of course. But what was the real world of serial killer versus cop?

"It's *not* cat-and-mouse. It's kind of like us against the public. We do what we're going to do based on luck. Our biggest concern is getting away from the crying eyes of the public. The police are not even in the picture, as far as we're concerned. It's all about *perception*. I don't think there's a killer out there that actually goes out and pokes at the police, like a rattlesnake, waiting for the police to strike back. We live on the basis of getting away with it."

I brought up his letters to the media. How would he explain those in the context he'd just described?

"When I sent those letters off, I just thought the police made a mistake. I was trying to tell them they needed to reinvestigate this case [Bennett]. I wasn't trying to egg them on. They took it as the cat-and-mouse thing, like here I was trying to play games. I *wasn't* trying to play games. I was trying to get them to reopen a case that was wrongfully prosecuted."

I STRUGGLED WITH GOING behind Jesperson's back. Cops are funny. I place them in two categories: down-to-earth and professional; guarded and by brass tacks. The latter are hard to deal with, not by any fault of their own. They're good people and loyal. I respect that. My anguish in going to Moody and Haley, two cops I trusted more than most I'd worked with, was not rooted in disappointing Jesperson over deceiving him. It was based on the anxiety I felt not being true to the journalistic screed I'd signed up for, a dilemma that brought me even more inner conflict.

After talking one day to Moody, a guy who made me feel like what I had to say mattered and my help was appreciated and productive, I sat in my office staring at a photograph of the dirty, tattered, and torn floral-patterned dress they'd found Jane Doe Florida's remains melted into. To look at what was left of this poor young woman, just a small lock of her hair on a skull sitting on the floor of the woods, unrecognizable (she'd not been found for three months), it occurred to me that my obligation was to Jane and her family. Not Jesperson. Not Moody. Not the FDLE. What if someone had information about my sister-in-law's murder that could help her case?

Screw journalistic integrity to a serial killer, I thought. *I want this girl to have a headstone, a name. I want her family to know where she is and what happened. She was loved by someone. She deserves to rest.*

Her family deserved answers. Any way I could get them. I needed to do whatever I could to make sure Jesperson manned up. Didn't matter what anybody else—or the freakin' academic, bow tie–wearing journalism police—thought. This was about Jane Doe, a victim, and her family. Lying to a murderer was part of the game.

I spoke to Moody soon after, asking him if there was more I could be doing. How could I help move this along?

"Well, we were hoping, at some point, Jesperson would draw a portrait of what he remembers Jane looking like," Moody said. "We've been trying to get that from him."

"I can get it done."

Next time I spoke to Jesperson, I told him to do whatever Florida asked. "Draw that fucking picture of her and do it as soon as possible. End of story. If not, I will never answer another phone call from you."

"I trust you, Phelps. I do. They've been pushing me on this. Moody wants a sketch or a painting. I've been putting it off."

"You're an artist. *Do* it."

KEN ROBINSON AND I spoke. We'd become close friends. I'm not one to keep "pals." I have acquaintances, sure, but no "best buddy," nothing like that. My cameraman on *Dark Minds,* Peter Heap, and I became best "mates." But Peter lives in Australia. With Ken, I could share theories and ideas, and Ken would always be honest to a fault with me. Plus, all that law enforcement experience Ken brought to the table—access to that doesn't hurt in my line of work. If I needed to find someone, maybe certain information about someone, I'd give it to Ken and he'd come back with details I could've never uncovered on my own.

Last time we chatted about Jane, Ken mentioned an idea. He explained: "I've been searching databases for missing women that fit the Jane Doe profile. I've come up with several candidates."

These would be actual photographs and narratives from the Doe Network and other online resources missing people are put into. With a few good matches from Ken, I could stick in a few placebo girls I knew weren't connected to Jane and send Jesperson a photo lineup.

"Send those girls to me," I told Ken.

"One of these girls, Ylenia Carrisi, her story, her look, match up pretty well with what we know about Jane from Jesperson and those reports," Ken explained. I could hear in Ken's voice a modicum of hope. He was excited about Ylenia. I'd not heard Ken sound like this before. He had something.

"No shit. You found one?" That name: *Carrisi*. I'd heard it somewhere before.

"Yeah, but there's one anomaly I'll have to explain. Still, all else fits nearly perfect—including the damn dress she was wearing and where she was heading."

42

JANE DOE, FLORIDA

"For there is nothing lost, that may be found, if sought."
—Edmund Spenser, *The Faerie Queene*

S HE WANTED TO KNOW WHERE HE WAS HEADING.

"North," he said.

"Where, exactly, north?" she asked.

"I don't know yet."

It was August 1994. The exact date is in question, but it had to be between August 7, after Jesperson left Waterbury, Connecticut, at 6:45 A.M. (according to his log), and August 15, the next entry he listed, putting him heading north out of Tampa. My guess—and Dennis Haley agrees—is somewhere near August 10, plus or minus a few days. Jesperson told me he'd driven from Waterbury back to Spokane, then back into the South. The dates line up with his memory.

In Tampa, Jesperson dropped off a load of Kaiser Aluminum coils. According to him, after making the Tampa delivery, he parked at the 76 Truck Stop on U.S. 301, outside downtown Tampa. There were two separate areas for parking: to the south, a traditional lot with diagonal, overnight spaces; to the north, a fuel island with slotted spaces; beyond that, showers and a convenience-type store with a restaurant. He parked in one of the designated eighteen-wheeler spaces to the south. His plan was to call dispatch in Spokane and get his next pickup.

Jane Doe stood by the 76 Truck Stop door into the store, talking to a security guard. Later, Jesperson mentioned "karma" and "fate" being at play here as they crossed paths, a familiar situation in his opportunistic victim-selection process.

In her right hand, Jane gripped a metal trolley (a device similar to a handcart). It had a long handle and two small wheels. A piece of carry-on luggage was bungeed to the trolley, and she pulled it along wherever she went. She had an RCA boom box. Jane was a pretty girl, approximately five-four, petite, about 110 pounds, "brown-black hair . . . with bleached streaks," running past her shoulders. She wore a "Windbreaker jacket, a long dress imprinted with large patches of brown and greens, as well as [a] floral pattern." Hemmed at the ankles, the dress had "groups of buttons . . . arranged in a decorative rosette pattern." Jesperson thought: *Late twenties, early thirties.* The medical examiner's report (the least accurate, according to investigators) indicated forties, maybe thirty-five to fifty-five. In addition, "She smelled," Jesperson told me. "I wasn't really interested in giving anybody a ride—especially someone that reeked so badly."

After Jane asked, he pointed to his new truck, a 1992 blue Peterbilt monster of a machine, #2392, with a forty-eight-inch sleeper cabin, forty-inch bed, where he spent most of his time.

In one of his eleventh-hour admissions to me after Les died, Jesperson said he kept a length of rope and a roll of duct tape inside the sleeper cabin. "To strap things down and plug up holes in tarps."

"What else?"

"To bind the hands, mouth, and feet of my victims, Phelps. It's true."

This had been something he hadn't wanted to admit to me. Up until then, he'd said the press and police played up this portion of his story.

"That's my truck right there," Jesperson told Jane. "But I'm not leaving right now. Won't be for another hour and a half to two hours. I have to find out first where I'm headed."

After their brief conversation, he walked into the truck stop and called dispatch. "The boss isn't in yet," the operator in Spokane told him.

He turned around after hanging up, and there she was, standing in back of him.

"Where the hell are you *really* going?" Jane asked. In one 1996 report, Jesperson said she might have spoken with a slight Latina accent, which could be mistaken for Italian, Greek, or Cuban. She was so dirty, he thought she'd been sleeping outside; her curly hair was ruffled, snarled, and frizzy. Her dress was wrinkled, worn, and torn up. He thought she might have been homeless, even running away from someone, or getting out of a bad situation.

"Probably to the West Coast or into the Northwest," he told her. "I'm not sure yet." Frustrated, he walked over to a table and sat down. "I need to eat breakfast."

She sat across from him.

"Where are *you* headed?" he asked.

"I'm trying to get to Lake Tahoe (could be Reno)."[9]

After thinking it through, he gave her "the option" to go with him. Totally up to her. He never begged "them" to come along, he made clear. He considered Jane, like most of the others, to be a "lot lizard." These were women who hung around truck stops—the marginalized. He felt they all saw him as a "sugar daddy," he once told law enforcement. They wanted nothing more than to take what they could from him, and it made him angry.

While sitting with her, talking, eating, he thought about his "problem," that dark "history" following him around. He didn't "want to deal" with it anymore.

"I never went out and chased these people down," he told me. Same as this particular Jane Doe, *they* had walked into *his* life.

These people.

Jane got up and walked away. Then she returned to the table "two or three times" as Jesperson ate. She pestered him about when he was leaving, where he was going.

---

[9]Reno and Lake Tahoe are thirty-seven miles apart, less than an hour's drive.

He didn't answer. He ordered more coffee. She'd gone to the "phone room" after getting up without a word for a third time, though she never said who it was that she called. He watched Jane as she left the restaurant, before coming back in to use the phone a second time. She had "walked around the parking lot" as though lost and looking for someone.

"Tea," she asked for, sitting across from him five minutes later.

"We sat and talked and she seemed like she had a pretty head on her shoulders, as far as mentality," he told law enforcement. The "others" didn't carry luggage. Jane had a bag, which told Jesperson she was heading to, or leaving, someplace. When they have luggage, he explained, "You kind of wonder where they come from, where they live—and you *know* you can't do it [kill]."

Orders from dispatch came. Jesperson was told to head north into Cairo, Georgia, pick up a load of electrical conduit, and haul it to Boise, Idaho. His log ends at August 15, 1994, and doesn't pick up again until October 1, 1994, putting him in Sinclair, Wyoming. So there's no way to tell if Boise was actually on the schedule. One report claimed he was on his way to Nevada (Jesperson was seeing a woman who lived outside Las Vegas), while Jesperson recalled heading into "the Northwest."

"Look," he told me during our last prison visit when I asked about logistics, "I kept three, sometimes four, logs. You have to keep in mind, the log you have is the log my trucking company *chose* to give the police so *they* could stay out of trouble."

Totally plausible.

"That's where I'm going," Jesperson told Jane. "Georgia to Boise."

"Where is that as compared to Lake Tahoe (Reno)?" she asked.

"Once I get loaded and I head that way, you'll be *that* much closer to [Nevada] if you went with me than if you stayed here, but that's up to you." He offered to put word out on the CB when they were closer to Idaho to see if he could find Jane a ride with another trucker.

He walked off to get directions, leaving the decision up to her.

Armed with his route, as Jesperson headed toward his truck, Jane followed.

"All right," Jesperson said. "Get in."

He looked around.

"I made mental note that no one saw her step into my truck."

THAT CALL I MADE after returning from my Portland/Salem trip to see Jesperson was to a psychologist. I needed to get in and do some serious inventory. I'd just turned forty-nine, on my way to fifty, a scary milestone for a guy who considers himself young at heart, mind, body, and soul. When I was a kid, a man of fifty had gray hair, wore a thick sweater, and sat in *his* living-room recliner doing crosswords, his reading glasses down on the tip of his nose like Mother Goose. He took naps, smelled medicinal, and stunk up the house with BENGAY. He took hour-long shits with the newspaper, went to bed after *Wheel of Fortune* and *Jeopardy.* That was not me. Strange I was stressing over this—I know, age is just a number!—and I never saw it coming. Pile onto that some personal issues at home, all I'd been through with Jesperson and the temperamental feelings of sympathy I'd developed for him, a desire to hate and cut him out of my life, which wasn't beckoning, and, well, some therapy was in order. No one could argue that.

I wasn't on the verge of drinking, mind you, as some around me began to ask with that judgmental, eyebrow-raised, you're-an-alcoholic stare. I'd decided long ago this body and mind of mine is allergic to booze. It was a struggle early on for me, but as decades of sobriety added up and my abstinence became a part of who I am, I wanted nothing to do with drinking. Alcohol, I knew from experience, has no mercy. Once it secures its talons into you, and you submit, your life is a shitstorm—that is, *if* it allows you to live. I was treading water, trying to find a safe pocket of air, no doubt about it; but I had a handle on my demons. The therapy was a way to sort it all out and get on with life.

Near the end of my final prison visit with Jesperson, I brought up Les, mentioning how I'd never gotten the chance to interview him and regretted not acting sooner.

This comment made Jesperson pause, look down at the small wooden coffee table between us. I'd bought him a Mountain Dew and pack of peanut butter bars from the vending machines. He took a gulp, a bite, a deep breath.

"What is it?"

"My father . . . that whole thing. Let's not go there anymore."

Perhaps for the first time, I realized there was no dream left for Keith Jesperson. He was a man, like all serial killers, born incomplete. A psychopath, yes. But beyond that clinical diagnosis, something else was missing from this man. All that rejection and ridicule he claimed his father projected onto him—real or imagined—had fed into an obsessive desire for power and control: over me, the public, the cops, his lawyers, his victims. It was something he couldn't change and didn't understand.

I brought him around to the topic of who Keith Jesperson, the serial killer, is. Or, at least, my calculation after all the research I'd done. I'd noticed the five years we'd spent together produced growth in him I hadn't realized until this visit. Not that he'd suddenly become a sympathetic, morally adjusted human being, but he'd started to think about who he was in a bigger context and under a different light. I told him one of the most powerful stories he'd shared with me that explained how his mind worked was the divorce court scene, in which he witnessed how much pain his kids were in and stood in front of them feeling warm and fuzzy because of their suffering.

"You wrote about that?" he said, surprised.

"Of course."

"I have no idea why I felt that way, Phelps."

"Do you think you're broken?"

He looked down at the unwaxed floor below our feet. The visiting room was empty. Quiet, almost still. There was no guard breathing down our backs, no one listening on the phone, no one reading our mail. We could talk freely. He took a long minute. Then, still not looking at me, he began: "I remember playing blocks with my boy . . . you know, those wooden building blocks." He explained how his boy would excitedly build up the blocks, laughing, smiling, just enjoying a bit of childhood fun with his dad. Without the boy knowing, Jesperson said, he'd flick the bottom corner block and watch the wooden mountain tumble. His boy became more frustrated and upset each time his dad did this. As the child built up the blocks, Jesperson kept knocking them down. The boy finally had a fit and cried.

"It felt good," he told me, still staring at the floor. "I'd gotten a kick out of my son's pain. My daughter, Melissa, wants to paint me as some sort of evil dad who killed kittens in front of his children and held these deep, dark secrets about killing people. But that's just not how it was."

As he finished the story, he looked at me. His eyes welled up. He didn't cry. I'd never seen him look or sound so serious. I could sense that, in this moment, he had feelings.

"I didn't want to hurt my son," Jesperson concluded. "I never wanted to hurt people. Not anyone. I don't know why I am this way."

On this day, in that moment, I believed him.

WITH JANE DOE RIDING shotgun, Jesperson drove north on I-75 for eighty miles, entering Wildwood, Florida. He pulled into a truck stop, fueled, and parked.

"I'm going in to grab a shower. If you want one, you can grab one. If you want something to eat, get it now, because we have to leave."

He sensed Jane was worried he might take off without her. Her luggage was stowed inside the truck in a place she didn't have access to.

"She watched everything I did."

After showering, he noticed she didn't have any grooming implements that most women carry: comb, brush, makeup. She shook her hair out and sat down with him at a table inside the stop.

"You want to eat?" he offered. "You can have whatever you want."

She ordered the all-you-can-eat spaghetti—three plates.

"When was the last time you ate?"

She didn't want to talk about it.

"Can we go down to Miami before we get loaded up in Georgia?" she asked.

Although there was zero chance he would consider this, he asked why.

"I have some stuff down there I would like to retrieve before I go [west]."

"That's almost [six-hundred miles] round-trip! I don't . . . *Listen* to me. I can't go out of the way. Just because you're in here with me doesn't mean you can start running me here and there."

This one question from Jane made him think about the women he'd murdered: *They all want something from me.*

Realizing she'd hit a nerve, Jane backed off; she agreed to go to Georgia and then west from there, and never mention Miami again.

Jesperson drove into Cairo, Georgia, just over the Florida state line.

"She slept most of the way," he told the FDLE. She'd had a shower. Ate. She was clean and full. "I told her that the bed is mine, too. We got some kind of sleeping arrangement." Per his normal routine, Jesperson brought up sex. Was that going to be a problem?

"Sleeping arrangements?" she asked. "I have no problem with you in the truck with me in the bed—*with* your clothes on."

Jane's position was clear: no sex.

As Jesperson loaded his truck in Cairo, he watched as she stood near the telephone on the dock. At one point, she picked up the receiver, as if to call someone. Jesperson walked over. Tapped Jane on the shoulder, startling her, and she "gave a quick scream."

"It's time to go," he said.

Happy Face was under the impression that whomever she'd been trying to call, Jane could not reach. In fact, everywhere they stopped en route to Cairo, she used the phone. She was trying to call someone, he assumed (she never told him), in Reno/Lake Tahoe to let them know she was on her way.

With his load strapped down, Jesperson headed south, back

into the Florida Panhandle via Interstate 10. Heading west on the 10, he drove "for about an hour or so" and pulled into a rest stop. They were about two-and-a-half hours east of Pensacola. Looking for a spot to park the rig, he noticed "three cop cars," one parked next to the other.

"As a truck driver, I always know where cops are," he told the FDLE. "Not just because I kill people."

With no other available spaces, Jesperson parked behind the security kiosk, not too far from the cops.

"She was [lying] there up against the wall in the sleeper. And I just crawled right in, laid in right behind her, and just started to go to sleep."

Then, out of nowhere, he claimed that "she started screaming."

He was "very aware" of security and those cops parked nearby. "And I was also very aware of what my past history had been. And I didn't want no altercation, whether it was true or not. So I just put my hand on her to shut her up—to *tell* her to shut up."

Within "three minutes," Jesperson said, "she was dead."

He looked out his side window to see if security or the police had heard anything.

They hadn't.

He drove a few exits west toward Pensacola, pulled onto an exit ramp, stopped, and dumped Jane off the road in the wild weeds. She would be found in three months by an inmate who, collecting garbage on the side of the highway, walked into the brush to urinate.

Jesperson rifled through Jane's suitcase. He found a set of tarot cards and a few pieces of clothing, nothing more. He drove into town. Located the first Dumpster he could find in back of a strip mall restaurant and trashed the suitcase and trolley. He kept her boom box.

43

ALL IN

"Those who seek to do forensic art should accept the
responsibility with seriousness. . . . The victims of violent
crimes . . . deserve your full efforts."
—Karen T. Taylor, *Forensic Art and Illustration*

*P*AUL MOODY HAS ONE OF THOSE SOFT, PLEASANT-SOUNDING VOICES:
deep baritone, comforting, late-night talk radio–worthy. He projects an earnest air, conjuring the paternal, neighbor-next-door
type. With his receding silver-brown hairline and gentle overall
demeanor, there's a reticence about Moody. Being around him,
you feel safe, calm—and yet, at the same time, it's clear that the
tactical pencil in Moody's shirt pocket and the Glock .40 strapped
to his hip are weapons the six-foot, two-hundred-pound Illinois
native would have no trouble using with faultless accuracy if the
situation warranted it.

Moody's ties with the Jane Doe case date back to 2007, when he
was employed by the Illinois State Police (ISP). FDLE SA Ken
Pinkard had reopened the Jane Doe investigation and contacted
Moody, who was known nationwide as a forensic reconstruction
artist, and was also on the Certification Board for Forensic Art
with the International Association for Identification. Besides,
Dennis Haley knew Moody from both having started their law enforcement careers with the Danville (Illinois) Police Department.

Moody's path had taken him from the Danville PD to Kansas
City, before stepping away from police work for a period. It was

1985 when Moody moved back to Danville and went to work for the ISP, where he stayed for the next twenty-five years, filling the role of trooper, sergeant, and a host of other jobs—including SWAT—before retiring an acting master sergeant.

Throughout his tenure, Moody was "never really a big fan of forensic art." The old Smith and Wesson Identi-Kit, he explained, was something he had little use for, adding, "It seemed generic." But a friend in the ISP's crime scene investigation (CSI) division, however, learned how to draw and became part of the ISP's forensic-art detail. "You know what," that friend told Moody one day, "I'm buried. You think you could give me a hand with some of this work?"

Heading toward retirement, already an artist (landscapes and portraits), Moody considered the offer. Bringing unknown victims back to their families, Moody felt, along with helping to identify rapists, murderers, and predators of all types, was a noble cause.

Still, Moody thought brass would never allow him to leave his job and step into a forensic-art gig. As it happened, however, the state had recently created a mentoring program within the department. So Moody's friend began training him.

By 2008, now retired from the ISP, Moody relocated to Florida and went to work for the PBSO as a forensic artist. Any skull, Moody explained, "gives you about a seventy percent road map. So you have to take other things into consideration. It's not an exact science, but works well enough to have some success."

With Moody and Haley convinced that Jesperson, under my guidance, wanted to help, Haley sent Jesperson a black-and-white rendering of Jane Doe that Moody had completed in 2007 for SA Ken Pinkard while still with the ISP. Jane appeared to be middle-aged. Her hair pulled back, her nose large, her facial features slim and taut. She looked older than what Jesperson had claimed and what Moody knew after familiarizing himself with the reports and Jane's skull. What they didn't tell Jesperson was that the images created from this particular black-and-white rendering, between 2007 and 2014, had failed to yield any significant leads.

Jesperson sent the sketch back to Haley with an emphatic no: "Not even close. She's too old." She also looked Native American. Jesperson had been firm: Jane was white.

Haley called Moody and asked him to initiate a dialogue with Jesperson. Both being artists, Jesperson and Moody needed to devise a plan to generate an image Jesperson was comfortable with.

Whenever he sat down to create a computer rendering or pencil sketch of any Jane/John Doe, Paul Moody relied not only on the skull, but police and ME reports, interviews, and any other data he could get his hands on. Thus, it was unprecedented to have the actual murderer help identify one of *his* Jane Doe victims.

Back when Moody was with the ISP, FDLE SA Ken Pinkard had sent him all they had on Jane, including photos of a clay reconstruction done in 1994, just after Jane was found by that prison highway worker. As he fell back into the case, reevaluating those twenty-plus-year-old materials, the one fact that struck Moody was that Jane's skull and the medical examiner's report clashed. The ME claimed Jane was between thirty-five and fifty-five years old, but Moody was certain after a careful study—including complicated measurements—of her skull and mandible (lower jawbone) that she was much younger. Probably in her early or late twenties, as Jesperson had maintained.

As we discussed the reconstruction and drawing I'd convinced him to do for Moody, Jesperson said during a call near this time, "One of the worst things they could do is put the wrong drawing of her out into the public forum." His fear was that once an incorrect bell had been rung, there would be no way to stop the reverberation. In fact, Jesperson was onto something—that 1994 clay bust of Jane had not generated one lead.

"The clay reconstructions do work and are still being used regularly," Moody clarified. "Some think they are the only way to go. Like anything else, some clay work is good and some is poor. Karen T. Taylor"—a world renowned forensic artist and consultant on CBS's *CSI*—"came up with the two-dimensional technique and I adapted it for digital work in Adobe Photoshop. I feel that digital work is faster. It doesn't alter the skull/mandible by adding a foreign substance (clay) to it. And I prefer the end result over clay."

As Moody continued his work, several issues arose. One, the 1994 bust portrayed, same as Moody's 2007 sketch, a Latina or Native American female, with features that failed to compare with the actual skull measurements Moody had since made. There was more "art" than science involved in the bust, in Moody's opinion. Plus, Jesperson had rejected it.

They needed to start over, from scratch.

Armed with help from the man who had stared Jane in the eyes and killed her, Moody needed a drawing from Jesperson to complete his work. The idea was to create an entire new set of digitally rendered images based on all of the (new and old) information, some of which included my interviews with Jesperson and my push to get him to help with a drawing of his own.

Jesperson sent Moody a letter, telling the cop he needed a picture as a baseline to begin his portrait.

Unbeknownst to me, Moody sent Jesperson a popular magazine, loaded with pictures of various female celebrities. Maybe Jesperson could find someone close to Jane and use that picture as a starting point.

As Jesperson worked on his first drawing, he and Moody exchanged letters. The plan was for Jesperson to deliver his best rendition based on his memory and the pictures Moody provided. Then Moody would take the drawing and, using it as a guide, along with Jane's skull and other investigative materials, turn it into a digitally rendered side and front profile, full-length body view (Jane wearing that floral-patterned dress; a Brandywine replica dress Moody had actually found on eBay), and a computer bust, all of which, including hair and eye color, would be signed off on by Jesperson. Both cop and serial killer, with me in the middle managing, wrote back and forth, the goal being to come up with a portrait of Jane.

* * *

THERAPY DID ME A world of good. Going in, I honestly felt lost, like I was swimming, searching for dry land. After a few sessions and some changes in my life, my head was above water; I was moving toward a new space. Where that space was going to take me, what would be waiting for me, became the unknown part of my journey. But I had a path and a plan. That's all I could ask for.

Part of understanding myself while sitting in the comfortable, safe office space of a therapist, sharing my feelings, made me realize that Jesperson's quest for evil was a way for him to avoid any anxiety and despair he'd suffered for being a failure, a man who could not keep a woman happy and take care of his family the way he should have. Within his marriage, Jesperson became the embodiment of what his wife did *not* love or need in her life at the time. Furthermore, Jesperson's victims were a means for him to explore, exploit, and maintain the control and dominance he lacked throughout his life. He struggled to correct what he believed his wife and father had stripped from him.

It all began to feel like an excuse to me, rather than an answer. A cop-out. Keith Jesperson couldn't face the fact that he was a disappointment to everyone in his life. He did not do anything to change who he was—even after he realized his flaws. He is a guy who, I've come to believe, suffers from chronic myopia where it pertains to his victims. Most of his writings attack the very foundation of justice, truth, morality, sympathy, and empathy. He would rather try to convert a reader to his twisted, wicked logic and ideals than try to understand why he killed and why he hates women.

Maybe it's *not* his fault. And genetics plays a role. Studying his recollections, I found Jesperson often played the fool, the child who was picked on and bullied (despite his massive size), the boy made fun of and ridiculed, further circumventing responsibility and shirking the blame onto his victims and the people in his life, especially Les.

"What's going to happen to Raven?" he asked during our last prison visit. He sensed I was almost finished writing the book.

I told him I didn't know.

As I began to reexamine my life, there was no way I could maintain any type of so-called friendship with a serial killer. I was slowly becoming another one of Keith Hunter Jesperson's victims. He was beating me down, willingly or not. I felt like a shell of a human being at times. Totally wiped. Emotionally drained.

I needed to get this psychopath out of my life for good.

44

THE MIGHTY MISSISSIPPI

"Not all those who wander are lost."
—J.R.R. Tolkien, *The Fellowship of the Ring*

KEN ROBINSON HAD NEVER BEEN A "MISSING PERSONS" INVESTIGA-tor, though he'd worked a handful of those cases with the NYPD: "I've actually found a few missing/kidnapped people myself."

Throughout his career, Ken had passed photos of missing people, mostly women and young girls. Seeing the flyers plastered on squad room walls of every precinct he went in and out of changed Ken. He'd stop and stare. Over the years, the photos became "like wallpaper" hovering over the framework of his life. It was a tragedy that *any* kid was abducted, went missing, or ran away, Ken felt. He'd look at one photo after the next and wonder if the child had ever made it home.

When I asked Ken to become my missing persons hunter, he went back to all those moments he felt he could help, but other law enforcement obligations prevented him, saying, "This was my chance."

We ate lunch in Palm Beach one afternoon after a meeting at the PBSO with Moody and Haley. We'd flown down to Florida to sit with both in the forensic investigator's Batcave that Moody works out of, there to talk it all through. Moody and Haley had also come to accept and appreciate the help Ken, a fellow cop, of-fered. The five of us—including Jesperson—made a great team for this task.

First thing Moody did during our meeting was hand me Jane's skull: "That's her—basically what's left, anyway."

Here was an exact scaled replica—right down to the look and feel—of Jane's skull and lower jaw. Her teeth were in perfect shape. Her cranium and cheekbones flawless. No bigger than a honeydew melon, her head felt small in my hands.

"Take that back to Connecticut with you," Moody said. "We want you to have it for all your help."

I was humbled by the gesture.

During our lunch after meeting with Moody and Haley, "You're an investigator, Ken," I said. "Robberies. Car thefts. Rapes. Murders. Missing people. You have that instinct. It's in your blood, brother. I know you can find a few solid leads here."

Ken took on the task of searching for candidates fitting the Jane Doe criteria so I could turn around and put them into that photo lineup and present it to Jesperson. As Ken began, the work brought him into a difficult place he'd not expected: the heartbreak of the families, not to mention the sheer numbers of actual missing people in the United States. The National Missing and Unidentified Persons System (NamUs) claims, on average, 90,000 people are missing at any given time, about 33,000 of those children under the age of eighteen.

"Story after story after story," Ken told me. "A person leaving and never being seen again. Reading all these narratives, searching for our Jane Doe, I became overwhelmed by the numbers and lost lives."

I could see the pain on his face. Ken is a big dude. Tough. Bouncer-type. He has kids himself. This work had rattled him.

"What have you found?"

Ken pulled up an image on his iPhone, passed it to me. Ylenia Carrisi: five-seven, 120 pounds. Carrisi had light brown/blond hair, green eyes, and brunette eyebrows. She was thin and in great physical shape. An Italian citizen speaking fluent English, Ylenia was twenty-three years old the last time anyone had heard from her. She'd walked away from a New Orleans "low-rent hotel," wearing a floral-patterned dress, leaving behind her personal possessions (identification, specifically). It was January 6, 1994. For about a week leading up to that day, she'd been staying with an older man, a French Quarter street musician. After she went missing, the man tried to pay the hotel bill using traveler checks made out in her name.

Ken explained how he'd found Carrisi and why he was interested in her as our Jane Doe. He'd discovered her months before our trip to Florida and had done a lot of research into her life. He explained that although she'd been living as a vagabond, her story was anything but that of a poor, homeless street girl.

"She was one of the first missing girls I came across," Ken said. "From all you've told me, from all the interviews I listened to between you and Jesperson talking about his Florida Jane Doe, from all I've learned about Ylenia, we might have found her."

In many circumstances, Americans who go missing have family members step up and submit familial DNA samples so a hit can be matched if a body turns up—like Jesperson's Jane Doe—somewhere. That DNA is then put into the system (Combined DNA Index System [CODIS] and other law enforcement databases). Because Carrisi was from Italy and had come to the United States on vacation, Ken found out, her familial DNA had not been put into the national American databases. That would explain why there had been no connection made between our Jane Doe and Ylenia Carrisi.

"New Orleans?" was my first question. It was not Florida.

"I found out Florida is where she *first* came to for vacation with her family, and it was stated somewhere she was possibly headed *back* to Florida from New Orleans because she was fleeing the city, terribly scared for her life."

That worked.

While researching her case, Ken and I obtained information that placed her in Miami just before that August date when Jesperson met Jane in Tampa. Jesperson's victim, who he claimed went by the name Suzanne, Suzie, Susan, Sue, Sue-Ellen, had told him she needed to go back to Miami in order to grab some of her belongings.

"Ylenia Carrisi told [someone]," explained a source Ken and I developed while looking into her life, "that a couple of men from Miami were looking for her. Not sure what for. Probably failed to pay for some[thing] (at least that's what was thought). Of course, then the mind runs scenarios and maybe they kidnapped her and took her to Miami to 'work' off the debt."

The other part of this was that while she was in New Orleans, she did not want anyone to know of her family origin, the Carrisi name, which held a celebrity, almost Hollywood royalty–like, status in Italy.

"So, because she didn't want people to know her family name, she went by 'Sarah' or 'Susan,'" the same law enforcement source said.

In his 1996 FDLE statement, Jesperson mentioned a Latina or Italian look to Jane. That floral dress. The hair. Her size and shape. Her eyes. The logistics. Now the name.

"The pieces are falling into place," I told Ken.

"I found her listed in the Louisiana repository for unidentified and missing persons," Ken said. "I knew nothing about the Carrisi name then, or who she was, other than the fact she was missing and wore a flowered-print dress, same as our Jane Doe."

Then we started looking at photos of Ylenia Carrisi. There were so many available online because of who she was—and every damn one of them seemed to match Jesperson's description.

Ken also found another missing girl from Louisiana.

"Either of these two could be Jane," he said.

"I like that you are not focusing on just one."

Making sure not to wear blinders, Ken continued searching missing persons databases, reading reports, and making calls to families of some of the women he found, asking questions (without projecting hope). Ken stayed up night after night, watched the sunrise more times than he'd like to admit while, he recalled, "my eyes bled from all the searching and sadness."

At times, he'd close his Mac and think: *How the hell can we find a needle in a haystack as big as the United States?*

It was true. Jane's DNA had been put into all of the databases long ago. No hit. We needed fresh leads. New familial DNA to test. Ylenia Carrisi and the other Louisiana girl were a start.

"More potential matches that haven't been put into the databases," Dennis Haley explained. "New people to come forward, in other words, and say, 'I think Jane Doe is my sister or wife or family member.'"

I e-mailed a lineup Ken had generated (with Carrisi and the other girl part of it) to Moody and Haley. I also prepared one for Jesperson. As that work got started, Ken created a second lineup. I e-mailed that one, too. And as we continued to study her life, more stars aligned. It was clear, for example, that Ylenia Carrisi could have dabbled in the occult, knew people from that "voodoo" culture so prominent in New Orleans, or she had been researching it for some purpose unbeknownst to anyone. This was significant because Jesperson had found tarot cards, along with some odds and ends (a few pieces of clothing) in Jane Doe's suitcase. Confirmed in the 1994 crime scene reports and photos, Jane wore jewelry with a square, two circles and triangle, which, when braised together in the way they were, could be interpreted as an occultist symbol. She also wore two bracelets and a ring: one was either occult-based or Native American, the other a charm bracelet without any charms, and a heart-shaped ring with symbols that could be considered connected to the tarot card, mystic/occult community.

We felt some momentum. Haley, Moody, Ken, and I were excited.

Then, as we dug deeper into her life in New Orleans, we experienced a setback. On January 30, 1994, a security guard at the Audubon Aquarium of the Americas claimed to have encountered a woman fitting Carrisi's description. On the same day she went missing, near 11:30 P.M., while he was conducting his nightly patrols inside Woldenberg Park, on the west bank of the Mississippi River, the guard spied a blond, thin woman sitting on the edge of the pier. About eighteen to twenty-four years old, she wore "a jacket and a floral dress that fell just below the knees."

"Hey, you cannot be here in the park after hours," the security guard told her.

"It doesn't matter," the security guard reported the woman saying. "I belong to the river."

Just after that, without another word, she jumped into the Mississippi and swam into the current. As the security guard called it in, she "began to struggle and ask for help."

A barge came by, kicking up an incredible wake, and the woman was swallowed up into the dark water and never seen again.

Rescuers searched the river. A helicopter was brought in. When it became known to the Carrisi family back in Italy that this could be Ylenia, for whom they'd been searching for three weeks already, the river was dragged.

They found a body—but it was male.

The day after this Mississippi River event was reported, the man Carrisi had roomed with in the low-rent hotel was arrested in connection with her disappearance.

He claimed ignorance. Said he had no idea where she'd run off to. With zero evidence, law enforcement was unable to hold him.

I was disappointed. It felt like Ylenia Carrisi had jumped into the Mississippi River for whatever reason—that this woman could be her.

"We have a report, though, that Ylenia was in Florida *after* January thirtieth," that law enforcement source confirmed.

"No kidding," I said over the phone. "Shit."

"We also found an old photograph of Ylenia wearing almost the same Brandywine dress Jane Doe died in."

45

THE BIG SLEAZY

"Why is it that the scoundrels of the world are
always remembered and the well-bred men completely
forgotten?"
—Don Diego, *The Mark of Zorro* (1974 TV series)

*D*ENNIS HALEY'S CAREER BEGAN IN 1971 WITH THE DANVILLE PD. UP
until he left Danville in 1985, Haley had worn just about every
badge: narcotics, major crimes, patrol. Haley and Moody became
close friends in college and wound up going through the Danville
Academy together. While it was no plan, both found themselves
in Florida later in life, working for different agencies.

After an undercover run in the Florida Keys and a stint during
the Miami "Cocaine Cowboy" days, cold cases became Haley's FDLE
forte. Common public opinion holds that Florida is a mecca for
murder, he said. "It's that we're a transient state. Hell, even serial
killers like to come here. Bundy. Gacy. Christopher 'Beauty Queen
Killer' Wilder. The Alphabet, or Double-Initial Killer, Joe Naso.
They all came here at some point."

As did Happy Face.

Elected Special Agent of the Year (2015), "I was up for Law Enforcement Officer of the Year for the whole state," Haley said, an
unmistakable coping mechanism of a laugh, filled with humility
and charm, within this comment, "but got beat out by a guy who
got shot twice."

Part of his job as an investigator of cold cases included traveling into different jurisdictions and picking up cases county investigators were no longer working on, which was how Haley connected with Jesperson's Okaloosa County Jane Doe. Reading through the reports, Haley felt the potential was there to identify Jane. The fact that the murderer was still alive and in prison, now willing to talk about the case and help with a victim's portrait, Haley concluded, made the potential to identify Jane a strong possibility.

As Haley and Jesperson corresponded during those early years, Jesperson told me in 2012, "All they want to do is identify her and then put me on trial and send me to the chair."

I'd since convinced Jesperson otherwise, of course, but that embedded bitterness against the FDLE still remained, even as he worked on a portrait of Jane Doe for Moody.

"It's not something you ever see," Haley commented. "Journalist, cop, serial killer, all working toward the same goal."

"I've never heard of a case where a serial killer is willing to help law enforcement on this level," Paul Moody added.

Haley got involved with a team that reviewed cold cases: a group of law enforcement from various sheriff's departments getting together on cases. Chuckling again, Haley added, "I pick out the ones I think I can solve." While looking into such cases, in one circumstance after the other, Haley found where simple evidence (DNA, fingerprints), for whatever reason, had never been processed. (There are thousands of these cases throughout the country; DNA and fingerprints sitting in files and drawers waiting to be manually put into the system to see if a hit can be generated.) Some of those cases became a matter of knocking on doors, Haley said, following up with interviews, submitting evidence into the databases and obtaining a hit. "I put in fingerprints from a case once. They'd never submitted them into AFIS (the Automated Fingerprint Identification System) because AFIS wasn't around at the time the case had gone cold. I got a hit right away. The guy was doing time in Texas for a murder there. I went down, sat with him. 'Yeah,' he said, 'I did it.'"

While Haley and Moody conversed, the first color, computerized rendering Moody generated based on Jane's skull, the reports, and Jesperson's interviews and letters looked more in line with the sketch Moody had created in 2007 after first becoming involved. Though different in several ways, Jane looked older than her early twenties and could no doubt pass for a middle-aged white woman, with possible Native American features. Moody created a full-color front profile down to her waist, a side view, and a full-body-length portrait. He put that square, triangle, circle piece of jewelry as a necklace on her and sent everything to Jesperson.

In a letter to me, including the original copies of the first color, computerized images Moody generated, Jesperson wrote, "So here is Paul Moody's *attempt* at Jane Doe." I could sense the sarcasm, scorn, and patronization.

"Well, what's the issue?" I asked next time we spoke.

"Just not her. Not even close."

"Well, get back to work on yours. Tell Moody he's off with this. No big deal. Start over."

"I actually have a magazine I asked for that Moody just sent. It's going to help."

"Then do it. Let me know when you have something."

I hung up and stared at the phone: *Freakin' guy is pathetic.*

WITHOUT TELLING JESPERSON, WE focused on Ylenia Carrisi—and what we learned was astonishing. Ylenia Maria Sole Carrisi was born November 29, 1970, the first child to A-list Italian celebrity singers Romina Power and Albano Carrisi. She was the granddaughter of American matinee actor—and household name—Tyrone "The Mark of Zorro" Power and his actress wife, Linda Christian (Romina's parents). Ylenia Carrisi was a celebrity herself: the Italian Vanna White, a letter-turner on the country's version of *Wheel of Fortune, La Ruota de Fortuna.* She was a singer and actress. YouTube videos show daughter Ylenia and mother Romina singing together, sounding both angelic and inspiring. Ylenia's passion, however, was writing. She aspired to be a serious literary novelist.

Romina was born and raised in Los Angeles, which led us to

consider that Ylenia Carrisi, if she was Jane, had good reason to head west with Jesperson.

"How the hell does a girl like Ylenia wind up living in a scuzzy hotel in New Orleans with that street performer?" I asked Ken. This baffled and bothered me. With her pedigree, how could her life have taken such a 180-degree turn?

"I asked myself the same question."

Carrisi landed in New Orleans a week before she went missing, Ken found out. She'd traveled to New Orleans for a vacation with her parents in July 1993. While on that holiday, she met a street musician she took a liking to, "a fifty-four-year-old cornet player with a Jamaican accent," the *New York Times* reported. When Romina and Albano continued their vacation from New Orleans into Miami, their daughter stayed behind in New Orleans, telling her mom and dad she "wanted to write and paint."

Two days after her parents left New Orleans, Carrisi fled the Big Easy to Miami, "telling her parents she feared two men were trying to drug and kill her," my law enforcement source was certain.

Carrisi had studied in London. During that 1993 holiday break (on December 30) from university, she headed back to New Orleans. She was a dedicated artist, who loved music and painting and that free spiritual movement of mysticism. Our source tracked down her best friend, who confirmed that "Ylenia loved flowery dresses, was into dark magic and tarot cards, and liked junk jewelry." All of which fit into Jesperson's Jane Doe scenario.

By January 1, 1994, she was roaming the streets of the French Quarter in New Orleans hoping to "find characters for a book she was writing," Romina told Italian media after her daughter's disappearance. Her mother said this was the only reason why Ylenia went back to mix it up with the homeless and street culture and live unassumingly as one of them. It was not because she wound up strung out, as some later claimed, but rather embedded herself in that world as research for a book and art project. While back in town, Carrisi hooked up with that street player she'd previously met. One shop owner in the French Quarter told the *Times* that Carrisi "worked 'very hard at being a street person.'"

Romina and Albano did not believe that the security guard— who later "tentatively" identified her in photos—had met up with their daughter; they once thought she was being held hostage somewhere. It would have been unlike her to jump into the Mississippi River. She had way too much going on in her life to abandon it. She wasn't reported to be depressed.

When later asked, the street musician said, "I believe she is safe."

One Elvis-like sighting surfaced in 2014. According to a German magazine, *Freizeit Revue,* an American sheriff reported that Ylenia Carrisi was living in a Greek Orthodox convent outside Phoenix, Arizona. Albano came out afterward and said it was nothing more than "shameful speculation containing not a bit of truth."[10]

Carrisi's body was never recovered from her possible jump into the Mississippi. Because of this, we could not eliminate her as a potential Jane Doe at that point, especially with all of the evidence pointing toward her being in Florida near the time Jesperson met "Suzanne."

"I read the descriptions about her and followed her trail and she keeps popping back up as my top candidate," Ken told me. "What has Jesperson said from the lineup you sent him?"

Jesperson, I explained, circled Carrisi in the lineup I'd mailed, not knowing anything about her and a possible connection. Ken had also found several other girls with Jane Doe potential, some of whom were named Suzette, Sue, Susan, Suzanne, which I had placed in the same lineup.

"'Could be her,' Jesperson told me, referring to Ylenia," I explained to Ken. "He didn't pick out any of the other girls."

---

[10]If you think you have information about Ylenia Carrisi's disappearance, or would like to learn more about her life and see photographs, please visit: http://www.doenetwork.org/cases/1107dfla.html. Contact info is available on the site if you think you have information about her whereabouts or disappearance.

"You're shitting me?" Ken responded.

"No. His entire focus was on Ylenia. He wasn't one hundred percent certain, but said he never could be based on how long it's been."

JESPERSON CAME THROUGH. THE first sketch of Jane he sent Moody was a black-and-white pencil-and-charcoal portrait drawn from just below her neckline, up past the top of her head. He wrote "white woman with blond hair" on the page, signed and dated it "?1994?," the question marks around the date indicating he could not recall when he'd killed her. Her hair was frizzy and thin, flowing wildly outward like fire. Her eyebrows were dark and resembled check marks. Her face oval, her eyes wide open.

Miss Anybody, I thought when I first looked at this image. But then studying it more closely, she had a strange familiarity about her I could not shake for days. I kept the image on my desk. She stared back at me as I worked. This woman looked like someone I knew. Someone I had seen before. I was certain of it. It bothered me that I couldn't figure it out.

The next drawing, a pastel, charcoal-colored pencil, a more in-depth and detailed creation, Jesperson sent to me. In this rendering, which looked similar to the black-and-white he had sent Moody, but with far more detail, her blue eyes looked up toward the sky.

"You realize that in all of the pictures he draws of Jane," Moody said to me during a call, "she is looking up? You know why that is, don't you? 'Cause he's so big, they all had to look up at him. That's how he sees his victims, [he's] looking down on them."

In Jesperson's portrait, Jane's hair was brownish blond. She wore a blue blouse. Her lips red, her skin tone and features Caucasian. He'd sent it to me in a large envelope. I opened the package, pulled the portrait out, and thought: *What the hell is he up to now?*

Next time he called, I lashed out: "Dude, you sent me a picture of Nicole *Fucking* Kidman. What the hell? It looks *just* like her. Is this some sort of a joke to you? Am I just wasting my time?"

I realized that was why the black-and-white sketch seemed so damn familiar, a drawing that could be mistaken for Kidman, but it's not what your mind gravitates to first; whereas, this color pastel he sent me was Kidman's doppelganger.

"All I had to go by was a *People* magazine," he said.

"What?"

Explaining further, he and Moody had talked about Jane looking similar to Kidman and that he would use a *People* magazine Moody had sent him as a baseline to generate ideas. Just so happened, there was a photo of Nicole Kidman in the magazine. However, neither Moody nor Jesperson had taken it upon himself to let me in on any of this.

"Are you messing with us?" I asked.

"No, no, not at all. I needed somewhere to start. I'm not that type of artist to go from memory alone. Kidman looks a lot like my Jane Doe."

This was dangerous ground where trying to develop a composite was concerned. People might only see Nicole Kidman. Jane would be lost forever. I was more than pissed.

"I told him *not* to draw me a likeness of Nicole Kidman," Moody recalled. "That wasn't going to help us. That *wasn't* part of the plan."

Although Jesperson's drawing did look like Nicole Kidman, Moody added, as he got serious about creating a computer digital rendering using the (Kidman) picture Jesperson painted for me and a second portrait Jesperson painted for Moody (another Kidman likeness), along with Jane's skull, all of it would be helpful.

Throughout the spring and summer (2015), Moody and Jesperson exchanged notes back and forth, while I watched over the situation as a quiet third party. Finally, Moody rendered a computer mock-up of Jane he mailed to Jesperson. By then, I had sent Moody the picture Jesperson had painted for me. When Moody superimposed that (Kidman) portrait over the new computer rending identikit he'd completed, correlating the sizes to match, as he focused in and out of the portrait Jesperson painted for me and the identikit he'd created, a near identical match emerged: Jesperson's portrait and the latest computerized identikit Moody created from the drawings and paintings and Jane's skull were one in the same. All of it done, mind you, without Jesperson seeing anything Moody had been working on. And what's more, when we matched those early mock-ups to Ylenia Carrisi, wow, the similarity was undeniable. We all believed—save for Jesperson, who still did not know anything about Carrisi—we were staring at Tyrone Power's granddaughter.

I stood inside Moody's office and gazed at these pictures as Moody focused on the computer model and then back out to the overlaying portrait Jesperson had made for me. I was amazed at how accurate Jesperson's drawing was and how it harmonized with Jane's skull. This, I concluded, was the best portrait of Jane we were going to see. The only thing we needed to do next was send the new images to Jesperson and see what he thought.

46

BRAIN SCAM

"Through others, we become ourselves."
—Lev S. Vygotsky

I EXPLAINED TO JESPERSON WHEN I VISITED HIM IN 2016 THAT THERE was a criminologist in England, now working out of the United States, who was doing some incredible work with the psychopath's brain and a quest to find a "cure for crime." This scientist had conducted brain scans on psychopaths and murderers in American prisons, and had been "among the first researchers to apply the evolving science of brain imaging to violent criminality," the *Guardian* reported. "He conducted PET (positron emission tomography) scans of 41 convicted killers and paired them with a 'normal' control group of 41 people of similar age and profile," the newspaper chronicled. The images "showed metabolic activity in different parts of the brain . . . striking in comparison." Murderers' brains, in particular, displayed "a significant reduction in the development of the . . . 'executive function' of the brain . . ." as "compared with the control group."

Interested in this research, I have always believed that psychopaths are born—or, rather, certain human beings, whatever genetic malfunction takes place, are brought into this world without the empathy or sympathy gene, per se. There's no doubt psychopathy is a developmental disorder. And this imperfection at birth sets up within the framework of that developing and evolving human mind the foundation for him or her to commit, later on, savage acts of repeated, brutal, deadly violence without feeling guilt, shame, or remorse.

The brain scan research and associated theories do not come without a fair share of controversy, and this particular researcher has had naysayers trying to spin his work into junk science. I was not at all concerned with any of that as I began to consider all the evil Jesperson had projected into the world. Thinking about all of the pain he'd caused families, not to mention objectifying, disparaging, and exploiting his victims (even after he murdered them), I cultivated the idea that if I could convince him to donate his brain to science upon his death, the least we could get out of him would be a bit of scientific data. It was not an olive branch, or a way for me to say "do some good for once in your life." Rather, it was a request he could agree to in order to help us further understand the mind of the serial killer.

"Don't say yes or no right now," I told him. "Think about it."

"I'll write you a letter," he said. "Explain how I feel."

"I'm sure you will."

I DROVE TO MY PO box one day after the back-and-forth correspondence between Jesperson and Moody, and the creation of the computerized identikit Moody had sent to Happy Face. Moody had been awaiting Jesperson's approval or any changes he might want to make. And that, along with the latest Ylenia Carrisi developments, gave us a feeling of closure.

There was a yellow card tucked inside my PO box.

What is he sending now?

After collecting the package from the postal clerk, I went to my car and opened it.

There she was: Jane Doe. The last (and final) image Moody had rendered and sent off to Jesperson for his approval. She no longer looked like Nicole Kidman, or a Native American; Jane was now her own person. She had a soul. That necklace—the triangle, circle, and square—wasn't around her neck anymore; it was attached to her waist as a sash, per one of Jesperson's earlier comments. Her hair was frizzy and blond, her features Caucasian.

She could easily pass for Ylenia Carrisi—along with a host of other girls.

Her final look wasn't what made me feel we had come together and developed a photographic image (or as close as we would ever get) of Jane. It was what Jesperson said to me later that week, when he asked during a phone call if I received the package. He was out of breath. One of those moments when he couldn't get the words out fast enough.

"You get the package?"

"Yeah, man, I got it."

"It's her," he said.

"You're sure?"

"Yes, Phelps. I sent all that shit Moody sent me to you because she haunted me. I couldn't keep it in my cell. Man. I had to get it the hell out of here. Looking at her—that's the woman I killed. It's her, Phelps."

This was interesting. He'd told me his victims did not spook him. Yet here he was, face-to-face with a woman he'd killed twenty years before, sweating.

In a letter to Moody, explaining his feelings about the image, Jesperson said as soon as he opened the package: "A cold rush fell over" him. "That's her," he told Moody. "No changes needed!" Further along, "I cannot keep her in my cell. I am disturbed by the images. I mailed the prints off to Phelps."

Jesperson looked at a lineup of photographs Moody had since sent depicting Ylenia Carrisi at different ages, wearing different clothes, her hair styled differently in every photo. Moody never told Jesperson her name, anything about her background, or why he'd chosen to send the photographs. With a black Sharpie, on the top of the page, all Moody wrote was: "Is this her?"

Jesperson sent back his explanation. He'd lettered each photo, pointing out "the hair of 'H' and 'L' is correct. Her face in 'K' is so very close. 'B' is also close. As long as her name"—referring to Susan, Suzanne, Sue-Ellen, etc.—"is correct, we have a very good match."

He seemed certain we had found Jane Doe.

"Now to confirm DNA will be one hundred percent," Jesperson concluded. "I hope it is. Put an end to this story."

DURING THE ENTIRE COURSE of this journey trying to identify Jane Doe, I'd been trying to sell a documentary based on my Jane Doe (California and Florida) work, with this new art form Moody had somewhat made trendy and mastered as part of that docu-narrative. It was going to be a homage to all the work I'd done on cold cases. Moody, the PBSO, along with Haley and the FDLE, were on board to keep the Raven secret until the documentary was completed, revealing to a national audience those images of Jane Doe that Moody and Jesperson had worked on with my help. I thought, if I could get that info—Jane's image, Lake Tahoe, Reno, Jesperson's story of meeting and killing her—on national television, Jane's family would come forward and we could bring her home.

The problem with the documentary became that the two networks first interested in coproducing wound up rejecting the idea (after months of development). I couldn't find any other takers. True-crime television had moved on to a more cut and paste, murder, chase, arrest, courtroom and conviction type of cookie-cutter programming, where open and uncertain endings—like on *Dark Minds*—were frowned upon and vetoed across the board.

I felt beaten. Terribly disappointed. This had never been about me; it was about getting that computer rendering of Jane Doe out into a national audience I could reach via cable TV. I picked up the phone, quite upset, and explained this to Moody. He expressed his disappointment in the network not to see the value of the documentary and thanked me for all the work I'd done.

A few weeks later, Moody called with a brilliant idea he and the PBSO had come up with to solve our problem.

47

VICTIM NUMBER SIX

"You can't go home again."
—Thomas Wolfe

*C*OMPLACENCY CAN SOMETIMES BECOME A DANGEROUS, LONELY, dark hole we can fall into from time to time. Such a false sense of security can then become a place where we fail to recognize life's warning system because we have become too jaded, cynical, accepting, or accustomed to a situation. There were many times throughout those years of dealing with Jesperson when I was in there, scratching at the sides of the hole, searching for a way out, no light to guide me.

Well into our fifth year, however, I felt a sense of empowerment, as though I had somewhat taken my life back. Therapy had helped me refocus and refuel. I realized I needed to wash my hands with Jesperson, Raven, the Jane Does, the Happy Face murders, and all the horrific details he'd shared and I had consumed. Our friendship over the years had taken me into places I thought I would have never gone, into depths of depression I never knew existed within me. I told myself when I started I could handle anything. John Kelly had warned me about inviting the Devil into my life, and he was right: Evil of this magnitude gets into your blood, rattles your spirit, shakes you to the core—and if you're not ready to defend yourself, you'll succumb to it without ever knowing what the hell hit you. Maybe it was the amount of time. Or the profundity and detail we discussed. I couldn't explain it. Nor did

I need to. I just knew it was there, poking at me, grinding me down, tossing me around on the floor of my office and bathroom, doubling me over in somatic pain. I'd suffered chronic bouts of anxiety, of course capped off by Jesperson's needy, selfish tendency to overwhelm and smother.

"You're describing demonic possession," a friend told me one day as I explained what was going on in my life, why I had lost so much weight and felt depressed.

"I need to be exorcised for sure."

The letter I received from Jesperson regarding his brain was everything I'd expected. It was a long and tiring explanation of why he was saying yes. Not only did he send a notarized letter giving me permission to use his brain any way I chose, but he gave me complete control—which I *did* not want—over his remains. He asked me to claim his body upon his death.

That was not going to happen. The brain I would donate to any researcher who wanted it. But I was done with him. For good. I was not about to give him a proper burial after he died in that shithole of a prison that has been his home. The State of Oregon could deal with the corpse of a serial killer.

THE IDEA MOODY CAME up with was to produce a mini version of what I had wanted to do. Titled *Who Am I? Victim #6 of the Happy Face Killer,* the PBSO produced a comprehensive, detailed, short documentary focused on Jane Doe, using the images Jesperson created and Moody's computerized renderings as the catalyst pushing the story into the public domain. To protect my Raven secret, Moody and Haley did a great job of keeping me out of it, save for a brief shout-out at the end of the video, which I must say caused me a bit of concern, thinking someone would put it all together.[11]

The six-minute and four-second YouTube video did not go viral, but the story took flight. Newspapers and websites picked it

---

[11]See that YouTube video here: https://www.youtube.com/watch?v=zRJ45dn0m-Q.

up. The PBSO received e-mail tips from Web sleuths regarding who Jane could be, over half of which included the name Ylenia Carrisi.

Word spread that Ylenia Carrisi was a potential Jane Doe match and the Italian media detonated this thread of the story, blowing it up. One story published on November 19, 2015, in *OGGI,* a weekly newsmagazine out of Milan, below the headline YLENIA CARRISI, SENSATIONAL BREAKTHROUGH . . . THEY FOUND THE BODY?, included a photo of Jesperson, Carrisi, and Moody's Jane Doe image melded together into one graphic. Reading the story, you'd think the case had been solved:

> *Keith Hunter Jesperson admitted killing a girl . . . determined to get to California or Nevada, a girl called Suzanne, just as, according to investigators, used to be called Ylenia [in] America.*

Some of those facts were speculative, notably the California addition. The *OGGI* report explained how Interpol had contacted the girl's father, Albano, in October (2015), and extracted a DNA sample to send to Florida for testing.

With that, the Carrisi/Jesperson connection was made.

After only one local Palm Beach story and those few in Italy placing Jesperson's face next to Carrisi's, websites and newspaper front pages all over the world, on top of television news reports and chat room and blog discussions, erupted into a frenzy.

At the time, Jesperson had no idea. We all agreed not to tell him.

The accompanying stories indicated it was likely Jesperson had murdered Tyrone Power's granddaughter, identified through DNA as Ylenia Carrisi. It was an international, sensationalized media event the Italian press and paparazzi could not let go of because of the star power Romina and Albano (and even Ylenia) had bred throughout their lives. The PBSO received scores of media requests, the language barrier adding fuel to the identity flame. The pace of Web sleuths and Internet surfers contacting the PBSO picked up as everyone seemed to have a potential Jane Doe match.

I sat back and allowed the narrative to play out, hoping that, in the end, Jane was heading home. It truly felt as if we'd done it: returned a soul to a body, and given her a name.

Ylenia Carrisi.

"We really believe it's her," Moody called to tell me one day. "It all fits."

I was enthusiastic and emotional. In tricking Jesperson to help with the drawing, making him think that capital punishment was off the table, there might just be a payoff, making it all worth the pain, suffering, and five years of dealing with him. If I could solve this *one* case, or even just help a family spread word about a missing loved one, in some respects I'd feel vindicated, maybe even redeemed.

In total, forty leads came in after the video was posted. Half pointed to Ylenia Carrisi. As the story went on into the winter of 2015 through 2016, Dennis Haley and Paul Moody zeroed in on her. As each new piece of information about her surfaced, especially from the Carrisi family, it seemed more plausible than ever that Jesperson had murdered her—which, if true, was going to no doubt put Jesperson inside a courtroom facing a prosecutor and the death penalty. The Carrisi family, all of us knew, would insist upon Jesperson paying the ultimate price for killing their child. Any family would.

"You win some, you lose some," I told Haley, Moody, and Ken one day as we discussed the likelihood of the Carrisi family putting pressure on the prosecutor to make Jesperson face death if their daughter was his Florida victim. "My first obligation is always to the victim."

They agreed. When negotiating with serial killers, breaking promises was part of the deal.

Neither Moody nor Haley was a believer in using psychics to aid in solving crimes. Still, one of Carrisi's family members had utilized a psychic in helping to find her during those days before the Happy Face story broke. The family sent Moody the report. The psychic had given the Carrisi family GPS coordinates, specifying where she believed the missing woman could be found alive, living her new, secret life. Because it was an official "lead," how-ever unconventional, Haley ran it down.

The provided GPS coordinates turned out to be "a block away from" Haley's FDLE office in Pensacola—incredibly not too far from where Jane's bones and dress and evidence had been stored since she'd been found. Even more fascinating (or maybe extraor-dinary), because the psychic had given the information to the family before Haley and Moody were involved with connecting Jesperson to Carrisi, none of it could have been gleaned from a Google search.

"Weird, just plain weird," Haley said. "I was certain we were onto something. Not because of the psychic. But we thought for sure we had this thing solved. It was all pointing to Ylenia."

"Yes, we did," Moody said.

That confidence had nothing to do with the psychic's informa-tion—a lead checked out by Haley himself, banging on doors in that GPS-suggested neighborhood, which went nowhere—but everything to do with Ylenia Carrisi's family filling in some of the missing blanks that made her story fit all the more seamlessly into the situation Jesperson had described. Dates, places, times, where Carrisi was heading and coming from, where she had been seen, what she was wearing, an alias she'd used, what she was into—all of it pointed to her.

The champagne was put on ice.

The only thing left to do was check the Carrisi DNA against Jane's. After a back-and-forth with Interpol and the Italian au-thorities, American law enforcement not wanting to use evidence sent from Italy that they hadn't swabbed and controlled its chain of custody, Haley and Moody contacted Romina, who was living in the United States and now divorced from Albano, and asked her to submit a DNA sample.

The lab promised Haley it would put a rush on the test.

48

GRAND OPTIMIST

"Even the darkest night will end and the sun will rise."
—Victor Hugo, *Les Misérables*

A DAY AFTER CHRISTMAS, DECEMBER 26, 2015, JESPERSON SAT IN HIS cell "watching TV, thinking about" his life and how it had culminated into what was, by then, more than twenty years behind bars. He wasn't upset, bitter, or angry, he claimed. He'd chosen this life. Instead, he wondered what "to leave behind as a legacy." The analogy he used to explain his predicament centered on country-western singer George Jones, whom Jesperson had seen roasted on television.

Reading this, I thought: *Narcissism oozes from this guy like sweat.*

Here we have the perfect example of that grandiose, exaggerated, fantastical thinking the psychopath reserves for his private thoughts: Jesperson was comparing himself to a country music legend!

Further along, in one of the more revealing letters he'd ever written, Jesperson claimed to have lied in some shape or form to just about everyone who had ever tried to tell his story—including me. But here he was, after five years, now ready to come clean, he explained. He was finished hiding behind any inhibitions.

This was his way of telling me he wanted to stop bullshitting about certain events and clear the record. He knew I was almost done with him. He sensed it. He was trying to fit everything he needed to say into what were his last moments of me being his sounding board, available to him.

"You know, in 2000, not all of my cases were settled and to be *so* completely honest with [the late Jack Olsen] (who wrote a book about Jesperson, published posthumously in August 2002) was not in the cards. Or *anyone* for that matter."

Jesperson said he still had "lots of court" ahead of him at the time he allowed Jack Olsen to interview him.

"I lied to Jack—a lot," Jesperson told me.

The fact that it was now twenty years into his life sentences— Happy Face being a sixty-year-old lifer—had left "little they can or will do to me," he said, adding how if Florida or California, the two states I'd worked hard at identifying victims, came calling, forcing him into court, he would not fight it. According to Jesperson, no more resistance. No more butting heads with the system. No more blaming others. It was time to man up.

In truth, he knew it would take fifteen years, at the least, to put him to death once the process got started. He believed he'd be dead by then, anyway.

From there, the letter, written as a series of answers to questions I was "going to get to, anyway," became another outlet for him to stream his interpretation of what the public thought of him. He addressed any *Dark Minds* viewers wondering why he agreed to become Raven and help me profile unsolved serial killer cases.

Friends: Week after week we talked on the phone discussing cases for Dark Minds. Talking to Phelps became an out for me to escape to from prison. He was genuinely concerned about my day-to-day wellness. Phelps is more family to me than my own family is. We are like very close friends that have been friends for a long time. I know that from our extensive talks he will investigate fully my story to give the world the truth about who is Keith Jesperson. Being Raven on Dark Minds allowed me to tell the side of being a serial killer without my crimes becoming the focal point to the show. We didn't want people to dwell on me.

Next, Jesperson pondered the notion that if Angela Subrize was alive when he dragged her underneath his truck, "Wouldn't that make a better story?" If he'd had sex with his victims after death, and went back to the dump sites to continue to have sex with them, "Wouldn't *that* make a better story?" What if "I was a cannibal and ate parts of my victims?" Wouldn't *that* be what the general public wanted (and expected) of him?

I had no idea where all of this was coming from. It didn't make sense. I felt, in a way, he was trying to interject more intrigue and mystery into his legacy: *Listen, Phelps, there's a lot I haven't told you,* because he realized our time was coming to an end.

"Thanks for that letter," I explained during our next call. "I'll have a look at it soon."

I had no intention of stepping back into what felt like a new beginning he was trying to impose on me. I needed all of it to stop. My focus was following through with the Ylenia Carrisi lead, hoping like hell that she was Jane Doe, and then cutting off this cancer that had been eating away at my humanity for five years.

49

BLANK CANVAS

"Everything just got messier and more consuming."
—Keith Jesperson, 2016

A MAN CANNOT OUTRUN OR OUTSMART HIS GHOSTS; THEY'RE EMBED-ded deep within the marrow of his soul. Sooner or later, however, without any prodding of his own, a resurrection occurs. If nothing else, this is the lesson I will take away from corresponding with Keith Jesperson for five exhausting years I can never get back: to be prepared when those apparitions reappear.

In the early part of our fifth year, Jesperson called one morning. As the phone rang, I considered picking up and telling him to stop. By now, I was resigned to answering every fifth or sixth call, allowing ten days, sometimes several weeks, to pass, with the thought of weaning him off me being there for him. It was early spring 2016, just after he'd sent me an eighty-page letter describing each of his murders with a self-imposed promise of "new" details and insights he'd not shared with anyone else. To which I rolled my eyes and told myself, *Not this time.*

"I could write out each murder to be what people would believe, coming from the killer," the letter began. I sensed he was in an odd place. As with any Happy Face explanation in letter form, he started this one with a soliloquy, putting what he was about to say into some sort of ideological, contextual logic, however twisted and self-serving. The guy feels the need to justify *every* action. Every admission. Every "new" disclosure. Maybe every single word and thought. With all of his banal platitudes, Jesperson holds on to a desperate compulsion to convince himself—more than any of us—that no matter what he says, the public should view it as relevant, not only to his overall story, but the grand serial killer narrative.

Jesperson then pointed out something he'd said on several occasions: How most people will believe whatever a serial killer says because it strikes at their worst fears and facilitates the public's core beliefs regarding what serial murder—and the psychology behind it—should involve. "Make it TV, sitcom-style—*Silence of the Lambs, Red Dragon*," he added, and they'll believe all of it. "The blank canvas is filled with stories and it's up to someone to pull out what really happened."

After a killer of his caliber is arrested, Jesperson explained, "We are schooled by the law and lawyers telling us what is important *to* and *not to* tell juries/prosecutors/police." Thomas Phelan had told Happy Face to "never admit to premeditated crimes." Ignoring that advice, Jesperson claimed there had always been an uncontrollable impulse inside him to search for a victim. Whenever I'd asked Jesperson about a "need inside him" to kill, he'd played it down, claiming it was not like that for him. That "story" had become a part of a legacy created by the media, further expedited by the Internet and his daughter years later, a carefully constructed narrative designed to demonize him and make him appear to be more in line with the Hollywood prototype. Jesperson's argument had been that karma put him and his victims together and, as such, that celestial path played into those lives coming to an end. The murders happened in a moment of rage after a trigger had been squeezed; they were never planned. He'd not once roamed the countryside in his truck, seeking out females to have sex with and then kill.

Now, suddenly, this was the big lie, he said: "Tell a story to whitewash it so it doesn't sound so bad." He'd hid behind that kismet mantra, he added, "To make murder sound softer. Take the sting out of it. There have been so many people talking about what I have done to my victims, the canvas is filled with several versions of each case. . . . I need to come clean."

Because of the holiday season, it had been more than two weeks since we'd spoken. I tried to make a habit of never accepting his calls on holidays, my birthday, or important personal days. I did not want that part of my life to become anything we shared. Whenever I'd slipped and mentioned a private "thing" I had to do, he'd begin the next call asking: "How'd it go?" After telling him not to go there, I'd receive ten pages of text in my PO box a week later describing how he knew and understood he was not my top priority in life and wanted to recognize I had a life beyond serial killers and talking to him and he needed to be more attentive to that boundary. His way of apologizing, I guess.

"What do you mean 'come clean'?" I asked next time we spoke.

"I have not been totally honest with you," he said.

"Okay."

He began (again) on the Bennett case, claiming a need to resolve a few minor discrepancies and clarify what actually happened inside his house on the night he murdered Bennett and those hours before.[12]

As he talked about his actual true motive and mind-set during the years he'd killed, the impression was that I'd hit on all of it about a year into our discussions. It was Jesperson's way of telling me I'd figured him out, had been right all along, without him having to admit total defeat.

"My girlfriend Pamela had left weeks before, out trucking and fucking her new man at every rest area and truck stop," he said of those days before he murdered Bennett. "What *I* would have been doing if *I* was trucking with her."

The image superimposed inside his head on the night he murdered Bennett: another woman who had let him down; another woman who had spurned and replaced him; another woman out having sex with another man. He allowed the anger the situation

---

[12]Much of his "new" narrative surrounding Bennett's murder is included in the opening section of this book.

infected him with to manifest: Pamela and her new man having sex. The jealousy ground him down. Ate at him.

Rose redux.

He blamed himself, now claiming his mind was "full of anger at how I had [screwed] up my life." He had "destroyed" a "perfect family" with Rose and his kids by acting on "lust," cheating on Rose, having "sex with different women."

After accepting Pamela had left him for the other man, Jesperson decided to go "searching for sex." Thus, for the first time, he admitted he did not simply bump into Taunja Bennett randomly that afternoon at the bar. He'd gone out to find a woman whom he could bed. To me, this admission is significant within his evolution as a serial murderer. He was motivated by lust, sexual urges, and sexual fantasies, which ultimately turned violent. Textbook serial killer stuff.

What's more: I'd always searched Jesperson's life for an addiction (a good portion of serial killers are addicted to something). I asked him about booze. Drugs? "So was it sex? Were you addicted to sex?"

"No," he said. "You got that wrong. It's gambling. I was addicted to gambling."

He explained how, after killing Bennett, he initiated a stalking routine by going out in his small world in search of females for a singular purpose: sex. He was driven by a compulsion to have sex and not have to pay for it. "I was always observing females for an opening to enter into their world to be able to offer up something they want/need, in hopes I'd get lucky."

On the road it became booze, cigarettes, a ride, food, even shelter.

His life post-Rose was a "roller coaster of sex and more sex." Searching for a new sexual partner to "replace Pamela" after killing Bennett, he assumed, was the initial objective setting him on a path toward committing additional murders. January 20, 1990, the last day of Bennett's life, Jesperson said, did not start out with him waking up and feeling idle, twiddling his thumbs, bored, sitting around the house, as he had told cops, writers, and journalists (including me). Now he said he left the house that morning to stalk women. He'd not killed anyone yet (so he claimed), but he'd been fantasizing about taking total control over females and being able to do whatever he wanted (sexually) to them. On this particular morning, he walked to the local mall "cruising, to see what I could see. Observing people. Studying people for a way into their lives."

Typical predatory behavior, no matter how Jesperson shined it up. He was a man looking to exploit the social vulnerabilities of women out and about, associating with community members, neighbors and friends. For example, while at a local supermarket, Jesperson sought out several women who fit his fantasy and stepped into their space by offering "help with their packages/groceries, open a door here, close a door there, carry [their groceries] out for them." As he did this, he spoke to them: "Have a nice day," while the tape loop inside his head repeated: *Do you wanna play?*

He couldn't spend too much time at the supermarket, Happy Face soon realized, because "that would be too obvious." So he split his time up among several public places: a local Jeep dealership, Radio Shack, a building center.

By noon, Jesperson found himself downtown, circling a few bars. He drank coffee, so as not to cloud his judgment and "make a mistake." He decided to "flirt" with the "first girl to smile" at him. By two o'clock in the afternoon, after meeting Bennett inside the B&I Tavern, making mental note she was available (that embrace initiated by her), he walked back to his house, now obsessed with sexing Bennett.

"I had learned," Jesperson said, "that my father's hit-and-run had made an impact on my thought process as I went. He got away with it, so can I. If nobody knows about it, then it didn't happen."

In this letter, Jesperson distilled each of his eight murders into single thoughts: "Killed Bennett, hurt Daun [Slagle], killed number 2 because she presented herself to me when I had time to play. Number 3 was there and I wanted her with me. Number 4 wanted a better life and I ended it. Number 5 was a conquest to a game to see if I could get her. Number 6 just wasn't being social. Number 7 overstayed her welcome, and number 8 had been a problem. I justified every murder on how I saw each person I dealt with. You call it playing God."

In a stroke of ruthless honesty, near the end of the letter, Jesperson described Angela Subrize: "I loved sex with her. Yes, the sex was great. But it had to end sometime. She had become a liability to me. I felt a need to be rid of her. She had to go. She had to die. There would be no rest for me from her if I let her go."

A ROME TELEVISION NETWORK flew into Palm Beach to interview Dennis Haley after the Ylenia Carrisi story broke internationally and media hounded Albano Carrisi and Romina Power. The language barrier among Moody, Haley, and the Italian media, once again, created more mystery surrounding any proven connection between Ylenia Carrisi and Keith Jesperson.

"They all had a hard time understanding that we were *not* saying we had found Ylenia. We just wanted to eliminate her from possibilities," Haley noted.

Early into our quest, Dennis Haley thought Jesperson was lying about Jane Doe the entire time; that Happy Face was holding on to information that could identify her. Through the Ylenia Carrisi investigation, along with several other possible victims now being checked via DNA, and corresponding with Jesperson, however, Haley saw a different side of Happy Face, concluding, "I now believe he has been truthful concerning victim number six."

The one aspect of the Carrisi case that concerned Haley, Moody, and me was all the attention Jesperson received in Europe. Jesperson was on the front page of many websites and newspapers. He'd become that infamous nicknamed serial killer all over again. The only silver lining in it all was that he knew nothing about it.

"They all ran stories on Jesperson and tied him to Ylenia Carrisi. I thought if I was open and honest with [the press there], they wouldn't screw things up, but they did," Moody said. "They even ran articles that we had identified our Jane Doe as Ylenia and that Jesperson had identified her."

As spring 2016 came, the Ylenia Carrisi story faded. Romina's DNA was put into the system and ran against Jane Doe. When the results came back, it shocked everyone.

No match. Ylenia Carrisi was not Jesperson's Jane Doe.

"We were surprised," Haley said.

"Well, with a striking number of similarities and bits of information coming together that seemingly linked Jane Doe with Ylenia Carrisi, we were both starting to get sweaty palms, thinking we may have had this case on the verge of closure," Moody added, speaking for him and Haley. "We both thought that so many uncanny and coincidental details could not possibly exist without our Jane Doe turning out to be Ylenia. And we also knew that everyone in Italy had been sitting on the edge of their seats, waiting to hear, while the Italian news media virtually had Jesperson tried and convicted for Ylenia's murder. It was rather intense."

To me, it felt like another death. I wanted so badly for Jane to find her home.

Haley and Moody were back at ground zero. Haley had exhausted all the leads that had come in, except for a couple of missing women who'd never been reported to NamUs, or any of the other databases. Her DNA had not been tested against Jane's. Haley ran down family members of those women and obtained familial samples. But those, too, turned out to be negative, compelling the Jane Doe mystery to continue.[13]

---

[13]I've put contact information for Florida law enforcement underneath the Paul Moody computer rendering of Jane Doe in the photo section of this book. If you think you have any information about this case after reading the book, or recognize Jane's photo and/or any of her clothing, jewelry, or her lifestyle seems familiar, please reach out to Dennis Haley or myself.

50

SAME OLD SUFFERING

"What is hell? I maintain that it is the suffering of being unable to love."
—Fyodor Dostoyevsky, *The Brothers Karamazov*

WHAT HAD ALWAYS SCARED ME CONCERNING MY FRIENDSHIP WITH Jesperson was finding out that there was a side of him I might like. When I began, I was determined to stay objective by putting up an emotional barrier between us, confident my hatred for him was enough to get me through it. There only had been one time in my career when I sided with a convicted murderer and argued her case for innocence in that book. That's not what I mean here. I understand Jesperson is evil, that he is guilty, that he lied to me and others and he fits into the Hare/Cleckley psychopath checklist as though it had been created for him. I also know psychopaths can love, but do it in their own way, on their own terms. Still, Jesperson could not get beyond his narcissism. Anytime he showed the slightest bit of interest in my life, or expressed a trace of morality, and the focus was not completely on him, he'd veer off into how whatever I was talking about reflected on his life or something that had happened to him. He couldn't suppress this impulse. Nor could he stop it. A psychopath is part of who this man is and always will be.

In his eighty-page letter sent to clear the record, beyond detailing all he'd done, stimulated to clean up many of the misconceptions and untruths said and written about him throughout the years, he talked about the type of killer he'd become at the end of his run. His thoughts became more complex and sinister, he said, during those final months, and once again he went back to, strangely enough, necrophilia, now offering cannibalism as part of the conversation.

"While they lay dead before me, I knew I could have had sex with their bodies. It just wasn't in me—not yet, anyway. What about eating them? Yes, the idea was there. The question of what does the meat taste like? How would it feel fucking a cold, dead body? My thought process hadn't driven me to do it, [but] there would have to be more time included with them . . . with *me*."

I took away from this that had he continued killing, with a need to increase the stimulation (which wasn't there anymore), necrophilia and cannibalism would've come into play.

"True?" I asked him.

"I think so."

These questions he posed were also, I soon realized, designed to keep me thinking about him. His way of trying to continue to stick to the inside of my head, to keep a hold on me.

"So now, Phelps, there you have it. Creative writing or a lie? Us killers have been known to lie to save our skins. But to lie to throw us into hell? Hell of a switch! Kill them for not wanting sex or even a kiss? Call your book, *Kiss the Girls*. Oh, sorry, that title is taken. You asked for answers. It is the best I got."

Here he was explaining that all of his kills were motivated by him wanting sex from these women and each of them turning him down at some point.

Near the end of the Ylenia Carrisi investigation, as I was immersed in all of Jesperson's writings, the recordings I'd made of our calls and Video Visits, I hit him with several hardball questions: Did you rape all of them? Bind them? Torture them? Beat them? He sensed I'd been interviewing sources related to his cases without telling him, and he was beginning to understand that perhaps I was not writing the book he'd envisioned and, from day one, had been desperate to control. One of the serial killer's most recognizable traits—one they cannot hide, no matter how hard they try—is the need to control every possible aspect of their lives. We've seen this time and again in Jesperson's complete need to reign supreme over his victims (when/where he picked them up, while in his custody, while murdering them, and even after, while disposing their bodies and even telling their stories). This is the same thought process certain serial killers unconsciously rely on as they store corpses inside their homes, go back to where they dumped bodies and spend time with them, and, in cases of necrophilia, have postmortem sex. In those instances, we have the serial killer wielding absolute power and control over his victim. Research indicates a tenable loneliness associated with this behavior: the solitary figure searching the world for his version of the perfect victim, killing, making sure to keep her within his grasp so as to feel as though he can, even in death, maintain that power and control. Jeffrey Dahmer took this to the extreme by consuming various body parts of his victims "in order to become one with them," Dahmer told authorities.

Dr. Willem Martens, a leading researcher studying psychopaths from within their own psychological perspective, explains that for the general public to comprehend the amount of isolation and loneliness these men feel is perhaps "unimaginable." We could never fully understand the separation from society the serial killer experiences and how that antisocial view of the world affects their decisions and crimes. A percentage of serial killers have, Martens contends, "describe[d] their loneliness and social failures as unbearably painful. Each created his own sadistic universe to avenge his experiences of rejection, abuse, humiliation, neglect, and emotional suffering."[14]

Five characteristics, among many others, I know for certain, completely and emphatically define who Keith Hunter Jesperson truly is.

[14]To read Dr. Martens's excellent article, "The Hidden Suffering of the Psychopath," from which this quote was used, go to: http://www.psychiatrictimes.com/psychotic-affective-disorders/hidden-suffering-psychopath#sthash.DxALG59P.dpuf.

"I accept my guilt," Jesperson concluded. "Embrace it. Not proud of it. I accept it as fact. I'm broken. But not making excuses. Whatever you come up with, Phelps, I'm sure it will be serving a purpose that reflects what you want people to know about me, my crimes—your suspicions. I've taken lives from those who deserved better."

In 2016, the FBI released its report on the Highway Serial Killings initiative, a comprehensive, twelve-year study that began when the Oklahoma Bureau of Investigation discovered "a pattern of murdered women's bodies being dumped along I-40 in Oklahoma, Texas, Arkansas, and Mississippi." That investigation led to the FBI compiling a list of 750 murder victims found near U.S. highway systems across American roadways, with nearly 450 potential suspects. Staggering numbers.

In a statement accompanying the report, the FBI stated: "If there is such a thing as an ideal profession for a serial killer, it may well be as a long-haul truck driver."

51

THE PAST AS RANSOM FOR THE FUTURE

"Life can only be understood backwards; but it must be
lived forwards."
—Søren Kierkegaard

*I*T HAD BEEN TWO DECADES SINCE I'D VISITED MY SISTER-IN-LAW DIANE'S
grave site. I knew I had to do it if I was to move on. I needed to
face those memories in front of her, forgive Diane, and especially
myself, for hating her the way I did at the time she was murdered.
Diane was not all bad. There was a kind, gentle, caring human
being inside her that addiction took possession of. I understood
this as I grew older. I could not have known it when she was alive.

My daughter and I were on our way to a volleyball tournament
in Hartford. We stopped for pizza down the street from the cemetery where Diane is buried.

"Come on," I said after lunch. "I need to show you something."

I drove into the cemetery and parked along the edge of the
grass, in a spot close to where I had at her funeral. When Diane
was buried, the cemetery was new; hers was one of the first grave
sites dug. I recalled it being on the border, by the entrance road
in, near the gate, in the first row of stones. How could I ever forget? The darkness of that day is a part of me.

We stepped out of the vehicle. There were hundreds of gravestones now. I was confused and flustered, kind of like when you're
looking for an address and anxiety kicks in while studying a map.
Everything looked so different.

"Start there," I told my daughter, pointing to the first row. "I'll look over here."

My daughter, sixteen at the time, is a smart girl. National Honor Society. Straight A's. Excellent student in every manner of speaking. She's an EMT. Extremely headstrong: a bull. Involved up to her eyeballs in everything under the sun at school and our parish. She is planning on going into medicine. She's a straight shooter. Tells it like it is. Has not an ounce of naiveté in her. She's a skeptic and does not take things as they are, how people say they are, but as she sees them. She, like me, appreciates evidence as a precursor to believing a story, such as the one we were about to experience.

We searched every row, every gravestone and ground plate, for twenty minutes.

"Can't find it," my daughter said. "You?"

"I swear it was right here," I said, walking up and down the first row of headstones and grave markers flush with the ground, this after scouring the entire cemetery, knowing damn well Diane had been buried in the first quadrant of gravestones that ran along the fence line by the entrance road in. I was certain of this.

We took another look.

Nothing.

Being January in New England, the cold was biting. The wind blew and our skin burned. We needed to get inside the warm car and to my daughter's tournament.

Sitting inside the vehicle, letting it warm up, I found one of those find-a-grave websites on my iPhone. There was a picture of Diane's gravestone, just as I had remembered it. The website, however, did not give any specific directions or coordinates in the cemetery indicating where the grave might be. I was disappointed.

As I scrolled up and down the Web page, my daughter leaned over and stared at the image without saying a word. She then looked up, as if lost in thought (or, come to find out, listening). She put her hand on the door to exit the car.

Still not a word, she got out, took a few steps toward the back of the vehicle.

I stepped out. "What are you doing?"

My daughter, standing fifteen feet from me, looked down and said, "Dad, it's right here."

"What?" I walked toward the back of the vehicle.

There it was. Not ten feet from the back end of my car, the first headstone in the cemetery, same as I'd remembered. There was a bush shading it from view, which must have been why we'd missed it.

"How did you know?" I asked.

My daughter stared at me, looked down. I'd never seen this expression on her face. Not ever. She wasn't scared, or spooked; she had a look of absolute clearheadedness, as though one of life's secrets had been revealed only to her.

"*What* is it, kid?"

"When I looked at the picture of the headstone on your phone, I didn't see it. I held this blank stare—and then I heard a voice."

"What? You heard a what?"

"The voice said, 'Sweetie, it's right over there, just get out and go look.' So then I said to her, 'But it's too cold out and we have already looked over there.' And she said, 'Just do it. Trust me, sweetie. I promise you. It's right next to the bush.' And then I said to her, 'Okay, but I am only looking there.'"

Diane used to call Meranda "sweetie." I can hear her say the word as clear as, apparently, my daughter heard her dead aunt explain where her grave was located.

ACKNOWLEDGMENTS

It's important for me to note that in all of my books previous to this one, I have spent a considerable amount of time on the victims' lives and stories, interviewing family and friends, trying to capture the essence of who each victim was, their dreams and goals, profiling their entire lives, taking each from being a simple headline to a sustainable memory. This has always been one of the driving forces of my work, a quality I'm known for. I get letters and e-mails and notes from readers expressing their deep appreciation for how I treat victims in the narratives I write.

I point this out because I did not do that in this book. I never intended with this project to write a straightforward true-crime narrative, where the space is available for me to detail a victim's life story. This is not that type of book. Therefore, it was hard for me to delve deeply into each of the eight victims' lives here. I don't apologize for that, but I want to make my intentions clear.

Thanking Keith Jesperson doesn't seem relevant, though there were times during the five years we spent talking that I did thank him for certain information. Today, as I write this postscript to the book, I feel as though I need a major break from Jesperson—months to process all that we discussed. Totally write him off? Not sure. For now, I am not talking to him. Not because of anything other than my emotional state and the toll this so-called friendship has taken on my emotional well-being and those around me.

Jesperson is an unfinished story; he is constantly unraveling and dissecting his thoughts, his purpose, who he was, who he is, trying to poke a hole in authority, yes, but also trying to say to the public: *You will never comprehend me fully because you are not me. You will never feel what I feel, therefore you couldn't possibly know me or understand what I did.*

Secrets, some say, are for keeping—and Jesperson will die with many. I am sure of that.

I would also like to acknowledge that I wrote a lot of the more personal sections of this book on my iPad, often lying in bed in the middle of the night, unable to sleep, or sitting in my living room after my afternoon reading, as the memories came. It gave those portions of my life a different perspective from me sitting at my office computer, demanding the memories take their place in the book. As the holidays of 2015 came, and my two living brothers were over, I spoke of those times when Mark, Thomas, Frank, and I were kids. We shared stories. The memories in this book are mine and mine alone. If nothing else, writing this book allows me to tap into a brokenness inside me I knew existed, but had been afraid to confront. And, to that end, Jesperson helped me find it.

I want to thank my mother, Florence Borelli, the Castellassi family, the Fournier family, the Phelps family, the Pavlocks, all my cousins, aunts, and uncles, many of whom were part of this book in memory without ever being mentioned in the text.

My editor, Michaela Hamilton, said this book would be a "game changer" for me. Michaela has been my biggest fan and championed every true-crime book. She has completely shaped who I am as a true-crime author and reporter and has been instrumental in making this book all that it has become. We worked so hard on every aspect of it. Thank you, Michaela, for all you do.

Equally as important to me as an editor is Norma Perez-Hernandez. Also, Kensington President and CEO Steve Zacharius and publisher Lynn Cully have been nothing but instrumental in backing me up throughout my career. I am grateful for their continued support. I am as equally grateful to Vida Engstrand and Morgan Ewell, the backbone of the Kensington publicity team. I am a lucky author to have such passionate and great people working on my behalf.

Matthew Valentinas, my lawyer and manager, has been a true friend, mentor, all-things-entertainment advisor, and incredibly patient partner in getting this project to the point it is. Matt was my biggest supporter as this project started as an idea. He saw my vision from day one and allowed it to transcend.

An immense, heartfelt thank-you to Sonya M. Cosumano, LMFT,

M. Ed., who continues to help me work through a lot of the pain and manage the stress of life.

Ken Robinson did so much more work on the Jane Doe cases (California and Florida) than the narrative reflected. Without him, I could not have completed work on either case, or come to the conclusions regarding Cynthia Wilcox and Jane Doe (Florida) that I have. Ken is a lifelong friend, partner in crime, mentor, one of a few people I can confide in.

Likewise, Paul Moody and Dennis Haley are like no two cops I have ever met and worked with. They accepted me without judgment and seemed grateful for my help, never questioning my intentions or motivations or integrity. They allowed me into the fold and I am forever humbled and honored. I will never stop searching for Jane Doe's identity, and these men know this about me.

The usual suspects seem redundant to thank—you know who you are.

In no particular order: Jim McIntyre, Thomas Phelan, Suzanne M. Aspy Ofs (for our conversation and your prayers), R. Dinca, OSP guards who were kind, and several people I met while in Portland, Salem, and Gresham researching Jesperson's life.

Markie, Tyler, Meranda, thank you for understanding. Thomas and Frank, my two brothers, thanks.

April and Regina, my family, what a strange trip this book has been.

John Kelly, man, oh man, were you ever right. I allowed the Devil in and he possessed me for a time and took control of who I was. I can never thank you enough for all you have done for me, Kelly. You're one of the most insightful men I know, like a father to me. I love you.

Readers, old and new, my immense gratitude and thanks. This one is for you!